The South Moves
into Its Future

The South Moves into Its Future

Studies in the Analysis and Prediction of Social Change

Edited by Joseph S. Himes

The University of Alabama Press
Tuscaloosa and London

Copyright © 1991 by
The University of Alabama Press
Tuscaloosa, Alabama 35487–0380

Library of Congress Cataloging-in-Publication Data

The South moves into its future : studies in the analysis and
    prediction of social change / edited by Joseph S. Himes.
        p.   cm.
    Includes bibliographical references (p.   ).
    ISBN 0-8173-0461-4
    1. Southern States—Social conditions.   2. Social prediction—
Southern States.   I. Himes, Joseph S.
HN79.A13S59   1991   90-10803
    303.4975—dc20   CIP

British Library Cataloguing-in-Publication Data available

Contents

Preface   vii

Acknowledgments   xv

1. Introduction: Background of Recent Changes in the
   South
   Joseph S. Himes   1

Part I. Population Dynamics   11

2. Population Change and Social Adaptation in the South,
   Past and Future
   Jeanne C. Biggar   13
3. Demographic and Economic Restructuring in the South
   John D. Kasarda, Holly L. Hughes, and Michael D. Irwin   32
4. The South and Its Older People: Structural and
   Change Perspectives
   Gordon F. Streib   69

Part II. Status Relations   101

5. Southern-Style Gender: Trends in Relations between
   Men and Women
   *Patricia Yancey Martin, Kenneth R. Wilson, and
   Caroline Matheny Dillman*   103

6. Trends in Ethnic Relations: Hispanics and Anglos
   W. Parker Frisbie   149
7. Trends in Race Relations: Blacks and Whites
   John J. Moland, Jr.   186

Part III. Social Orientations   223

8. New South or No South? Regional Culture in 2036
   John Shelton Reed   225
9. Southern Conservatism and Liberalism: Past and Future
   Paul Luebke   236

Part IV. Social Change, Social Prediction, Social Action   255

10. Summary: Societal Transformations and Social
    Predictions
    Joseph S. Himes   257
11. Making a Difference: The Role of the Social Sciences
    Abbott L. Ferriss   269
References   286
Contributors   310
Index   312

Preface

I

The American South can be thought of as having evolved through three stages—a traditional, autocratic "Old" or "Antebellum South," from the last quarter of the seventeenth century to the 1870s; an unstable, uncertain "Inter-Stage," from the 1880s to the Great Depression/New Deal–World War II decade; and a still developing vital and changing "New South," since 1945. The seismic forces that separated these stages gave each its distinctive social character and social direction. The literature of each stage provides a record of how the actors in that stage perceived the history of their times. This book examines the course of Southern history in the early years of the New South and predicts what it may be like in the foreseeable future.

The record of thought and discussion of serious social issues in the Inter-Stage was produced, in the main, by journalists, historians, ministers, and politicians. Immediately after the Civil War, the region faced a great dilemma. Current and associates (1983, 484) write that the South ". . . could attempt to transform itself into a modern industrial region able to compete with its former enemy . . . or it could attempt to rebuild its agrarian economy and restore some semblance of the comfortable civility that white Southerners had so valued in their civilization before the Civil War." Nevertheless, the leaders did not have access to social science methods to guide their choice.

Journalists and historians exerted the greatest influence in the debate. Henry Grady in 1904 and W. J. Cash in 1941 took opposite positions on this issue. Later, after the choice had been made, many journalists applauded the decision and disparaged the undesirable image of urban industrial life. Historians, being more empirical, often lamented this choice of direction and cited undesirable consequences.

Other policy actions of the region functioned to generate interracial prejudice and the "race problem." Jim Crow laws limited political activity by blacks, and the new tenant practices made competitors of poor whites and poor blacks. This interracial struggle accentuated the moral dilemma of the region and exacerbated the situation after the New Deal and World War II.

By the end of the 1930s the methods of the social sciences had become a major way of understanding social issues and contributing to the literature of the region. In the 1920s Robert E. Park and Ernest W. Burgess (1923, 734–83) at the University of Chicago had pioneered the scientific study of race relations. Soon thereafter sociologists in the South adopted this approach to race relations. The important saltation in the scientific study of general social issues in the region was made by the publication (1936) of Howard W. Odum's landmark research on *Southern Regions of the United States.*

Following these developments, sociological research began to make a significant contribution to the serious social literature of the region. Professional sociology burgeoned, and the Southern Sociological Society was launched in 1935 and 1936. At the same time, the other social sciences—economics, political science, and anthropology—were growing and contributing to this accumulating literature. As Odum had insisted, this research issued into social planning for the region. In Chapter 11 below, Ferriss discusses how this flurry of social-science activity became implemented by organizations that combined research, planning, and collective action.

The most important of these organizations were the Southern Regional Council (SRC), established in 1944, and the Southern Regional Educational Board (SREB), founded in 1949. The SRC sponsored extensive research and publication in the area of race relations. The SREB promoted higher educational opportunities for both whites and blacks in the South. The Southern Growth Policy Board engages in multi-purpose research and planning for the region; its strategy is to set goals and plans for their achievement by group action.

The interracial struggle that emerged in the early part of the century erupted into organized collective action in the 1950s. By 1964 the dramatic evidences of this struggle included the 1954 Supreme Court Decision banning school segregation, the Montgomery bus boycott of 1955–56, the Sit-in Action in Greensboro in 1961, the nationwide revolt of young people, and the Civil Rights Act of 1964. This activity filled the media with dramatic reports from all parts of the region. Moreover, this protest-rebellion activity produced a new sociology of social conflict.

In 1965 James C. McKinney and Edgar T. Thompson, editors, published *The South in Continuity and Change*. In the history of the era and in the face of the burgeoning conflict sociology, this is a surprising book. Although it was researched and written between 1962 and 1964, it makes little or no reference to the social revolution that swirled around the heads of the editors and chapter authors. On the contrary, the editors state that the perspective of the book ". . . takes cognizance of the past, examines the present, and looks to the future" (x). However, it does not stress the possibilities of future change. Instead, the editors assert further, ". . . change exists primarily, but not entirely, in continuity" (xi). They go on to state their case by declaring: "The assumption is that the persistence of social structures and of cultural patterns present the primary clues to the future of the Region" (xi–xii).

In the final chapter, Thompson explains what is meant by continuity. He asserts: that "whether we conform to this heritage of revolt against it, the plantation norm will continue to glorify or to stain the culture and the attitudes of the South's people" (458). As suggested above, this book fails to take account of the inchoate social revolution that was beginning to transform the social structure and culture—even as they wrote about it.

The South Moves into Its Future projects a radically different perspective on the study of social change. It uses research on recent social change as an instrument for predicting the future course of change. It accepts the rapid social change of the past half century as a central factor in both research and prediction. Although continuity facilitates projection, this book does not envisage it as a traditional bond slowing and impeding rapid change. Such a point of view is one consequence of recent developments in the discipline.

This book is relevant to the mission of sociology in several ways. Ferriss in Chapter 11 examines the responsibility and opportunities of sociologists to the task of guiding and controlling the stream of future change in the region. The application of both methods and findings to the well-being of society is a longstanding commitment of the profession. In addition, the set of studies that compose this volume issued from an Annual Meeting program of the Southern Sociological Society. In 1983 the Society asked the Program Committee to plan a series of sessions for the 1986 Annual Meeting to celebrate the Fiftieth Anniversary of the founding of the Society. These studies were a result of that invitation. The sessions went well and, thus encouraged, the scholar-authors decided to publish the collection as a monograph. And thus in the end the activity that began as a routine participation in the Annual Meeting of a professional society may constitute a contribution to the sociological literature.

II

This book is about the South and Southerners. What do these terms mean? *The South* is defined and perceived in three related ways. First, the South is defined in terms of its past, its traditions. By reference to politics, it is called "the Confederate States"; by reference to tradition, "the Old South." The relevant list of states are shown in the columns below.

Confederate States	Old South
Florida	Florida
Alabama	Alabama
Georgia	Georgia
Louisiana	Louisiana
Mississippi	Mississippi
*Texas	*Kentucky
Virginia	Virginia
Arkansas	Arkansas
Tennessee	Tennessee
North Carolina	North Carolina
South Carolina	South Carolina

In 1937 Vance, and in 1970, Killian spoke of the Old South that contained a list different from the Confederacy (see asterisks). These lists recognize both the importance of the Confederacy and the consistency of traditional Southern culture.

Second, the U.S. Census employs another definition of the South that contains seventeen states in three subregions. The three sub-regions are shown in the following lists.

South Atlantic	East South Central	West South Central
Delaware	Alabama	Louisiana
Maryland	Mississippi	Texas
District of Columbia	Tennessee	Arkansas
West Virginia	Kentucky	Oklahoma
Virginia		
North Carolina		
South Carolina		
Georgia		
Florida		

As used in this book, the term *The South* refers to many conceptions. For example, although a specific definition is not designated, in Chapter 1 the text refers to an area most like the Old South. In Chapter 2 the Old South is specified as the referent. In the third chapter the Census definition is employed because the analysis relies on official quantitative data. In Chapter 4 the use of statistical data from an important study dictates a different conception of the South. In all these cases, though, the term South refers to a commonly understood geographic area that is characterized by a unique tradition and history.

The term *South* has a third meaning, often overlooked. It is a quasigroup, a self-conscious collectivity capable of acting as a unit. The people of the region tend to think of themselves as "we" united by shared memories, hurts, values, possessions, longings, and aspirations. They can resent perceived slights, grow angry over alleged mistreatment, exult over symbolic victories, and work for collective goals. In this telic sense the South is often a gigantic social movement.

Southerner is another term that needs clarifying. Just who are Southerners? In general it can be said that Southerners constitute a class of individuals who are differentiated from others by various social and kinship characteristics. Killian (1970) and Reed (1983) identify two defining characteristics of Southerners: first, having lived a substantial portion of one's life in the South, often including being born and growing up in the region; and second, the act of self-identifying as a Southerner. A person who identifies as Southern need not have been born in the region. However, Huff-Corzine, Corzine, and Moore (1986) believe that socialization in the South is the critical delineator of Southerners. Dillman (1986) regards as "truly" Southern only those with several generations of Southern-born and -bred ancestors who are acquainted with Southern history and culture. These characteristics are overlapping and mutually exclusive. Functionally, it can be said that the best criterion is self-identification, which implies some experience in the region.

III

For a long time, observers and scholars have been prophesying and predicting the future course of social change. In general terms, prediction is understood to designate beforehand the outcome of an ongoing course of social change that must or can be expected to occur. In this connection Blackburn (1972, 1) wrote that "we expect uniformities in our experience to be representative." For this reason, he continues, "we award ourselves the right to believe that at least in some respects the future should resemble the past and the unobserved should resemble the observed" (p. 1). Prediction is an act of sociological imagination and is understood to constitute a form of hypothesis. The enterprise of prediction employs conditions known from past experience or novel ones not yet experienced but clearly anticipated. It is thus the process of using known or hypothesized information to describe the changes that are expected to achieve the anticipated outcome.

A pattern of recent change is operationally involved in the act of predicting the foreseeable future. In the South, for example, the transformation of the past and of creating the "present" was a consequence of major dynamic factors—for example, federal social engineering by New Deal and World War II legislation, in-migration of investment capital and industrial leadership, and movement of poor white and black rural workers into the burgeoning urban industrial sites. Predicting future change requires turning the process of past change around. Dynamic change factors must be hypothesized and their consequences inferred.

In this book, such logical exercise offered the scholars two major options. They could assume that change-producing conditions would continue in the future much as they had been in the recent past. In this case, prediction consisted of projecting ongoing processes and patterns of change. The other option was to assume that things in the future would not be the same as they had been in the past. Instead, they would be forced to assume that unknown and unanticipated dynamic factors would cause change in the future. (This option is called "developmental prediction.")

It is evident that both options are available in every predictive situation. Prediction by projection is sometimes a commonsense act of logical inference about the future from knowledge of the past. Projections can be made exact by the use of quantitative data. Nevertheless, McCleary and Hay (1980, 110–12, 206–15) demonstrate that predictions of time series phenomena can also require technical scientific methods. In projective prediction, the stream of change itself is the major dynamic factor.

Developmental prediction may be more complicated than the projective process. The dynamic factors involved may be only casually known and not yet subject to measurement. The novel change factors that affect change at one time are later accepted and integrated in the social system. They then become part of the stream of change that later routinizes the process itself. A substantial portion of future change in any situation will result from the deliberate action of the people concerned. The self-conscious motives of the people, the efforts to plan and control change, the drive to be mainstream, the efforts to solve problems and improve conditions will activate people to engage in social change efforts. (This telic character of the south as a region was discussed above.)

IV

It may be helpful to point out to the reader the fact that this book is organized in several different though related ways. The various differentiations and categories are sometimes deliberate, sometimes required by the data used, and sometimes a function of the methods of the scholars. Whether revealed by an outline or built into the text, the differentiations and categories that are the material of organizations should be fairly evident.

The Table of Contents reveals the formal organization of the book. The Introduction, Chapter I, mentioned above, sets the historical background and moves the reader into the substance of the book. In terms of content, the book consists of eight empirical chapters (2 through 9) that examine social change in specific social areas. These chapters are arranged into three parts and differentiated and characterized by subtitles indicating the methodological perspective of each—"Population Dynamics," "Minority Status," and "Socio-Cultural Orientations." Population dynamics provide the framework to examine increase and diversification, urbanization and industrialization, and aging. Male-female, Hispanic and Anglo, and black and white relations are studied in terms of status differences. Social-cultural patterns are the conceptual context for exploring traditional-mass and Traditionalist-Modernizer orientations of the culture.

The last two chapters, 10 and 11, Part IV, summarize findings and terminate the book. Chapter 10 is a summary of research findings and an inventory of major predictions set out in the empirical chapters. Chapter 11 calls attention to the opportunity and task of planning and controlling future social change in the region and examines the role of sociologists and other social scientists in performing this service. It concludes by asserting that "it [such effort] does make a difference."

Operationally, each of the eight empirical chapters performs two functions that are essential to the goal of the book. First, it examines the processes of social change that transformed the latter-day Old South into what, by the time the book was written, constituted a New South. For the chapter authors, this research function constituted a necessary prelude to reading and predicting the future, the second essential goal of the book. Each chapter undertook to predict, for the foreseeable future, what one aspect of Southern society would be like. These operations are inseparable aspects of the same inclusive process.

JOSEPH S. HIMES

Acknowledgments

Many individuals and organizations have made contributions, large and small, to creating and writing this book. It goes without saying that the multiple authors are grateful for these acts of assistance. As editor, on behalf of these different authors I write this acknowledgment and express thanks to all those who made a contribution to the writing task.

Many graduate students in the various universities represented here assisted the chapter authors and me in a variety of ways. A few of their names are included among the Contributors. They performed a wide range of services for the professors who wrote and edited the manuscripts. Since I do not know all their names, I will refrain from naming the few whom I know. Nevertheless, they should all be reassured that their services are sincerely appreciated and regarded as crucial to the completion of this task.

On behalf of the authors I express thanks to colleagues who counseled and assisted them in various ways. Everyone in academia knows how important and precious this colleagial relationship is to any creative or writing project. For all the authors I communicate their gratitude to colleagues.

In notes, several authors thanked research agencies and other organizations for support given in this writing task. On behalf of all these authors I repeat and support the expression of gratitude for assistance.

In 1985 the Blumenthal Foundation of Charlotte, North Carolina, gave us funds to support the book-writing project. This grant provided crucial financial assistance to make this project come to fruition. On behalf of the authors I express our heartfelt thanks to the Blumenthal Foundation for this timely aid.

The sociology departments of all the authors have made significant contributions. Routinely they have provided typing and word processing service, stationery and other supplies, postal costs, as well as the time of their professors who researched, created, and wrote the various chapters. Speaking for all these authors, I thank the sociology departments of these several universities.

Most important are the contributions of Professors Everett K. Wilson, University of North Carolina, Chapel Hill, and Abbott L. Ferriss, Emory University, for their skillful service in editing the manuscripts. Both men are experienced journal and book editors. Professor Wilson had the time and patience to read and critique all the manuscripts, once meticulously and in some cases twice. Their comments, insights, suggestions, and criticisms have gone far toward transforming first-run manuscripts into finished book chapters. I can say that every author in this book expresses thanks for this critical and creative assistance. And, finally, our appreciation goes to Tarlough Wiggins of the Academic Computing Center of the University of North Carolina at Greensboro for making the tables "camera ready" and for collating and typing the Index, and to the Geography Department of the University of North Carolina at Chapel Hill for technical assistance in preparing the charts for publication.

Again, the several authors of this book express through this statement their gratitude to the persons and organizations who have helped them in ways described above. However, they wish to assure these persons and organizations that they are not held responsible for the judgments and opinions expressed in this book. What is said in any chapter is the responsibility of the author.

JOSEPH S. HIMES
University of North Carolina at Greensboro

The South Moves into Its Future

1

Introduction:
Background of Recent Changes
in the South

Joseph S. Himes

The Civil War was the most traumatic event in the history of the American South, for it separated the Old South from a newer version of the region. It is customary to refer to the region before that calamity as the *Old South,* the *antebellum South,* or the *Traditional South.* Such titles recognize characteristics of the region that are no longer customary.

This chapter will examine some of the changes that differentiated the Old South from this more modern version. The central focuses of this analyses are the changes of social structure and relations that distinguish the transformation of the region.

The Civil War imposed at least three lasting changes on the structure of the region. First, it abolished the legal institution of black slavery and thereby in a single stroke altered the work structure and swept away a major portion of wealth in the region. Second, it necessitated creation of a new labor system of free workers that was based on several credit patterns—sharecropping, the company store, and the advancement of seeds, tools, and supplies to tenants. And third, these changes alienated poor whites and blacks, made them competitors for economic and political values, and established the structure of intergroup competition and controversy.

Growing tired of controlling, punishing, and edifying the traditional leaders of the region, in the late 1870s the Congress withdrew the occupying Union Army; repealed the Reconstruction legislation; liquidated the Freedmen's Bureau; and pardoned the leaders of the Confederacy and the Confederate Army. This action permitted the pre-War leaders of the region to operate again. Rejecting the option to copy the industrial North, the leaders preferred to restore the "Old South" insofar as possible (Current et al. 1983, 484). What they could build was a new version of the old model.

Restoring the Old Structure

Many of the pre-War planters still had or could acquire land, tools, and equipment. They created various novel credit systems with which to hire the jobless blacks and poor whites. Soon they moved to control the entire economy and the state and local governments. In this way they confirmed their claim of being the autocratic cavalier class of the region. Proper social distance was established and maintained between these aristocrats and the lower orders of Southerners.

The new middle-class sector was composed of plantation and factory managers, free-standing and institution-related professionals (doctors, lawyers, ministers, and journalists), and large tradesmen. Although some of these middle-class individuals maintained social contacts with the elites, most were relegated to a distinct lower circle of social activities. Middle-class persons and families also lacked the wealth and power that characterized the aristocracy.

The remainder of the population was regarded as lower-class, even though they occupied several different ranks in the stratified system. Many whites and some blacks in this category owned property and were politically active, voting and holding minor elective and appointed offices of government. The poor whites were often excluded from political participation by the Jim Crow laws, particularly those requiring payment of poll taxes and ownership of property as qualifications for voting. Further, as poor whites many worked as sharecroppers and hired hands on the plantations. They were exploited by plantation owners and threatened by competitive black workers.

Most blacks were relegated to the base of the status ladder and virtually excluded from membership in the polity. The systems of Jim Crow laws, enacted in the late nineteenth century, achieved these ends (Franklin 1980, 266). They could not register and vote, run for or hold public office, serve on juries, or participate in the political parties. They were largely excluded from working in the factories and commercial enterprises of the region. Thus most were confined to tenant work on plantations under the credit systems that kept them impoverished. To protest or resist such treatment constituted open invitation to police abuse or collective violence. Prejudice and custom functioned to separate blacks from all classes of whites.

Under this structural pattern, women were almost as greatly suppressed and abused as in the antebellum South (see Chapter 5). Although they were ceremonially placed on social pedestals and revered, many white women had little or no position in the economic and political affairs of the region. Poor white women fared better than their aristocratic sisters, however. They worked and shared along with their laboring husbands, and they enjoyed respect and consideration. On the plantations many black women became the heads and leaders of their families. They enjoyed high respect and great power in the family and community systems of black society.

The black and white masses in this reconstructed South were typically poor. Incomes of all workers were among the lowest in the nation. Poverty conditioned the housing, subsistence, and clothing of all people. These Southerners belonged to the sector that President Franklin D. Roosevelt in the early 1930s called the most "ill fed, ill clad and ill housed" third of American Society. In the half century before the Great Depression this condition of poverty changed very little.

In the early years of this era, Southern governments and philanthropies provided few public and private services for the citizens. Just after the Civil War some effort was made in this direction. Although the Reconstruction legislatures of the South, including many black representatives and senators, acted to initiate public school systems, after the national government withdrew its control of the region in the late 1870s, little money was appropriated—and most of that went to the service of whites. State governments and local governments made little attempt to provide health and social services to their residents. Some private service was provided by wealthy Southern women, and Northern philanthropy supported public or free schools for poor whites and blacks—for example, the Rosenwald Schools. As a consequence, the experience of poverty in the region was only slightly alleviated.

The Business of Race Conflict

Stabilization of this new class-race social structure was accompanied by extensive interracial controversy and conflict. In the late 1870s and early 1880s the whites established a series of aggressive organizations—for example, the Ku Klux Klan and the White Camelias—to "put the blacks back in their place." For nearly half a century these organizations left a trail of floggings, lynchings, and riots in their wake—and in our national history.

In the 1890s powerless and economically distressed whites and blacks began to find a common cause and tried to cooperate politically under the Populist movement (Frazier 1957, 151–53). In this episode the race struggle was played out as a class struggle. Nevertheless, although the movement was widespread in the region, it achieved little in substantive improvement of social and economic conditions, and it intensified interracial hostility.

Widespread aggressive actions by whites compounded the fear of blacks and led them to perceive their situation as desperate. As far back as the 1890s they began to consider strategies and organizations to protect themselves and improve race relations. In 1898 in a famous speech, Booker T. Washington took a first significant step in this direction. He asserted of blacks and whites: "In all things that are purely social we can be as separate as five fingers, yet one as the hand in all things essential to mutual progress." He urged blacks to obtain useful training as workers and to be respectful, courteous, prudent, and restrained in relations with whites. This speech had a dramatic impact in the region and expressed the philosophy of the pragmatic education that distinguished Tuskegee Institute where Dr. Washington was principal.

However, some members of the black community thought that Washington's strategy was passive and deferential. These spokesmen argued that blacks should demand full participation and democratic justice. Under the leadership of W. E. B. Du Bois, a group favoring this point of view met at Niagara Falls in 1909, discussed the problems, and issued a list of social demands.

These ideologies, together with these and other leaders, generated a series of implementing action organizations, the most successful of which are the National Association for the Advancement of Colored People (NAACP) and the National Urban League (NUL). Even before the First World War these organizations initiated a kind of liberation movement in the black community. Control and repression of this resistance by blacks became a focal preoccupation of Southern whites. It was said that Howard Odum once commented that whenever two or more people gathered, obsession with race relations always dominated their conversation.

World War I

World War I (1914–1917) interrupted this preoccupation of Southern whites with control and exploitation of blacks. We can see clearly now that it marked the end of an era in Southern life and began rotating the region toward the future. The war demanded the attention of all people, both whites as well as blacks, with issues of defense and survival. Wartime conditions affected traditional structures and patterns of Southern life. For the first time since the Civil War, the South was opened to the remainder of the country. Southern young men were sent North, and the Northern recruits were shipped South for military training. This was a novel experience for many of them. In addition, these young men were sent to Europe to fight and there encountered still another cultural shock. Most Europeans had little knowledge of or concern with the Jim Crow practices and exploitative tactics of the South. For many this was a rude awakening. War-related experiences drew other whites and blacks to the North for opportunities that were limited in the South, i.e., industrial jobs, higher education, cultural opportunities, and business enterprises.

Wartime conditions affected traditional structures and patterns of Southern life. Pulling millions of young men up by their social roots had a profound effect on family life and structure in the South, both of their parental families and of their own future families. The Southern economy was transformed into a military institution for the duration of the war. After the fighting, this institution had to be reoriented for peacetime operations. Many blacks left the South, stripping cotton agriculture of its work force and providing Northern industries with a new labor supply.

The war also had important psychic effects on the South. It shook the region out of its traditional lethargy and began to project it into the energetic activity of the industrial North. Under wartime circumstances many of the pleasant customs of the traditional South could no longer be practiced. After the war, it was hard to revive and restore this fabric of comfort and culture. Moreover, many thoughtful people began to question the legitimacy and morality of international war in general and aggressive conflicts in particular. Arendt (1963, 3) reported that as a consequence of the war, many serious people concluded that national aggression is fundamentally criminal and that war is justifiable (if at all) only to ward off or prevent aggression, and that aggressive wars are morally indefensible. At the same time, the South could enjoy the heady gratification of believing that "we" had helped to save the world for democracy and ensure peace of generations to come.

The war also caused a number of novel economic problems. Millions of working-class people experienced a forerunner of "Recession" (Current et al. 1980, 294–95). Mobilization and demobilization severely affected the established labor forces of the South. Structural unemployment was widespread. The full effect of this downward economic slide was not felt until the fall of 1929.

Fundamental change of the South had already begun by the end of World War I. The regional population was in the process of massive change—rural blacks were industrialized in the North and the South's agrarianism declined. Traditionalism of culture, social organization, and power was challenged. The South was opened to let native residents out and "curious Yankees" in. The migration of large numbers of black farm workers to cities worsened race relations in the North. Riot violence increased in the North while lynching and assaults declined in the South. Prejudice and discrimination intensified in Northern cities as Jim Crow abuses and practices tended to abate in the South. As a consequence, the contrast between North and South became perceptively less striking by the onset of the Great Depression (Williams and Jaynes 1989, 60).

The Great Depression and World War II: Toward a New South

World War I prepared the South for fundamental change. However, it required two further world-shaking events to break the South loose from its roots and its past and to propel it into the American mainstream. The two historic events that had this effect were the Great Depression of the 1930s and World War II from 1939 to 1945. Pulled and pushed by the seismic forces issuing from these phenomena, the traditional closed, autocratic, racist, agrarian Southern system gave way to a new-style, large-scale, industrial, bureaucratic, and urban pattern of social organization (see Falk and Lyson 1988).

The Great Depression, and especially the New Deal, affected the South in several crucial ways (Leuchtenburg 1963). Initially, the New Deal stimulated and helped to stabilize the reeling Southern economy. Public assistance through work programs (Works Progress Administration, N.Y.A., etc.) pumped massive injections of ready cash into the financial arteries of the region. These projects supported and extended the urban and general infrastructure of the region—by means of streets and roads, water and sewer systems, and public buildings of many kinds. Workers, families, young people, and the elderly were immediate beneficiaries of these programs. The money they received as wages made its way into the retail system and thence back into the primary structures of the economy.

Of even more importance, the federal legislative engineering actions of the government functioned to bolster and regularize the South's social and economic structures. Labor-relations laws imposed order and dependable regularity upon the intercourse between employers and workers. Wages-and-hours laws and the anti-racial segregation posture of the government signaled a new respect for workers and their services. Blacks were heartened and their opportunities were expanded by the Fair Employment policy of the national government. Unemployment insurance and the Social Security Program gave thousands of Southern people a sense of confidence and feeling of hope they never believed possible. Through the Tennessee Valley Authority the government salvaged, reorganized, and stabilized a vast section of the region that had been peopled in the main by poor, non-slaveowning whites.

The involvement of the United States in World War II at the end of the New Deal functioned to "cure" the Great Depression. The military activities of both the Allies and the United States dramatically increased the demand for agricultural and manufactured resources. As a consequence, unemployment was virtually eradicated. All aspects of the economy—agriculture, industry, transportation, and so on—were operating at peak level. This activity stimulated rapid change in all aspects of national society.

World War II reinforced "the rediscovery" of the South by Yankees and other outsiders (Woodward 1986). As in World War I, Northerners were sent to the South and Southerners were sent North for military training. Adventitiously, training in the South was important for Northerners because it afforded them the chance to observe and learn firsthand about the region. They were impressed in various ways—by the Sunbelt, the traditional hospitality of locals, the courtesy and openness of public officials, the abundance of untapped raw materials, and the vast unused labor force and unexploited market (see Newman 1984, 1). Many of the thoughtful young officers decided that as soon as they were discharged from military service they would return to examine and exploit some of these opportunities.

Indeed, many did return after 1945, bringing with them investment capital, executive and technical personnel, good economic connections in the North, and plans for immediate action. The first-comers acted to expand, update, and utilize existing industries—textiles, tobacco, furniture, and the primary extractives. Another wave of in-migrants came in the late 1960s and 1970s and initiated high-tech industrial development (see Weinstein and Firestein 1978, 19). They stimulated a way of in-migration for the new jobs and opportunities. The third innovative front was in service and sales. Both high-tech and service industries required trained personnel. As a consequence, there was increased in-migration of workers and intensified education of local personnel for the new jobs.

The far-flung travel experiences of both Northern and Southern persons affected the social characteristics of the region. In-migrants brought with them the mass culture of the older urban-industrial sections of the nation. Southerners acquired this cultural veneer as part of their work experience. Traditional, rural-based Southern culture was slowly relegated to remote and isolated enclaves of the region. (See Chapter 8, below.)

In addition, the far-flung military experiences of Southern-bred soldiers affected their racial attitudes and values. Southerners were sometimes uneasy and disturbed by the casual racial relations and contacts they found in Northern localities. Yankee soldiers were also shocked or disturbed by the racial patterns they found in Southern communities. Both learned a good deal from these experiences.

Experiences abroad often affected racial and class attitudes and practices brought from home. For example, aristocratic Southern officers were sometimes required to be respectful or even submissive to a black or other nonwhite head of state; or expected to comply with commands issued by Indian or Malaysian senior officers. Still other soldiers observed or were forced to engage in actions that seemed to contradict and disparage hallowed American values—principles of fair play or civil rights practices.

These and other social forces and conditions tended to push the uncertain South of the early twentieth century off its traditional moorings and turn it toward the mainstream of economic, political, and social life in the rest of America. By the end of World War II, the South was becoming substantially a "new South," as Reed calls it (see Chapter 8). It was a rapidly changing mix of the old and the new, on its way to becoming more new and much less old. This brief historical background is intended to bring the discussion to the point where the other authors will take up the analysis.

Part I

Population Dynamics

In these three chapters the process of urban industrialization of the South is intertwined with the processes of population dynamics. In Chapter 2 Biggar focuses on population dynamics, exploring the issues of relative growth in size, diversification of characteristics, source of increase, and social consequences of these processes. This is the essential overview of the following analyses. In the next chapter Kasarda et al. feed the analysis of urban industrialization into this process and explain why it all happens. In this analysis the emergence and stabilization of the New South are revealed. This approach enables Kasarda and associates to make substantial predictions about the future development of the region. Streib (Chapter 4) draws attention to the fact that rapid growth of an elderly population sector is one major aspect of the change of the South. The study of this process of regional aging is set in the context of the structure and character of Southern life. From this perspective, Streib can make several trenchant predictions of future change.

2

Population Change and Social Adaptation in the South, Past and Future

Jeanne C. Biggar

Fifty years ago, in *Human Geography*, Rupert Vance portrayed the South as a stable population in a regional mosaic of subregions closely tied together by elements of a common culture. He quotes Carl O. Sauer: "South of the Ohio a sense of continuity with the past persists because change has been slow and the tempo of life has not been much accelerated nor its measure syncopated" (Vance 1937, 21). The post-World War II development, along with the invasion of the Yankee migrants (see Chapter 1), has speeded up that earlier tempo of life and brought a synchronization of functional activity quite foreign to the South that Carl Sauer knew. Along with this change has come a continuing increase in population numbers and an altered population composition.

The 1930 South that Vance describes had a population of slightly fewer than 2.5 million, about one-fifth (20 percent) of the nation's total. Despite the net out-migration of both blacks and whites over the next fifty years, by 1980 the South's fifty-one million was a slightly larger proportion (22.4 percent) of the total population. If the national population redistribution patterns of the past three decades persist, the South may increase to approximately one-third of the national total over the next fifty years.

This chapter examines the projections of recent growth patterns in the South; the possible changes in state population numbers; racial, gender, and age compositions; and the possible economic, social, and cultural consequences of these changes.

Methods

The *South* is defined here as Rupert Vance defined it—"The Old South"—including eleven states (see Preface). This definition clusters states that participated in the Civil War and are further unified by the traditional Southern culture.

The data were collected from the 1950, 1960, 1970, and 1980 U.S. Census State Reports (PC series) to provide total, male and female, and black and white population data by five-year age groups.

The first attempt at projection used the standard annual growth rate formula. The population totals for 2036 were so large that even the most enthusiastic Chamber of Commerce representative would be forced to reject them. A simple compromise of demographic sophistication generated three straight-line projections. The first set of estimates is based on a projection of the average of three decades, 1959–80. The second set of estimates projects the growth rate of the most recent decades (1970–80). The third set projects the growth rate of the past thirty years (1950–80) to the next fifty-six years. All three methods depend on assumptions of stable birth and death rates. Furthermore, the methods assume stable net migration rates. This, of course, is a most serious limitation to the research design. At the same time, though, the relative stability of migration streams over time may lend some credibility to these estimates. Because the first projection method gave the most conservative estimates overall, it is the primary method employed here.

Population Estimates for the South, 2036

The earlier national out-migration patterns, South to North and West, were reversed in the late 1960s to bring the balance of net migration flows from other regions into the Southern states. By 1980, the South's population was more than twice the 1930 figure. All three projections estimate even higher growth rates in the next fifty years (see Table 2-1 and Figure 2-1). The most conservative estimate (a) shows a 113 percent increase; the most liberal (c), a 155 percent increase. This means that after fifty years (1930–80), with a stable population of about one-fifth of the U.S. total, the South has real promise of approaching a third of the estimated national total population by 2036.

The projected estimates vary a good deal among the eleven states

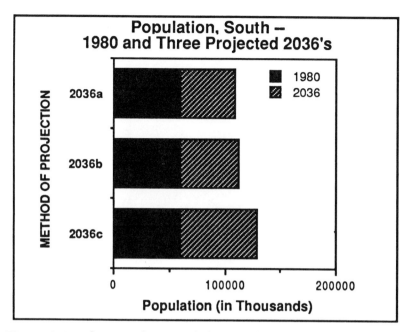

Figure 2-1. The Population of the South, 1980 and Three 2036
          Projections.

in the region (Figure 2-2). In all three estimates, Florida's growth was
the most spectacular. The lowest estimate would multiply its 1980
population by more than four—the highest, by more than five. The
2036 estimate for Virginia, North Carolina, and Georgia all show
sizable increases that will nearly double their 1980 populations.
Nevertheless, the amount of growth and ultimate size-rank among
the states varies by the projection method used. For example, as
noted above, the projected growth rates of Florida are spectacular. By
contrast, Arkansas and Mississippi reveal extremely low future
growth rates.

Projected Changes in Population Composition

Racial Composition

Population estimates (Projection a) for the 2036 black population
in the Southern states reflect consistent increases in total numbers
(Figure 2-3). Note, however, that except in Florida, the fifty-year in-

Table 2-1. Populations (in thousands) of the Southern States, the South, and the United States, by decades 1950-1980 and with three Projections to 2036

GEOGRAPHIC AREAS	1950	1960	1970	1980	2036[a]	2036[b]	2036[c]
STATES							
Virginia	3,319	3,967	4,648	5,347	10,507	9,838	11,445
Kentucky	2,945	3,038	3,219	3,661	5,221	6,469	5,323
North Carolina	4,062	4,556	5,082	5,882	10,208	11,052	10,799
Tennessee	3,292	3,567	3,924	4,591	7,626	8,962	7,975
South Carolina	2,117	2,383	2,591	3,122	5,551	6,706	5,891
Georgia	3,445	3,943	4,590	5,463	10,552	11,276	11,440
Florida	2,771	4,952	6,789	9,746	38,740	33,546	55,533
Alabama	3,062	3,267	3,444	3,894	5,724	6,753	5,872
Mississippi	2,179	2,178	2,217	2,521	3,244	4,455	3,260

Table 2-1. continued.

Arkansas	1,910	1,786	1,923	2,286	3,143	4,705	3,127
Louisiana	2,684	3,257	3,641	4,206	8,021	7,857	8,656
SOUTH	31,786	36,894	42,068	50,719	108,537	111,619	129,321
UNITED STATES	150,687	179,323	203,302	226,541	371,240	371,240	371,240 [d]
SOUTH AS PERCENT OF UNITED STATES	21.1	20.6	20.7	22.4	28.6	30.1	34.1

[a]Projection of average of 1950-60, 1960-70, and 1970-80 percents of population growth.

[b]Projection of 1970-80 growth rate.

[c]Projection of 1950-80 growth rate.

[d]Projection of population reference bureau growth rate (1985).

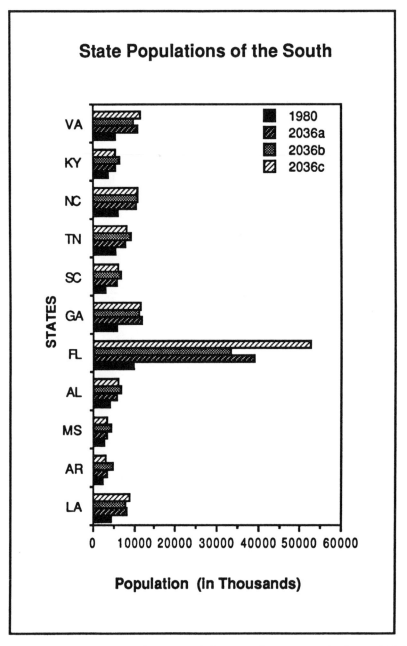

Figure 2-2. State Populations of the South, 1980 and Three 2036 Projections.

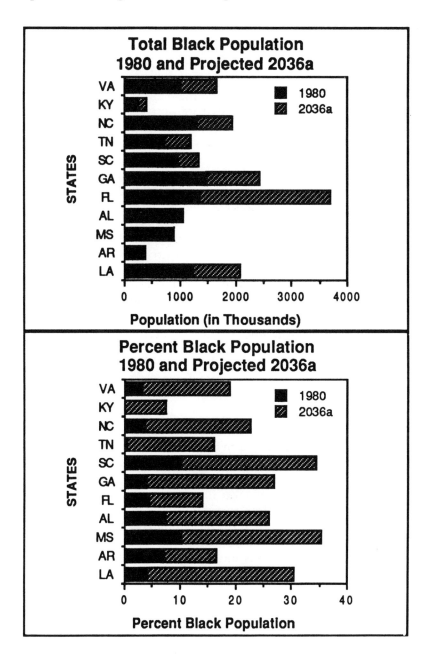

Figure 2-3. Numbers and Percents of State Black Populations, 1980 and Projection 2036a.

crease for blacks is more modest than those for the total population. The data suggest a slight decrease in black population in Mississippi and Arkansas. On the other and, the Florida projection shows nearly a threefold increase in the black population by 2036.

The smaller projected increases for the black population will have a significant impact on the racial distribution of the Southern states. Note in Figure 2-3 that the percent of black population is expected to decline significantly in all states except Kentucky, where no change is apparent, and in Tennessee, with only a small loss in the percent of black population. Even in Florida, which projects close to a 200 percent increase in the number of black residents, the relative proportion of black population will decline by one-third. A similar pattern of decline in the relative racial compositions is apparent in the other two projections as well. This differential is, no doubt, the result of the very sizable white migration streams into the Southern states. While there is now a net in-migration of black population in most states, the size of this stream is still not large enough to equal the white in-migration (Longino et al. 1984). Unless the racial composition of in-migration streams changes radically over the next fifty years, an increasing dominance of white population numbers can be expected.

Gender Composition

The state patterns of projected increases in the female population over the next fifty years are much like those of the projected changes in the black population (see Figure 2-4). While each state shows some growth, only Florida, Alabama, and Mississippi can expect increases that more than double the number of females. The projected change for Florida suggests a threefold increase during the period. On the other hand, in relation to the estimated 2036 population totals, the overall increases for women do not reveal much change in the proportions of the various states. While there is some indication of a feminization of the South, the degree of change is slight.

Age Composition

The projected changes in age composition are another matter (see Figure 2-5). Here we see radical changes in age structure, particularly

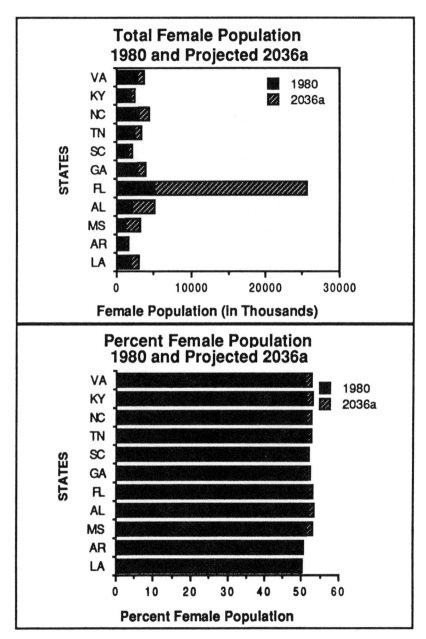

Figure 2-4. Numbers and Percents of State Female Populations, 1980 and Projection 2036a.

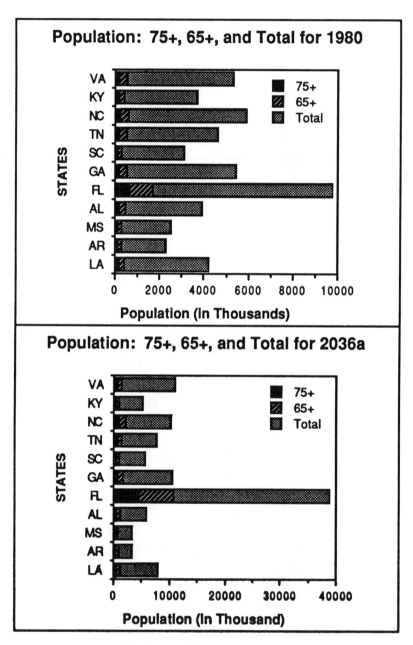

Figure 2-5. State Elderly Populations, 1980 and Projection 2036a.

in terms of the numbers and proportions of the older members in relation to the total population (all ages) over the period. Throughout the 1980s the old-old group—those 75 years and older—have been the most rapidly growing of all age segments (Longino et al. 1984). The 1980–2036 comparisons of the size of the darkest segment of each state's bars bear out that prediction—that is, at least a doubling in the 2036 projection for each state. This is also true in most instances for the changes in the size of the figures of the young-old—those 65 through 74. Particularly dramatic is the estimated increase in both of these segments in Florida, where the most conservative projection indicates more than a fourfold growth. This state may well become the retirement center of the nation, perhaps even of the Western Hemisphere.

The projected changes in age composition for the black population show a similar pattern (see Figure 2-6). The change in the proportion of blacks over the period shows a doubling of elderly blacks in relation to other ages in Alabama, Mississippi, and Arkansas. Surprisingly, however, proportional changes for elderly blacks in Florida are lower than in any of the other states. This is doubtless a consequence of white domination of the in-migration streams (Biggar 1984).

Considering the gender differentials in mortality rates, the differences in male and female increases among the elderly over the next fifty years are not surprising (Figure 2-7). Nevertheless, both the size of the increases and the degree of gender differentials are greater than we would expect. In each state the relative size of both male and female elderly components more than doubles. Florida once again shows a radical change. The male component of the elderly population is estimated to increase fourfold; the female, more than sixfold. Additionally, the relative balance of males and females among the 1980 elderly may be changed radically according to all the 2036 estimates. In no state is the 2036 sex ratio larger than two males for every three females. In Florida the fifty-year sex ratio is even lower. This is somewhat surprising in light of the fact that the majority of migrants from the north come as couples to this "Fun and Sun" state (Biggar 1984).

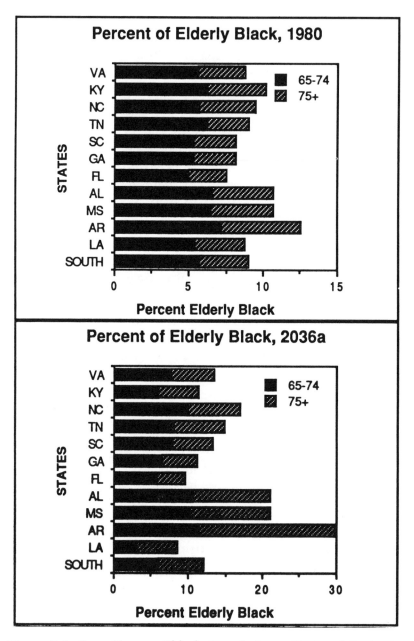

Figure 2-6. State Percent Elderly Populations, 1980 and Projection
2036a.

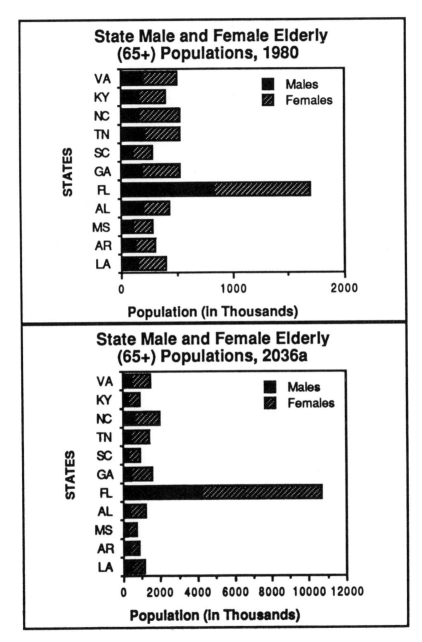

Figure 2-7. State Male and Female Elderly Populations, 1980 and Projection 2036a.

Alternate Projected Population Age-Sex Structures for Florida

The extremely high growth patterns reflected in the projections just discussed make Florida an interesting case study for estimating its age-sex composition for 2036. To understand the results of such an exercise in projection, however, we need to examine the patterns of growth in Florida since World War II.

In 1950, Florida was one of the smaller states in the South (see Table 2-1). The population of 2,750,000 placed it in seventh place among the eleven Southern states. However, its phenomenal growth (78.7 percent) over the next decade moved it into the top rank when the population reached nearly five million. Florida maintained this dominance in the South by adding almost two million people in each of the next two decades, so that by 1980 it could report nearly ten million residents.

Comparison of Florida's population pyramids for 1950 and 1980 shows the extent of that growth as well as the radical impact of in-migration on the state's age-sex structure during the intervening thirty years. Two distortions in the 1980 age-sex structure exerted significant effects on the 2036 projections. The first was seen in the young-adult age categories. Some bulge was revealed here, since most in-migration streams include many young adults who are entering the labor force or making early career moves. No doubt the sons and daughters of recent in-migrants as well as out-of-state students in Florida's major educational institutions add to the distortion of these younger age segments.

The second distortion was found in the upper part of the pyramid, where the pre-retirement categories (fifty years and older) move out from the middle career age segment, and the first retirement age group (65–69) holds the larger population segment. The distortion in the older ranks of the pyramid stems from the long-term gains from elderly in-migration to Florida. For the last two decades, Florida has attracted more than one-fourth of the nation's interstate elderly migrants. In 1970, one of every five of Florida's older persons (60 and older) had moved into that state within the previous five years. By 1980, this had increased to nearly one of every four of the elderly population (Longino et al. 1984). The changing age structure over this period doubled the 1950 Aged Dependence Ratio from 133.5 to 27.2 in 1980. This means a change from one older person for every eight persons in the labor force ages to one older person for every four of younger ages.

A radical change in Florida's age structure since 1950 would move the fifty-six-year projections into the realm of fantasy. To explore this possibility, two radical projections of the age-sex structure were employed. The first was the straight-line projection of the 1970–80 age-sex specific population increases (2036b, see above). This was chosen because Florida's 1970–80 growth rate was lower than the three-decade rate or the three-decade average rate and, therefore, produced the smallest projected increases. The second was the projection of the 1950–80 growth rate, which for Florida showed the highest increase of the three projections (2036c). In a sense, then, we may have a lower and upper limit of population increase over the next half century.

Applying these projection models in two age sex pyramids enabled us to project possible future sizes of the state's population and to perceive some of the socioeconomic consequences of such radical population growth. The 2036b age sex structure radically affected relations among population segments. It produced an age dependency ratio of 38.5, which is about 50 percent higher than that of the 1980 age structure. Such an Aged Dependency Ratio would mean about two older persons for every five persons in the working ages.

The 2036c projection tends to exaggerate even more the distortions of the 1980 structure. This age structure yields an Aged Dependence Ratio of 87.8, i.e., nearly nine older persons for every ten persons between the ages of 15 and 64. This 2036 ratio more than doubles that of the first projection discussed above.

Whether the more conservative or the more radical projection is viewed, clearly Florida is likely to experience extraordinary population growth over the next fifty years. Furthermore, the state can expect serious distortions in both the younger and the older segments of the age structure. In the following section it is pointed out that this situation is producing a serious politico-economic dilemma for the state.

Implications of Future Population Growth in the South

Realization of Predicted Trends

The fifty-year projections of recent growth rates among the Southern states in relation to the projected U.S. totals indicate a radical shift toward increasing dominance in the size of the Southern population. The factors that might intervene in the projected growth rates to alter the degree and direction of growth are examined here. The first factor to consider is the possible changes in the trends of the components of population growth. Marked changes in the birth or death rates would change both total numbers and the shape of the age-sex structures. However, at present, such changes seem unlikely. The South, once known as the seedbed of the nation because of its high fertility rates, is now very similar to the rest of the nation in terms of both natality and mortality (Hamilton 1964). Even racial differentials in births and deaths have virtually disappeared over the last two decades. Because of the stability of these vital rates in both the South and nationwide, population change has come through population redistribution. In the South such change has resulted primarily from net in-migration.

If the fertility and mortality norms of the in-migrant urban residents exceed the vital norms of the more traditional rural population, the increase of population will come from growth through migration. However, an increase in national fertility norms will generate more radical population increases than these projections indicate.

A second factor that may invalidate these projections involves unforeseen decreases in the recent in-migration trends. Such trends in migration would reduce the population increases projected here. Finally, despite the persistence of migration streams once they are established, changes in industrial structures as described by Kasarda et al. (see Chapter 3) will alter occupational structures in ways that will bring changes in age-specific rates, particularly among those of the young adult years. Such changes, however, would alter the age-sex pyramid more than the projected population size.

Whatever structural changes may lie ahead, there are no clear indications at this time that in-migration rates will soon abate. The net in-migration rates from the Northeast and the North Central to the Southern states have been increasing since 1960, particularly among the young-adult and retired white populations (Biggar 1979). Since 1970, North Carolina, South Carolina, Georgia, and Tennessee have followed close behind the rest of the South in terms of growth, particularly among the elderly.

Environmental Consequences

Despite the vagaries of these population projections, clearly the South can expect continued growth in the numbers of its residents.

Continually increasing population numbers will bring an increased press on the natural environment—the availability of open rural areas, water supplies, and even fresh air. "The rural southerner now finds his hunting fields covered with subdivisions, and his favorite bass-fishing lake churned by water skiers all summer so that the fish don't bite anymore" (Thatcher 1978). Further, Southern states and localities will find increasing demands for public utilities—construction and maintenance of streets and highways, the expansion of sewer and water facilities, improvement of street and air traffic controls, and the development of regulations to retard air pollution from increased automobile emissions and industrial toxins. The expansion of government to meet environmental hazards will be associated with increased demand for public services—education, welfare, and protective programs. During rapid increases in such demands, "meticulous long-range planning yields to crisis bandaid responses" (Biggar 1979). However, this increased burden on state and local governments will be associated with parallel demands for housing and retail services, as well as shifts in the industrial structure (see Kasarda et al., Chapter 3). The balance between demands on and increased revenues to local and state governments will vary from place to place.

Race, Sex, Age Implications

Projected changes in population composition present further challenges. The preponderance of young adult and older white migrants in the South suggests a changing racial balance in future years. Moreover, the movement of new migrants into suburban areas exacerbates socioeconomic and racial segregation in Southern metropolitan areas, as the central cities are abandoned to black residents while suburbs increase their number of white residents. The South must be vigilant lest the increasing white plurality in population numbers, as well as the racial redistribution in metropolitan areas, be translated into the political domination of the black population, which typified the preintegration period. Such a new segregation pattern, frozen into a visible apartheid, would create grievous problems affecting every sector of Southern life (see Chapter 7). Furthermore, the projected changes in the sex ratio, particularly the increasing feminization of the elderly population, may bring new demands for social services for the dependent frail elderly in the coming years (see Chapter 4).

Clearly, the age biases that characterize the projected population increases in Florida suggest that public demands will shift to meet the needs of young tax-paying adults and the older service-demanding elderly. The projected changes of the demands by the elderly population will challenge the growth rate of retail and protective services provided. At the same time, the probable increase in the age dependence ratios suggests a more conservative political climate (which may discourage the very changes demanded to serve this new population). Further, the bimodal distribution in age structures, which may develop from the projections discussed here (i.e., the extraordinary growth of the young and old age segments), creates an environment ripe with the possibilities for conflict between generations. The proportionally shrinking middle-age sector may be challenged to work out ways in which to buffer such conflicts.

The Changing South

Finally, the impacts of in-migration have increased and will continue to increase the social and cultural heterogeneity of the region. For example, a broad spectrum of speech types is already evident in most Southern metropolitan areas. However, as Reed points out (Chapter 8), the "Old South" continues in the traditional pockets of the rural areas. At the same time in which many different cultural styles have proliferated within the region, the social and cultural South as a whole has increasingly come to resemble the nation as a whole. Whatever social indicator is chosen—education, income, or occupation—measures of the Southern population move closer and closer to the national average. The development of the performing arts, particularly in the metropolitan areas, have generated orchestras, ballet, and drama companies that rival those found in the Northeast. In the process of these social and cultural changes, the distinguishing characteristics of both Yankees and Southerners have, then, been blurred in the blending of earlier regional styles of living.

The South as Carl Sauer knew it has changed radically in the past fifty years. If the projections of recent growth and changing composition have any modicum of validity, the South will change even more radically in the next fifty years. The nature of the alterations in the social and industrial fabric that may accompany such population changes is described in the following chapters.

Acknowledgment

Thanks to Kelvin Pollard for initial preparation of the graphs and tabular presentations—and to N.I.A. for grants that supported earlier work on elderly migration cited here.

3

Demographic and Economic Restructuring in the South

John D. Kasarda,
Holly L. Hughes, and
Michael D. Irwin

In this chapter we tell the remarkable story of the South's metamorphosis from a rural-oriented, economically stagnating, people-exporting region to a metropolitan-dominated employment dynamo presently attracting millions of migrants. We commence with an overview of the region's demographic and economic trajectory since the colonial era. We then document the trends in contemporary migration and industrial development that are shaping the region. The chapter concludes with a set of projections that forecast the size, composition, and distribution of the South's population and its economic base over the next half century.

The South in Historical Perspective

As early as the colonial era, the Southeast had developed regional, social, and economic patterns. Like the rest of the Atlantic seaboard, the colonial economy of the Southeast centered on primary resource production. But, unlike the Northern colonies, the climate of the Southeast was suited to the production of cash crops especially valuable to England (Jackson et al. 1981). In Virginia, South Carolina, North Carolina, and Georgia, relatively autonomous plantations produced rice, silk, tobacco, and cotton for export, while importing staples and manufactured goods directly from England (Hawley 1981). The Northern colonies harvested furs and fish, products neither so lucrative nor so plentiful as Southern agricultural products. This led to an unfavorable balance of trade between the Northern colonies and England, which encouraged their development of manufactured goods for domestic consumption along with the reexportation, through their port cities, of the South's agricultural products to England and other European countries. The main Southern port, Charleston, South Carolina, operated primarily as a regional distribution center, importing slaves from Africa and exporting agricultural products through Northern gateways to England.

The economic specialization of these two colonial regions resulted in markedly different patterns of population distribution. The South remained deconcentrated with few major cities, while the Northern colonies developed large maritime commercial cities, most notably Boston, New York, and Philadelphia. Although initial advantages favored the growth of Southern cities, by the end of the colonial period these advantages were waning. Northern cities, oriented to the North Atlantic trade routes, were better situated to capture national population and economic growth.

With the nation's independence, commercial ties with England were severed and Southern trade was reoriented to the North, both for the sale of crops and for acquisition of staples and manufactured goods. The new Southern market provided an economic boost to Northern cities as did the movement of people to midwestern territories, whose commerce was channeled via canals and other waterways through the Northeast corridor. Southern cities, on the other hand, continued to function as distributional centers for their hinterlands, so that their development was limited largely to growth in Southern agriculture.

During the first half of the nineteenth century, Northern states developed their manufacturing base, specializing initially in cotton textile production. Southeastern states increasingly concentrated their agricultural production in cotton, and the newly settled areas of Alabama, Mississippi, and Louisiana followed suit. By 1850 the South was one of the world's leading producers of cotton and was the preferred source of this fiber for textile production (Hammond 1897).

The effects of this shift toward a single-crop economy increased regional uniqueness. With the locus of economic activity concentrated on the plantation, the South remained rural, while growth in the Northeast became increasingly urbanized. In addition, the exigencies of cotton production led to markedly different forms of class and economic relations, which further differentiated Southern and Northern social systems (Fligstein 1981).

The development of rail transportation and the Civil War widened these regional differences. The rail system followed existing water routes, reinforcing the North's locational advantage for urban and industrial growth (Duncan and Lieberson 1971). Moreover, the Civil War left the South in a state of economic distress, undercapitalized with transportation lines disrupted and many cities destroyed.

Following the Civil War, Northern capital and world demand for textiles continued to encourage Southern specialization in cotton. Whereas the uniquely Southern system of plantation production ended with the Civil War, it was replaced by the equally specialized social innovation of tenant farming. The social and economic changes associated with tenant farming spread to Oklahoma and Texas as these states were incorporated into the expanding cotton belt economy. By the end of the nineteenth century, the South exhibited a social, economic, and ecological character that clearly distinguished it from the rest of the nation.

The same factors that solidified the South as a region encouraged the social and economic development of the West. Before the Civil War, the West was largely undeveloped. While its agricultural potential and mineral resources were identified, the region lacked an effective transportation system to exploit them.

The Civil War encouraged the U.S. government to underwrite two transcontinental rail lines, one through the Southwest and the other through the mountain states to San Francisco, both bypassing the South (Duncan and Lieberson 1971). The effects of the rail lines on Western development were dramatic. In 1850, the West had less than 1 percent of the U.S. population, and virtually all of its territory was unsettled frontier. By 1900, the Western frontier had largely disappeared, and the region had captured nearly 6 percent of U.S. population. Although much economic development was dependent upon mining, the West's economy also began moving toward a diversified agricultural base (Perloff et al. 1960).

In the Northern tier of the nation, the transformation from a rural to an urban society was proceeding apace. Most of the work force had shifted from agriculture to manufacturing and services, and the population was increasingly concentrating in urban places, especially larger cities. Whereas overall urbanization and manufacturing were less developed in the Midwest than in the Northeast, the rate of expansion was far more rapid, with cities such as Chicago, Milwaukee, Pittsburgh, and Cincinnati replacing many of the Northeastern cities as major centers of population and industrial growth (Duncan and Lieberson 1971). Chicago, for instance, which was incorporated in 1833 with just 4,100 residents, had grown to more than two million residents by 1910.

The South, accounting for nearly a third of the nation's population, was a bystander during America's urban-industrial explosion. No large city in the South developed a significant manufacturing base, and cotton production continued to dominate its economy. The lack of industrial diversity left Southerners largely dependent on Northern goods, and much of the limited manufacturing industry that did exist in the South was controlled by Northern capital (Fligstein 1981; Woodward 1974; Woodman 1968). Thus, while the South experienced significant post-Civil War growth in cotton production, the aggregate wealth of its population increased relatively little.

Twentieth-Century Developments

As far back as 1900, the West showed signs of following Northern trends in urbanization and industrialization. Forty percent of its small population base had settled in urban areas, much of this in a few large cities such as San Francisco. Unlike the South, though, Western agriculture became increasingly diversified, complementing its strong mining and burgeoning manufacturing and service industries. With efficient rail transportation lines crosscutting the region and linking it to the East, the basic requisites for rapid demographic growth of the West were in place.

Table 3–1 shows that, in the first half of the twentieth century, the West more than doubled its share of the national population. This gain came at the expense of the Northern tier, which declined from 62 percent of the population in 1900 to 56 percent in 1950. The population of the South remained relatively unchanged during this period, at 32 percent of the national total.[1]

These distributions, however, conceal major differential migration flows among regions. From 1910 to 1960, the South experienced significant net migration losses to the North and West. The largest number of out-migrants were poor whites and blacks, responding to agricultural distress and stagnating local economics in much of the South. The Southern share of the nation's population remained constant because of the high fertility rates of its rural population (Taeuber and Taeuber 1971, 396). The North was also a net exporter of

Table 3-1.   Number (in thousands) and Percent of National Population by Regions,[a] 1900–1985[1]

Year	Frostbelt		South		West	
	Number	Percent	Number	Percent	Number	Percent
1900	47,380	62.4	24,524	32.3	4,091	5.4
1910	55,802	60.7	29,344	31.9	6,826	7.4
1920	63,682	60.2	33,126	31.3	8,903	8.4
1930	73,021	59.5	37,858	30.8	11,896	9.7
1940	76,120	57.8	41,666	31.6	13,883	10.5
1950	83,939	55.7	47,197	31.3	19,562	13.0
1960	96,297	54.0	54,973	30.8	27,194	15.2
1970	105,612	52.3	62,795	31.1	33,731	16.7
1980	108,001	48.0	75,372	33.5	41,805	18.6
1985	109,055	46.0	81,877	34.5	46,046	19.4

[1]Sources: Bureau of the Census, Census of Population, 1900 to 1980 and 1985 Current Population Survey machine-readable files.

[a]"Frostbelt" (Northeast and Midwest), South, and West (excluding Alaska and Hawaii).

people, primarily to the West; and, since its large urban population maintained relatively low fertility levels, the region's share of national population declined. The West made consistent proportional gains during the first half of the twentieth century—primarily through in-migration—while maintaining levels of fertility only slightly higher than the North.

During the second half of this century, the West continued to grow at a rapid rate, more than doubling its population between 1950 and 1985. The South, though expanding in absolute numbers, actually grew at a slower rate than the nation during the 1950s. It wasn't until the 1960s that Southern growth exceeded that of the nation as a whole. Between 1970 and 1985, the Southern population surged, with the region adding more than fifteen million residents, compared with 12.3 million in the West and only 4.4 million in the Northeast and Midwest combined.

The regional economic changes, alluded to previously, greatly influenced patterns of population change. Table 3-2 presents the post-1900 growth and redistribution of employment, by region, in primary resource production, manufacturing, and all other industries combined. The transformation of the nation's employment structure is clearly seen. In 1900, primary resource employment (agriculture, forestry, fisheries, mining) constituted 42 percent of national employment, 31 percent of employment in the North, 40 percent in the West, and nearly two-thirds of total employment in the South. In 1940, the corresponding percentages were 20 for the nation, 13 in the North, 19 in the West, and 33 in the South. By 1985, primary resource employment had declined to 3 percent of total employment in the North and to less than 5' percent of all employment in the South and West.

Throughout the first forty years of the century, manufacturing employment exhibited relatively more stable proportions of national and regional totals. These ranged from 31 to 38 percent in the North, from 12 to 19 percent in the South, and from 13 to 25 percent in the West. Basic economic restructuring followed from steadily declining shares of employment in primary resource industries, which were more than compensated for by gains in the construction and service industries of each region. Thus, between 1900 and 1940, the percent employed in construction and services expanded in the North from 38 to 61 percent, in the South from 24 to 52 percent, and in the West from 39 to 68 percent.

Since World War II, a number of economic, political, and tech-

Table 3-2. Trends in Number (in millions) and Percent of Workers by Region and Industry

Region & Industry	1900 #	1900 %	1920 #	1920 %	1940 #	1940 %	1960 #	1960 %	1980 #	1980 %	1985 #	1985 %
US												
Total	29	100	42	100	53	100	65	100	94	100	107	100
Primary[a]	12	42	12	29	10	20	5	8	4	4	4	4
Mfg	7	25	13	31	12	22	18	27	22	22	21	20
Others	10	33	17	40	31	59	42	65	72	73	81	76
Frostbelt[b]												
Total	19	100	26	100	32	100	36	100	47	100	49	100
Primary[a]	6	31	5	19	4	13	2	6	1	3	1	3
Mfg	6	31	10	38	8	27	11	32	12	26	11	23
Others	7	38	11	43	19	61	22	62	33	72	37	74

West

Total	1.7	100	4	100	6	100	10	100	19	100	21	100
Primary[a]	.7	40	1	29	1	19	.7	7	.8	5	.9	4
Mfg	.3	20	.9	25	.8	13	2	21	3	18	4	17
Others	.7	40	2	46	4	68	7	71	15	78	17	79

South

Total	9	100	12	100	16	100	19	100	32	100	36	100
Primary[a]	6	64	6	49	5	33	11	21	2	5	2	5
Mfg	1	12	2	19	2	15	4	21	6	21	6	18
Others	2	24	4	32	8	52	13	68	24	75	28	77

Sources: Perloff et al. 1960, Bureau of the Census 1970, Census of Population, Bureau of the Census 1980, Census of Population, Bureau of the Census 1985, Current Population Survey, machine-readable files.
[a] Agriculture, forestry, fisheries, and mining.
[b] Frostbelt includes Northeast and Northwest regions.

nological forces have combined to accelerate industrial restructuring and shift the nation's employment growth pole—first to the West and then to the South. The rapid postwar growth of aerospace, defense, solid-state electronics, and other advanced technology industries not tied to deep water sites (together with expanding construction and services), spurred the economies of the far West, especially California. Growth of these industries was instrumental in attracting more than three million migrants to California alone from 1945 to 1960 (Bureau of the Census 1975).

With diversified economic expansion continuing in the West, the region's total employment doubled between 1960 and 1985. Nevertheless, the South emerged in the 1960s as the nation's leader in absolute employment gains. From 1960 to 1985, the South added eighteen million jobs to its economy, compared with a growth of slightly less than eleven million in the West and the same number in the Northeast and North Central regions combined.

The South's attractiveness for industrial growth is a function of dramatically improved accessibility to national and international markets via newer interstate highway systems and expanding air transportation, shifting energy sources and costs, more modern physical plants, a benign climate, and relatively lower taxes and wage rates interacting with a changing structure of the national economy and negative features of the concentrated northern metropolis (e.g., congestion, strong unions, high land costs, and taxes—see Chapter 1). To these technological and financial considerations were added healthy doses of progrowth attitudes and industrial boosterism on the part of Southern states and communities (Cobb 1982, 1984; Goldfield 1982; Kasarda 1980). Thus Table 3-2 shows that, while manufacturing employment in the Frostbelt (Northeast and North Central regions) declined by more than 500,000 jobs between 1960 and 1985, manufacturing employment in the South grew by more than two million. This table further reveals that employment growth in Southern manufacturing was far overshadowed by remarkable increases in construction and services, which added more than fifteen million jobs to the South's economy between 1960 and 1985.

Comparison of the regional employment distributions in 1900 and 1985 shows that the South has experienced the most dramatic economic metamorphosis. It is the only region to exhibit a larger percent of its labor force in manufacturing in 1985 than at the turn of the century (18 versus 12). Moreover, the South has exhibited the greatest declines in percentages employed in primary sector industries (from 64 to 5) and largest increase in percentages employed in construction and services (from 24 to 77). These transformations have resulted in structural convergence of the regional economies, as may be observed by the close interregional correspondence in percent employed across the industrial sectors in 1985.

Recent Migration and Demographic Shifts

The expanding economies of the West and South during the past three decades attracted major streams of migrants. The net regional migration exchanges shown in Table 3-3 clearly reveal the nation's shifting demographic growth poles—from the West to the South. Before 1970, the West was the net beneficiary of migration streams from all census regions. These streams were especially large during the 1950s. During the 1970s, more persons from the West began moving to the South than vice-versa, while net flows from the Northeast and Midwest to the South rose dramatically. Between 1970 and 1980 overall net migration to the South more than doubled that to the West. Spurred by a dramatic increase in net flows from the Midwest, net migration to the South nearly tripled that to the West between 1980 and 1985. During the past fifteen years, both the Northeast and Midwest experienced net migration losses of nearly three million, with the South becoming their chief beneficiary.

What accounts for such large interregional net migration shifts, especially the dramatic turnaround of the South from a net exporter of people (as late as the 1950s) to the powerful human magnet it then became in the 1970s and 1980s? As suggested in Chapter 1, there are a number of reasons, economic and non-economic: (1) a growing footloose retirement population who have private pensions, Social Security payments, and other sources of income not tied to specific locations and who have sought the milder winter climates that the South, in particular, provides; (2) the introduction and spread of central air-conditioning systems, which allow far more comfortable summertime living and working conditions; (3) life-style changes oriented to more recreation and year-round outdoor activities; (4) changing racial attitudes permitting blacks and Hispanics new opportunities to participate in mainstream economic and social institutions; (5) a more progressive political orientation and an increasingly cosmopolitan atmosphere in the metropolitan South that

Table 3-3. Net Interregional Migration Flows, 1955 to 1985

Regional Migration	Net Migration (in thousands)					
Exchanges	1955-60[a]	1965-70[b]	1970-75[c]	1975-80[d]	1980-85[d]	
South with						
Northeast	314	438	964	945	737	
Midwest	122	275	790	813	1,100	
West	-380	-56	75	176	60	
Total	56	657	1,829	1,935	1,897	
West with						
Northeast	285	224	311	518	234	
Midwest	760	415	472	634	475	
South	380	56	-75	-176	-60	
Total	1,425	695	708	976	649	

Midwest with					
Northeast	40	53	67	146	50
South	-122	-275	-790	-813	-1,100
West	-760	-415	-472	-634	-475
Total	-842	-637	-1,195	-1,302	-1,525
Northeast with					
Midwest	-40	-53	-67	-146	-50
South	-314	-438	-964	-945	-737
West	-285	-224	-311	-518	-234
Total	-639	-715	-1,342	-1,609	-1,021

[a]Bureau of the Census. 1960. Census of the Population, vol. 1, Table 237.
[b]Bureau of the Census. 1970. Census of Population, vol. 1, Table 274.
[c]Bureau of the Census. 1975. Current Population Reports, "Mobility of the Population of the U.S."
[d]Bureau of the Census. 1980, 1985. Current Population Survey machine-readable files.

has altered the antiquated redneck image many Northerners and Westerners had of the South; (6) generally lower land, living, and amenity costs; (7) a dramatic improvement in the quantity and quality of consumer services brought about largely by rising personal income levels; and (8) the emergence of the South as the nation's leading economic growth area for reasons discussed previously (for additional discussion, see Biggar 1979 and Kasarda 1980).

What about the demographic composition of Southern migrants? Table 3-4 presents the South's net migration exchanges with other regions, by race and ethnicity, between 1975 and 1980 and between 1980 and 1985. These exchanges, computed from the Census's Current Population Survey tapes, show that nonhispanic whites account for nearly 90 percent of recent Southern migration gains from other regions. Indeed, both the absolute number and percentage of net migrants to the South who are nonhispanic white rose from the 1975–80 period to the 1980–85 period. Of related interest, the migration of nonhispanic blacks from other regions to the South declined from 195,000 between 1975 and 1980 to 87,000 between 1980 and 1985, with most of this slowdown resulting from a 59,000 drop in black migrants from the Northeast. Furthermore, the nonhispanic black migration stream from the South to the Northeast increased by 50,000 between the 1975–80 and 1980–85 periods. Conversely, nonhispanic black migration to the South from the Midwest increased by 45,000 over these two periods.

Another migration stream of growing importance to the South is movers from abroad, especially Hispanics and Asians. Movers to the South from abroad have increased from 505,000 between 1955 and 1960 to 1.2 million between 1980 and 1985. Today, the South and West absorb most of the immigration to the United States. Since 1975, more than 2.8 million movers from abroad have settled in the West; 2.3 million in the South; 1.7 million in the Northeast; and 1 million in the Midwest. More detailed analysis of these data by race and ethnicity reveals that during the last ten years the South has exhibited major increases in Hispanic immigrants, falling closely behind the West. The South has also shown increases in Asian immigrants but still substantially trails the West as the regional destination of this group.

With increased migration from abroad supplementing substantial net interregional migration flows to the South and West, recent population growth in these regions has dwarfed that of the Northeast

Table 3-4. Southern Interregional Net Migration Exchanges (in thousands) by Race, 1975–80 and 1980–85[a]

| Race | Regional Migration Exchanges with the South | | | |
	Total	Northeast	Midwest	West
Non-Hispanic White				
1975-80	1,638	731	762	145
1980-85	1,695	630	981	84
Non-Hispanic Black				
1975-80	195	139	30	26
1980-85	87	30	67	-10
Hispanic				
1975-80	105	64	21	20
1980-85	108	51	51	6
Asian and Other				
1975-80	-1	12	2	-15
1980-85	8	28	0	-20

Sources: [a]Bureau of the Census. 1980. Current Population, machine-readable files.

Bureau of the Census. 1985. Current Population, machine-readable files.

and Midwest. Between April 1, 1980, and July 1, 1985, the population of the South expanded by 6,654,000; the West by 4,486,000; the Northeast by 724,000; and the Midwest by 331,000. In other words, the South and the West accounted for more than 90 percent of the nation's 12.2 million population increase during the first half of the 1980s.

Recent Employment Shifts

A fundamental reason for the substantial growth of the South during the past decade has been the region's ability to weather recessions better than the economies of other regions. Economists have argued that areas dominated by employment in older, cyclically sensitive industries (such as automobile parts, machine tools, textiles, and steel) will experience more severe downturns in their local employment during recessions than areas where the employment mix is predominantly newer service-sector industries. Others have argued that factors such as local business climate, federal fiscal involvement, and local ecological conditions—for example, population density and transportation access—contribute substantially to an area's ability to compete for jobs during recessions as well as periods of economic growth.

In fact, both industrial mix and unique competitive factors contribute to the economic performance of a region. To determine the relative importance of these factors to the emergence of the South as an employment growth pole, we have analyzed county-level employment changes within each of the four census regions using shift-share analysis (Dunn 1960, 1980; Perloff et al. 1960). This technique disaggregates employment change for any area into that resulting from (1) national growth; (2) the area's industrial mix; and (3) unique features of the locality. This final term—labeled the *shift component* or *competitive effect*—is the residual in an area's employment change that cannot be explained by national employment change or by an area's industrial composition.

Shift-share analysis allows us to assess the relative importance of each component of regional employment change during the two most recent national recessions (1974–76 and 1980–82) and during two growth periods (1976–78 and 1978–80).[2] To shed further light on the employment shifts, counties within each region were categorized along an urban-rural continuum, ranging from the largest, metropolitan central-city counties to counties containing no place of 2,500 or more.

Changes in Employment

The Northeast and Midwest experienced considerable employment losses during the most recent recessions. The Midwest was hit particularly hard during the 1980–82 recession, losing more than 1.2 million jobs. Employment declines were pervasive across all types of Midwest counties. The Northeast, on the other hand, lost only 64,000 jobs during the 1980–82 recession, down sharply from its 762,000 decline during the 1974–76 recession.

The South, which lost 96,000 jobs during the 1974–76 recession, actually gained 612,000 jobs during the 1980–82 recession. During this latest recession, small job declines in the nonmetropolitan counties were more than offset by large employment increases in all metropolitan counties. In addition, during the national business cycle upswing from 1976 to 1980, the South added nearly four million jobs.

Employment in the West, which grew during both recessions, also increased substantially during the economic upswing. But the West's economy during the 1980–82 recession was weaker than the South's. Whereas the South gained more than 500,000 jobs, the West added only 18,000 jobs between 1980 and 1982. Furthermore, the West lost jobs in metropolitan areas during this recession, while Southern metropolitan areas gained large numbers of jobs.

Industrial Mix

The Northeast weathered the 1980–82 recession much better than it did the 1974–76 recession primarily because of the increasingly favorable industrial mix in its more populous counties, especially its large metropolitan areas. These areas were successful in restructuring their employment bases away from goods processing toward information processing and other services. In the smaller metropolitan counties and all nonmetropolitan counties of the Northeast, a large share of the labor force remains in slow growth industries.

The Midwest had a generally disadvantageous industrial mix throughout the business cycle. During the most recent recession, the industrial mix in all Midwestern county types (except large, central-city counties) hurt the region's economy. A loss of 52,000 jobs during the 1980–82 recession can be attributed to the region's slow growth industries.

Likewise, the overall industrial mix of the South was not conducive to employment growth. However, the more urbanized Southern counties did have an industrial mix that contributed to employment growth during both business cycle downturns and upswings. The robust industrial mix of its larger urbanized areas, nevertheless, did not compensate for the disadvantaged industrial structure of its nonmetropolitan counties.

The West's industrial mix was favorable to employment growth in all types of counties during economic booms and busts. Western metropolitan core counties had the best mix of high growth industries of all central-city counties in the nation. Interestingly, there was relatively little difference in the industrial mix of the small, medium, and large metropolitan counties in this region.

Competitive Factors

Competitive patterns of growth are the result of numerous factors. These include, among others, wage rates, taxes, union strength, congestion, federal investment, business regulations, physical climate, and local attitudes toward growth. As competitive factors change, some regions fall behind, while others surge ahead.

Before 1978, the competitive edge of the Northeast was weakened by a poor business climate and other negative features of its large and medium-sized metropolitan central cities. After 1978, however, the competitive position of the region improved. By the 1980–82 recession, the Northeast's overall competitive effect had become positive. This switch in the competitive effect indicates important changes in defense expenditures, business regulations, taxation rates, and ecological structure as the decentralization of population and industry acted to mitigate problems of congestion and density in the central cities while boosting economic growth in the suburbs and smaller metropolitan areas.

Trends in competitive effects in the Midwest were counter to those of the Northeast, with the Midwestern situation steadily deteriorating between 1974 and 1982. This deterioration occurred in most types of counties but was especially severe in metropolitan core counties. Such factors as high wage rates, union restrictions, aging infrastructure, and a negative balance of tax payments with Washington have compounded problems of the Midwest's disadvantaged industrial mix, substantially weakening the region's ability to compete for jobs.

The South's competitive edge increased sharply between 1978 and 1982, then slowed down. During the 1980–82 recession, all types of counties—from the most rural to the most urbanized—gained substantially more jobs than can be accounted for by either national growth trends or the industrial structures of Southern counties. Smaller metropolitan central-city counties showed particularly strong competitive effects during the 1980–82 recession, as did the central-city and suburban counties in the region's largest metropolitan areas.

It should be noted, however, that with agricultural problems, falling oil prices, and foreign competition striking the South's rural manufacturing industries, negative competitive multipliers rippled through the region's nonmetropolitan areas during the mid-1980s. At the same time, an office and condominium glut and energy industry-related problems severely dampened a number of large metropolitan core counties such as Harris County (Houston) in Texas. Between 1982 and 1984, the combined competitive effects of metropolitan core counties in the South were less than the Northeast and almost as weak as in the Midwest's metropolitan core counties—a dramatic reversal from the strong competitive position of the South's metropolitan core counties during the 1980–82 recession (Kasarda and Irwin 1987). With employment growth in the South slowing in the mid-1980s and substantial in-migration continuing to swell the region's labor force, the number of unemployed actually rose in the South from 1984 to 1986, making it the only census region to experience a rise in its unemployment rate (Kasarda 1987).

The competitive patterns of growth in the West were strongest during the 1976–80 economic upswing. Whereas the region maintained a consistently positive advantage throughout the business cycle, its competitive edge weakened during the 1980–82 recession. The Western economy is dominated by California and such large cities as Los Angeles, San Francisco, Phoenix, and Denver. These cities are now showing signs of developing many of the adverse features previously associated with major Northern cities. Increased congestion, aging infrastructure, rising land costs, and community growth controls are beginning to dampen their once ebullient economies.

In summary, our shift-share analysis of county-level employment trends shows that the dramatic expansion of jobs in the South between 1974 and 1982 resulted exclusively from its strong competitive features. These features (which did deteriorate after 1982) more than compensated for the poor industrial mixes of its nonmetropolitan counties. The large employment declines in the Midwest have resulted from a disadvantaged industrial mix, coupled with weak competitive effects relative to other regions. The Northeast has improved its competitive features and its industrial mix in recent years, increasing its ability to hold and attract jobs. Finally, the West has been blessed with a favorable industrial mix and with competitive features that have resulted in that region's steady employment growth.

The Next Half Century

Regional patterns of employment and population growth are well established, but will they continue into the twenty-first century? Extrapolating trends in a straight-line fashion has put egg on the faces of many demographic and economic forecasters in years past. Even with sophisticated algorithms that modify future estimates, unforeseen events can upset the most scientifically based projections. Our projections are best regarded as illustrative outcomes, based on events of the 1980s and our assumptions about developments that are likely to shape the demographic and economic structure of regions into the next century.

With the above caveat in mind, we adjusted the Bureau of Economic Analysis (BEA) models using current data to project employment and population for the four census regions, by decade, through the year 2030. The BEA models—called OBERS—are the most geographically detailed and demographically sophisticated long-range projections available.[3] In a similar manner, we constructed our own models to project racial and ethnic mixes and the urban and metropolitan distribution of population within the four regions over the next half century.

Employment

Our projections of employment for the South and the other census regions are provided in Table 3-5. The total number of jobs in the United States may be expected to increase at a moderate rate throughout the next fifty years, from 109.5 million in 1986 to 140.5 million in 2030. Despite the recent resurgence of the Northeast, many of the Sunbelt's present competitive advantages will continue to operate well into the twenty-first century. As a result, the South and West may be expected to account for the greatest proportion of the nation's estimated employment growth of 31 million jobs. By the year 2030, the South's share of total U.S. employment should surpass the combined share of the Northeast and Midwest regions, adding some eighteen million new jobs. The West will also disproportionately gain employment, adding slightly fewer than ten million jobs and increasing its percent of total national employment from 19.8 in 1986 to 22.2 in 2030.

The economic base of the South, like that of the United States, has clearly shifted from the production of goods to the production of services. Table 3-6 shows that over the next half century, most of the employment growth in all regions may be expected to occur in the service sector, with secondary employment (manufacturing and construction) growing slightly in the South and West and declining slightly in the Frostbelt (Northeast and Midwest). Whereas the absolute number of Southerners employed in manufacturing and construction will rise by more than two million by 2030, the percent employed in these industries will decline from 21.4 to 18.3.

The national importance of primary sector employment (agriculture, forestry, and fisheries) is projected to continue its long-term decline. The percentage of Southerners currently in the primary sector is expected to be cut nearly in half in the next fifty years, falling from 4.5 percent in 1986 to 2.5 percent by 2030. These proportional declines in primary and secondary sectors are the result of the continued dynamism of the South's tertiary sectors. By the year 2030, four out of every five Southerners will be employed in the tertiary (service) sector. For the coming generation of Southerners, employment as a data processor or hotel clerk will be far more likely than employment as a textile worker or farmer.

These optimistic projections for Southern growth must be mediated by the manner and extent to which business leaders and gov-

Table 3-5.   Total Regional Employment (in thousands) and Percent of Nation, 1986
and Projected through 2030

Region	1986	1990	2000	2010	2020	2030
SOUTH						
Number	37,994	41,423	47,014	51,604	53,876	56,008
Percent	34.7	35.6	37.2	38.3	39.2	39.9
WEST[a]						
Number	21,688	23,543	26,568	29,062	30,197	31,267
Percent	19.8	20.2	21.0	21.6	22.0	22.2
NORTHEAST						
Number	22,743	23,337	23,569	23,819	23,355	23,209
Percent	20.8	20.0	18.6	17.7	17.0	16.5
MIDWEST						
Number	27,117	28,208	29,236	30,092	29,933	30,020
Percent	24.8	24.2	23.1	22.4	21.8	21.4
UNITED STATES						
Number	109,542	116,511	126,387	134,577	137,361	142,017
Percent	100.0	100.0	100.0	100.0	100.0	100.0

[a]Includes Alaska and Hawaii

ernment officials implement future-oriented policies that capitalize on Southern advantages in a rapidly changing environment. While such factors as benign climate, locational advantages, and access to deep water ports will remain constant, other advantages may erode in the face of national and international competition. Increases in population and density will increase frictional costs of transportation and decrease the attractiveness of many natural amentities. Moreover, traditional Southern regional advantages in wage levels, housing costs, and taxation rates are likely to disappear as the Southern economy expands and competition in manufacturing from developing nations accelerates. Indeed, the South's long-term competitive edge in gaining labor-intensive industry, resulting primarily from the ready supply of labor willing to work for relatively low wages, could prove a disadvantage in the future. These industries will become increasingly vulnerable to international competition. The burgeoning labor force in countries such as Korea, China, and Brazil are likely to make these places the most cost-effective sites for labor-intensive production well into the next century. It is unrealistic to think that Southern industries can compete in the wage arena with such nations.

The future growth of the Southern economy thus depends largely on (1) the region's ability to foster an information age public infrastructure that supports service sector growth and (2) investment in quality education at all levels. Apropos the former, just as the construction of canals, rail lines, roadways, and electric power lines facilitated industrial-age growth, employment growth in the information age will increasingly rely on a computer-age infrastructure that facilitates newer means of information exchange and transit access. The South's metropolitan areas must be fully wired with fiber optics and broadband cables to help their businesses receive, store, and transmit immense amounts of data and information. The region must also continue to develop its national and international airline accessibility by expanding and modernizing existing airports and constructing new ones. Apropos education, with brainpower replacing horsepower as the driving force of the postindustrial economy, increased investment in public schools and Southern colleges and universities will generate substantial future returns. For reasons stated above, a well-educated, flexible labor force will increasingly become "the" crucial business climate factor for future employment growth, superseding the region's earlier attractions such as below average manufacturing wage rates, limited unionization, and low taxes.

Table 3-6. Regional Employment (in thousands) by Industry, 1986 and Projected to 2030

Industries	Total	Northeast	Midwest	West	South
1986					
Primary[a]					
Number	4,410	428	1,218	1,066	1,698
% of Industry	4.0	1.9	4.5	4.9	4.5
% of Nation	100.0	9.7	27.6	24.2	38.5
Secondary[b]					
Number	23,836	3,650	7,971	4,097	8,118
% of Industry	21.8	16.0	29.4	18.9	21.4
% of Nation	100.0	15.3	33.4	17.2	34.1
Wholesale and Retail					
Number	23,701	4,875	5,881	4,630	8,315
% of Industry	21.6	21.4	21.7	21.3	21.9
% of Nation	100.0	20.6	24.8	19.5	35.1
Services[c]					
Number	57,593	13,789	12,046	11,895	19,863
% of Industry	52.6	60.6	44.4	54.8	52.3
% of Nation	100.0	23.9	20.9	20.7	34.5
Total Employment					
Number	109,540	22,742	27,116	21,688	37,994
% of Industry	100.0	100.0	100.0	100.0	100.0
% of Nation	100.0	20.8	24.8	19.8	34.7

	2030				
Primary[a]					
Number	4,031	349	1,059	1,230	1,393
% of Industry	2.9	1.5	3.5	3.9	2.5
% of Nation	100.0	8.7	26.3	30.5	34.6
Secondary[b]					
Number	27,152	3,334	8,269	5,290	10,259
% of Industry	18.0	14.4	27.5	16.9	18.3
% of Nation	100.0	12.3	30.4	19.5	37.8
Wholesale and Retail					
Number	31,015	4,865	6,523	6,541	13,086
% of Industry	22.1	21.0	21.7	20.9	23.4
% of Nation	100.0	15.7	21.0	21.1	42.2
Services[c]					
Number	78,305	14,660	14,169	18,205	31,271
% of Industry	55.7	63.2	47.2	58.2	55.8
% of Nation	100.0	18.7	18.1	23.2	39.9
Total Employment					
Number	140,504	23,209	30,020	31,267	56,008
% of Industry	100.0	100.0	100.0	100.0	100.0
% of Nation	100.0	16.5	21.4	22.2	39.9

[a] Industrial group consisting of agriculture, mining and forestry, and fisheries.
[b] Industrial group consisting of construction and manufacturing.
[c] Industrial group consisting of F.I.R.E, public utilities, services, and government.

Population Growth and Redistribution

Regional trends in population growth over the next half century are projected to parallel those of employment growth. Our projections, presented in Table 3-7, indicate that the South's population is likely to increase by 42 million, from 81.9 million in 1986 to 124.1 million in 2030. During this period, the West is projected to grow by more than 28 million; the Midwest by nearly 7 million; and the Northeast by more than 2 million. Employment opportunities in the South, combined with the amenities of Southern life, will continue to attract population during the next 50 years.

It is interesting to recall that until 1975, the Frostbelt (Northeast and Midwest) contained more than half the nation's population. By 2030, the Frostbelt's percentage will drop to 37.7 and, as with total employment, the South will exceed the Frostbelt in population size. The West will also disproportionately expand from 20 percent of the nation's total population in 1986 to nearly 24 percent in 2030.

As the South's population expands, it will continue to be redistributed from rural and small town areas to urban and metropolitan locations. Perhaps nothing better illustrates the South's internal transformation during this century than its rapid rate of urbanization. In 1900, the proportion of the South's population living in census-defined urban places (i.e., places of 2,500 or more) was less than 20 percent. In contrast, at that time more than 70 percent of the Northeastern population was concentrated in urban places.

Between 1900 and 1950, the South continued to lag behind other regions in its rate of urbanization. Following World War II, the South commenced its transition from a rural to an urban region. By 1980, the South was approximately 70 percent urban, nearly converging with other regions. Our projections across regions (shown in Table 3-8) indicate that urbanization, driven by population growth, will surge ahead during the next half century, transforming the Southern region from the least urbanized in 1980 to the second most urbanized in 2030.

Patterns of urbanization in the South may differ radically from those observed in the Northeast and Midwest regions. The growth of cities such as Chicago, Boston, and New York took place under technological and industrial conditions that favored large, dense settlement. Smaller cities were directly oriented around a handful of large cities. The postindustrial economy, less dependent on physical proximity and operating under far more efficient transportation and communication technologies, favors more moderate, less dense, urban development. Future urban growth in the South is likely to occur as a system of highly interconnected medium-sized cities. Such a pattern should reduce many of the problems associated with mega-urbanization in the Northeast and Midwest regions.

Nevertheless, the South will likely confront a number of serious challenges associated with population growth and urbanization. For instance, the relationship between local employment and population growth is frequently uneven, leading to local area labor surpluses and high unemployment (as experienced by New Orleans and Houston during the mid-1980s).

Several factors link structural unemployment with rapid growth. Movers from the de-industrializing Frostbelt and from Latin America, lured by the promise of economic growth, bring few appropriate skills to the more white-collar, service-oriented Southern economy. In addition, much of the current population of the South, often rural and poorly educated, will not be able to take advantage of the rapid expansion in high-skilled, information-based employment. Even jobs that have not required additional education in the past are likely to demand greater education in the future. This is seen clearly in the transformation of agriculture in the past forty years. The small, labor-intensive farmer has given way to specialized, capital-intensive agrobusiness. The most financially successful farmers have developed skills in agronomy, animal husbandry, financial planning, and marketing. Without significant improvements in Southern educational systems and programs to develop skills useful in the postindustrial era, large numbers of Southerners may be left behind in the dust of a regional employment boom. The South may find itself burdened with a permanently disadvantaged segment of population, facing conditions roughly analogous to the urban poor in today's large Northern cities.

Poverty is not a new problem to the South, however. In fact, poverty has been a significant problem in the region throughout the twentieth century. At mid-century, half of the nation's poor were living in the South. Additionally, in 1959 the poverty rate in the South was more than twice that of any other region; the Southern poverty rate was 35.4 compared with 16.0 in all other regions combined. Following the economic transformation of the Southern economy, however, the poverty rate began to converge with that of other regions. By 1986 the poverty rate in the South was 16.1, compared with 12.3 for all other regions (Bureau of the Census 1984, 1988).

While poverty levels in the region have begun to converge with

Table 3-7. Regional Population (in thousands) and Percent of Total Population, 1986 and Projected through 2030

Region	1986	1990	2000	2010	2020	2030
SOUTH						
Number	81,877	87,848	98,404	107,991	117,091	124,126
Percent	34.3	35.0	36.3	37.4	38.4	39.1
WEST[a]						
Number	47,628	51,682	58,973	65,529	71,416	75,707
Percent	20.0	20.6	21.8	22.7	23.4	23.8
NORTHEAST						
Number	49,859	50,575	50,891	51,174	51,709	52,036
Percent	20.9	20.1	18.8	17.7	16.9	16.4
MIDWEST						
Number	59,197	61,134	62,575	63,764	65,010	65,913
Percent	24.8	24.3	23.1	22.1	21.3	20.7
UNITED STATES						
Number	238,561	251,239	270,843	288,458	305,226	317,782
Percent	100.0	100.0	100.0	100.0	100.0	100.0

[a]Includes Alaska and Hawaii

Table 3-8. Percent[a] Urban and Metropolitan Population[b] by Region, 1900–1980 and Projected to 2030

		URBAN		
DATES	SOUTH	WEST	NORTHEAST	MIDWEST
1900	18	40	66	39
1950	49	70	80	64
1980	67	84	79	70
2000	76	86	80	78
2030	85	88	80	82
		METROPOLITAN		
DATES	SOUTH	WEST	NORTHEAST	MIDWEST
1900	23	47	71	36
1950	41	68	79	57
1980	67	82	85	71
2000	76	84	85	78
2030	83	85	85	82

[a]Rounded to nearest percent.

[b]Metropolitan areas 1900 to 1950 constructed from 1960 counties.

national levels, the geographic distribution of poverty in the South remains distinct. Unlike other regions, a majority of Southern poor have traditionally been concentrated in rural and nonmetropolitan areas. In areas outside the South, a larger proportion of the poverty population resides in central cities and metropolitan areas than in nonmetropolitan areas. In 1969, 58 percent of the Southern poor lived in nonmetropolitan areas. In comparison, only one-third of the poor living in other regions resided in nonmetropolitan or rural areas. Additionally, only 26 percent of the Southern poor lived in central cities, compared with 40 percent of the poor in other regions (Bureau of the Census 1973).

Nevertheless, as with the general poverty rate, the spatial distribution of poverty in the South has begun to converge with the national pattern. In 1986, one-third of the Southern poverty population lived in central cities, and 40 percent lived in nonmetropolitan areas. On the other hand, nearly 50 percent of the poverty population in areas outside the South lived in central cities, and only 23 percent lived in nonmetropolitan areas. Although it appears that poverty in the South is following the national trends and becoming an inner-city problem, the Southern poverty population also remains disproportionately concentrated in the rural and nonmetropolitan areas.

To some extent, the concentration of poverty in rural areas reflects the later economic development of the South. Nevertheless, there can be a certain advantage to this economic lag. If the South was left behind during the nation's early industrial development, it was also relatively untouched by the Northern urban economic deterioration in the years following World War II.

In the postwar period, waves of the South's rural poor poured into the industrial cities of the North to flee stagnating local economies, only to find entry-level job opportunities disappearing as industry moved out of the cities. Racial discrimination, lack of low-income housing in industrially expanding suburban areas, and relatively better public assistance programs in the cities anchored millions of Southern black migrants in Northern inner cities. The declining urban blue-collar employment base further diminished opportunities for successive generations. Additionally, a declining tax base continued to undercut the quality of education available to the inner-city poor, further removing this population from the economic mainstream. By the 1970s, sociologists began to talk of the Northern inner-city poverty population as an "urban underclass": a population of structurally displaced poor—whose parents were poor and whose children would also be poor—with little hope of escaping their economic plight.

With few exceptions, Southern central cities, unlike their Northern counterparts, have not yet reached maturity. In fact, Southern economic growth is tied directly to the vibrancy of its metropolitan economies. Most larger Southern cities did not experience blue-collar job declines of the scope of large Northern cities. And, while Southern cities do have substantial poverty populations, few exhibit massive urban underclass features.

In the coming decades, Southern urban and metropolitan areas will eventually experience the infrastructure and density problems Northern cities have been experiencing for the last fifty years. Additionally, the continued decline of the Southern agricultural economy and the concentration of economic development in the urban and metropolitan areas will guarantee a stream of migrants from the rural countryside to the metropolitan areas. Similarly, immigrants from Mexico, South America, and the Caribbean will continue to move into Southern cities in the years to come. These in-migrants will generally have less education and fewer job skills appropriate to the urban service economy. The eventual increases in inner-city problems could combine with the in-migration of less skilled workers to create a Southern urban underclass similar to that found in Northern cities.

The South, however, is in a unique position to take advantage of hindsight, by looking North and back fifty years. By evaluating the failures and successes of poverty programs and industrial policies in Northern cities, the South has the potential to avoid numerous problems of the urban North. Unfortunately, not all aspects of Southern poverty can benefit from such hindsight. The South will still have to address its unique problems of substantial rural poverty and the possible development of a rural underclass.

The rural areas in the South, areas long in the economic backwash of the national economy, are not experiencing the same economic transformation as the Southern urban and metropolitan areas. These areas are likely to remain economically less developed for decades to come. As the small farm continues to give way to corporate agribusiness, the family farmer could be left without the means for subsistence or the skills required for the new service-oriented occupations in urban areas.

Thus, rural poverty will remain a significant feature of the South as rural people remain isolated from anticipated metropolitan economic growth of the region. Furthermore, the increasingly cosmopolitan nature of the Southern metropolis, as well as the multiethnic diversity of major urban places, could create a geographic dimension for social and political schisms, with traditional Southern culture largely confined to nonmetropolitan areas. Such social differences, coupled with problems of rural poverty, could create a twenty-first-century rural Southern underclass anchored in economically stagnating, isolated communities. This may result in particularly severe social problems, such as a powerful resurgence of racism and political extremism among large segments of the rural underclass.

Along with such possibilities, the South will certainly experience difficulties in allocating and protecting natural resources. For example, continued urbanization may affect water quality and availability. The necessary expansion of buildings, roads, and parking lots seals groundwater from natural replenishment. Water that would otherwise seep through the soil is carried through sewers and drainage systems to streams out of the urban locale. This urban runoff increases stream flow rates, and sedimentation often damages plant and animal populations, as well as recreational facilities located downstream from urban areas. Unless addressed through appropriate planning, such environmental degradation could prove damaging in many areas.

Population Composition

In addition to changes in the size and distribution of the region's population, there are likely to be substantial shifts in racial and ethnic composition. Table 3–9 provides projections of the regional composition of nonhispanic whites, nonhispanic blacks, Hispanics, and Asians and others, in 2030. Our projections suggest that percent of nonhispanic whites in all regions will decline substantially between 1986 and 2030, with the nonhispanic white population in the South declining from the current level of 73 percent to about 60 percent in 2030.

Several current demographic trends make this decline highly probable. First, natural increase will be greater in minority populations than in nonhispanic white populations. Fertility rates among nonhispanic whites have declined dramatically during the past three decades and are likely to remain at low levels throughout the next half century. Fertility rates among all other racial and ethnic groups, while declining, are likely to remain relatively higher than for nonhispanic whites. Their higher birth rates more than offset the higher mortality rates of these minority groups (see Chapters 6 and 7).

In addition, blacks, Hispanics, and Asians have significantly larger proportions of their populations in child-bearing years than the nonhispanic white population. These differences in age structure further increase the differential in natural increase between nonhispanic white and minority populations. This discrepancy in age structure will become more pronounced throughout the next fifty years as the white baby boom cohort ages and following smaller cohorts have fewer children.

Finally, immigration will continue to increase disproportionately the number of Hispanics and Asians in the United States throughout the next fifty years. Since the turn of the century, nonhispanic white immigration to the United States has declined markedly. On the other hand, political unrest, rapid population increases, and poor wage conditions in much of Asia, Central America, and South America have increased the flow of legal and illegal immigrants to the United States. With little hope in sight for relief from social and economic problems, major immigration streams from these areas will likely continue well into the twenty-first century.

Such disproportional increases of various minority groups over the next half century will profoundly affect the nation's overall racial and ethnic mix. By 2030, Hispanics, with the highest fertility and in-migration rates, will be the largest minority group in all regions except the South. The proportion of U.S. population made up by Hispanics will increase from the present 7.2 percent in 1986 to a projected 15.8 percent in 2030.

The nonhispanic black population is projected to increase from 12 percent of the U.S. population to 14.8 percent by 2030. In recent years, black fertility has declined, and it is likely that this decline will continue. However, the much younger age structure of the black population will sustain significant absolute population increases, adding more than 18 million to the current nonhispanic black population of 28.6 million.

The South is likely to experience the greatest absolute increase of nonhispanic blacks, traditionally its largest minority group. In 2030, nearly 60 percent of the nation's black population is projected to be living in the South (compared to 53 percent at present), constituting

Table 3-9. Regional Population (in thousands) by Race, 1986 and Projected
to 2030

Races	1986				
	Northeast	Midwest	South	West	Total
White[a]					
Number	40,794	51,320	59,852	34,054	186,020
% of Regional Pop	81.8	86.7	73.1	71.5	78.0
% of Racial Pop	21.9	27.6	32.2	18.3	100.0
Black[b]					
Number	5,248	5,729	15,322	2,381	28,680
% of Regional Pop	10.5	9.7	18.7	5.0	12.0
% of Racial Pop	18.3	20.0	53.4	8.3	100.0
Asian and Other[c]					
Number	716	716	1,197	4,048	6,677
% of Regional Pop	1.4	1.2	1.5	8.5	2.8
% of Racial Pop	10.7	10.7	17.9	60.6	100.0
Hispanic[d]					
Number	3,101	1,432	5,506	7,145	17,184
% of Regional Pop	6.2	2.4	6.7	15.0	7.2
% of Racial Pop	18.0	8.3	32.0	41.6	100.0
Total					
Number	49,859	59,197	81,877	47,628	238,561
% of Regional Pop	100.0	100.0	100.0	100.0	100.0
% of Racial Pop	20.9	24.8	34.3	20.0	100.0

Sources: 1986 data are from the 1986 CPS tapes. Baseline racial
estimates for 2030 are from Current Population Reports,
Series P-25, no. 952.

[a]Racial group consisting of non-Hispanic whites.

[b]Racial group consisting of non-Hispanic blacks.

2030				
Northeast	Midwest	South	West	Total
35,952	51,653	74,794	40,546	202,945
69.1	78.4	60.3	53.6	63.9
17.7	25.5	36.9	20.0	100.0
6,623	8,239	28,008	4,118	46,988
12.7	12.5	22.6	5.4	14.8
14.1	17.5	59.6	8.8	100.0
1,577	1,901	3,183	11,087	17,748
3.0	2.9	2.6	14.6	5.6
8.9	10.7	17.9	62.5	100.0
7,884	4,120	18,141	19,956	50,101
15.2	6.3	14.6	26.4	15.8
15.7	8.2	36.2	39.8	100.0
52,036	65,913	124,126	75,707	317,782
100.0	100.0	100.0	100.0	100.0
16.4	20.7	39.1	23.8	100.0

[c]Racial group consisting of non-Hispanic Asians and others.

[d]Ethnic group including Hispanic whites, Hispanic blacks, and Hispanic Asians and others.

Note: The proportions of the table sum to 100%, indicating that Hispanics have been allocated to the Hispanic category from each of the racial categories.

nearly 23 percent of the region's population (compared with nearly 19 percent at present). However, the percent of Southern regional population constituted by Hispanics is projected to more than double from the current 6.7 percent to nearly 15 percent in 2030. Thus, while the rate of increase of the South's Hispanic population is greater than that of the nonhispanic black population, its current size (5.5 million) is not large enough to overtake the dominant minority position held by blacks.

The nation will also add significantly more people from the "Asian and Other" category. Given present demographic trends, this category is likely to increase from the current 2.8 percent to 5.6 percent of the nation's population in 2030, with the absolute size of this minority group projected to rise from 6.7 million to 17.7 million. The South, historically less attractive to Asians, is projected to add approximately two million, increasing its Asian component to 2.6 percent. The West, continuing its function as an immigration gateway from the Far East, is projected to be the largest growth region for Asians. In the course of the next half century, the West could add as many as 5.6 million Asians, who would constitute 15 percent of this region's population in 2030.

The Metropolitanization of the South

Metropolitanization involves far more than changes in population size, distribution, and composition; metropolitanization is the diffusing of modern urban life-styles and economic interdependencies on a regional basis. It involves two countervailing forces, centrifugal and centripetal, each trend creating major changes in the social and economic fabric of newly integrated areas.

Centrifugal forces involve the spread of urban social and economic processes and relationships into the hinterland. Urban institutions expand and reorient the social and economic patterns of outlying small towns and villages. Health care and government services spread from urban areas to address the needs of rural population. Standard retail outlets and consumer service establishments disperse throughout the hinterland. The result of this urban centrifugal drift is the incorporation of once isolated communities and rural populations into the daily pattern of metropolitan life.

Centripetal trends involve the centralization of administrative and organizational control in the metropolitan core. The general store in the hinterland community is replaced by the chain super-market, administered from offices in the metropolitan center. The local hospital is incorporated as an auxiliary clinic of a major metro-politan health complex. Small-town newspapers, movie theaters, banks, and other service facilities are absorbed or replaced by large core-based corporate institutions. Central-city television stations dominate the daily intake of regional news and entertainment. One outcome is a substantial territorial expansion of metropolitan influ-ence that will continue to erode the demarcation between rural and urban activities and life-styles.

Indeed, the metropolitanization of the South marks a fundamen-tal transition from its traditional rural and small-town life and its functional integration into urban society. The demographic scope alone is immense. At the beginning of this century, three out of every four Southerners resided outside areas of major urban influ-ence. By 1980, two-thirds of the region's population resided within metropolitan areas as defined by the Bureau of the Census.[4] Our projections suggest that by the year 2030, four out of every five Southerners will reside in metropolitan areas (see Table 3–8).

Despite an overall abundance of open land, many farmlands and forests will be replaced by housing subdivisions, shopping centers, and roads, servicing a far more geographically dispersed population. Small communities on the urban periphery, once populated by fam-ilies whose community ties extended back generations, will become commuter suburbs within the expanding metropolis. Increased geo-graphic mobility, associated with metropolitan development and newer urban occupations, will reinforce in-migration of non-Southerners. The orientation of growing urban populations will shift from ties of place to ties of profession, thus loosening traditional bonds to the South and reducing cultural distinctiveness.

As we look to the future, we speculate that the Southerner of the twenty-first century will be far different from the Southerner of the mid-twentieth century, more involved with the nation and world at large. The typical Southern community will be the metropolitan area, multi-ethnic, service oriented, and inextricably tied to the global economic system. The challenge for the South's next fifty years will be to implement environmentally sensitive growth pol-icies, educational programs, and computer-age infrastructures to help the region adapt to its new role in a rapidly changing national and international arena.

Notes

1. For our empirical analyses and projections, we shall define *the South* to match the U.S. Bureau of the Census definition. See Chapter 1.

2. In our analysis, we examined ten industrial categories: (1) agriculture and mining; (2) construction; (3) durable manufacturing; (4) nondurable manufacturing; (5) utilities/communications; (6) wholesale trade; (7) retail trade; (8) finance, insurance, and real estate; (9) low-skilled services; and (10) high-skilled services. We defined the skill levels of the service industries by the average years of schooling of job holders in each industry in 1970. The service industries in which workers averaged thirteen or more years of schooling were classified as high skilled; all others were classified as low skilled. The county employment data are from the Census Bureau's *County Business Patterns.*

3. For more information about OBERS models, contact the Bureau of Economic Analysis at the U.S. Department of Commerce.

4. Metropolitan areas typically contain a central city of 50,000 or more residents, plus the county of which the city is a part and adjacent counties that are urban in character and shown to be economically integrated with the central city's county.

4

The South and Its Older People: Structural and Change Perspectives

Gordon F. Streib

The lives of the elderly in the South are characterized by sociological ambivalence (Merton 1976)—a concept that describes how social relations are influenced by incompatible social expectations and opposing normative tendencies. The ambivalence arises because the contemporary South is marked, on the one hand, by roles and relationships found in urban, industrialized communities and, on the other hand, by values and norms that Odum calls "the way of the folk." These traditional ways view the treatment of older people as benign and proper, dignified, and honorable. The elderly lived among their own kind of people in small towns and rural areas in which religious beliefs and practices were important, and kin-centered relations formed the core of social relations. These core factors were the basic shapers of social structure and defined the proper way to live and fulfill one's obligations to family and community. The middle- and upper-class elderly had a particularly supportive situation because local relatives were expected to rise to the occasion and give needed assistance, and domestic help could be found easily for nursing and custodial care.

Sociological ambivalence does not affect all Southerners to the same degree. Middle- and upper-class persons are probably influenced to a greater extent by the urban, industrialized parts of American culture than are rural and small-town residents (see Chapter 8). But even the most sophisticated middle-class Southerners encounter occasions in which competing norms and expectations define the situation for them and affect their behavior. Those who have less education and have spent most of their lives in the same location in the South are more apt to favor traditional ways, according to Reed (1982). He notes that persons who live in the preindustrial parts of the South are more likely to have traits labeled "localism," "fatalism," "familism," and "resistance to innovation" (Reed 1983).

Structured ambivalence is apt to manifest itself in family and kin situations; hence it may involve older family members. Rural and small-town Southerners (who have never ventured far from home) have attitudes and behaviors shaped by sociological ambivalence because the ways of the larger society touch their lives, through the mass media and particularly through government bureaucracies. These influences may be filtered out to some degree through the traditional cultural sieve. But the elderly themselves and their relatives are constantly aware that we all live in a bureaucratic society, particularly because of the importance of Social Security, Medicare, Medicaid, and other government-sponsored programs.

In urban industrialized societies, the care of the elderly becomes more formalized or institutionalized, as illustrated by the number of frail older persons who live in nursing homes and depend upon public tax money for support. The decline in the number of family caregivers occurs because of family mobility, decreased family size, and a larger proportion of women in the paid labor force—all consequences of industrialization. These factors are involved in the transfer of the care of the elderly to bureaucratic institutions.

It must be added that although only a small proportion of the elderly—about 5 percent at any one time—receive nursing home care, nearly 25 percent of all older persons over the life course will spend some time in a nursing home. The overwhelming majority of the elderly live in the community and receive help, when needed, from a variety of family, neighborhood, and community services, some of which may be funded by public monies.

The ambivalence between local, personalized, familistic solutions and impersonal, bureaucratic control of programs for the elderly takes on a striking form in the case of what Gans (1962) has called "urban villagers"—persons living in cities and metropolitan areas who cling to a life-style oriented to traditional folkways yet earn their living in the bureaucratic, industrialized world that has come to dominate the economy of the South (as described in the previous chapters by Himes and by Kasarda et al.).

If one takes a broad and factual look at the past, both at the South as a region and at the elderly as a major social category, one must conclude that much has changed—and changed for the better. Fifty years ago, the elderly were not considered to be a population demanding special attention, for they often worked until they died. If they became sick or incapacitated, they were taken care of within the family (Achenbaum 1978; Fischer 1978). The situation has changed radically during the last fifty years, for now retirement, Social Security, pensions, and Medicare are institutionalized and fully accepted as part of the normal process of aging. Many elderly can look forward to ten to twenty years of independent living after their work years have been completed. Most elderly prefer to maintain separate residences rather than move in with their children. The elderly now are the focus of considerable attention because they require a large proportion of the federal and state budgets. They are a growing political force, and in the years ahead they will probably become more influential. Aging as an important phase of life has "come of age" in the nation and in the South.

This chapter analyzes the present situation and the future trends affecting the elderly in the Southern region of the United States. The discussion is divided into three areas: demographic patterns and trends; institutional and organizational issues; and forecasts regarding the future of the elderly in the South and their relationships to American society.

In discussing a demographic category—such as the elderly—one must constantly consider the position of that category in the broader national context. Events that occur in Washington, D.C., are highly significant for the daily lives of the elderly and for their long-range activities and well-being.

The demographic trends in the South indicate that this region is generally a growth area, although there are pockets of population decline (see Chapter 2). The region is also marked by a number of states with populations that are "old," for they have a percentage of the elderly that is higher than the national average. In-migration has been a part of the demographic picture and has been particularly significant for Florida.

This chapter also describes and analyzes how the major organizations and institutions affect older persons, and how older persons in turn affect these institutions. The institutional structure provides a basic framework for analyzing the relationship of older people in the South to government, the economy, religion, and the family.

The institution that has the greatest effect on the lives of Southern elderly is the government of the United States. The government has priority both in numbers of persons served and in dollars expended by the Social Security Administration as pensions and as Medicare payments.

The economy of the South has been undergoing tremendous change, and some of these developments will continue into the future (see Chapter 3). The Southern textile industry is disappearing, and the tobacco industry is in a process of slow decline. There has been an influx of new industries in some areas, and places like the Research Triangle in North Carolina have fostered new kinds of economic activity and growth in the South. These economic trends leave their mark on some older persons, who may lose their jobs, live in declining mill towns, be forced into early retirement without pensions, and have little hope of new kinds of employment.

The religious institutions and the family have had a special significance for Southern culture and society (Hill 1985). Both have changed and probably will continue to change as a result of secularization, the restructured nature of the economy, and the way in which government programs become integral to the lives of older people.

Special attention must be given to Florida because Florida is "different" (Flynn et al. 1985; Reed 1982; Dauer 1972; Hill 1984). Some Floridians are proud of the tie to the old Confederacy, and the residues of traditional Southern culture are still found in North Florida.

In the study of Florida's older population, one must measure and evaluate its heterogeneity. Other social characteristics are important in their effect on the present and the future situation of all age categories. Florida has a large older population—exceeded in absolute numbers only by California and New York. More important, it has the largest proportion of persons older than 65—now almost 18 percent.

Looking ahead to the future of the South and its older people, we confront a complex mosaic. As one attempts to forecast the future, the major factor will be the nature of the welfare state in its present undeveloped and uncoordinated form as found in the United States. At the present time, there are vigorous attempts to reduce or eliminate programs that have taken a half century to develop. How these trends will continue into the twenty-first century is a speculative endeavor, but one worth pursuing.

Demographic Patterns

What Is the South?

An introduction to the demographic patterns and the institutional analysis of the South requires the demarcation of the South as a region. The sociological literature on the South has great depth, richness, and variety. Indeed, the South is undoubtedly the most studied region of the United States. Sociologists in the South were among the pioneers who have looked at their own region and have tried to understand the South as part of a general study of regionalism in the United States (Odum and Moore 1938).

What constitutes the South? As suggested in Chapter 1 above, the South has been defined geographically in many ways. Some writers have said the South is composed of the states that constituted the Confederacy. Lewis Killian (1970) included eleven states in his study of the South, bordered on the Northern side by Virginia and Kentucky, and on the Western side by Arkansas and Louisiana.

In this chapter the South is defined in two ways for different purposes. For a demographic analysis of the older population of the region, the South is defined in terms of the Census usage. This is the inclusive South described in Chapter 1. For the analysis of social experience of the elderly, the South is defined as Administrative Region IV as specified under the Older Americans Act. This includes eight states: Alabama, Florida, Georgia, Kentucky, Mississippi, North Carolina, South Carolina, and Tennessee. Choice of this region is justified for two basic reasons. First, these eight states are an essential part of the traditional South, and within them we have observed the traditional Southern culture and recent changes of the region. In this respect, they are a "typical" part of the South. George Myers (1981) points out that sometimes in social analysis it is fallacious to demarcate precise boundaries where none exist. Second, Region IV is designated as our unit of analysis—because it links together the eight states for the administration of important government programs and the allocation of large sums of money. These eight states are a cohesive cluster of geographical units linked together historically in the Confederacy, and economically and socially by ties to one another through a myriad of federal agencies and private organizations. Moreover, the eight states constitute a cohesive part of what has been loosely referred to as the Sun Belt—an

Table 4-1. Age of Population of the South by Divisions and States, 1980

Regions	All Ages	60 to 64	65 Years and Older	Median Age
THE SOUTH	75,349,155	3,274,365	8,483,516	29.7
SOUTH ATLANTIC	36,943,139	1,713,924	4,363,492	30.7
Delaware	595,225	26,852	59,284	29.7
Maryland	4,216,446	180,374	395,594	30.3
Dist. of Columbia	637,651	29,453	74,202	31.1
Virginia	5,346,279	221,136	505,204	29.8
West Virginia	1,949,644	92,657	237,868	30.4
North Carolina	5,874,429	254,825	602,273	29.6
South Carolina	3,119,208	128,675	287,287	28.2
Georgia	5,464,265	215,901	516,808	28.7
Florida	9,739,992	564,051	1,684,972	34.7

Table 4-1. continued.

EAST SOUTH CENTRAL	14,662,882	626,339	1,656,672	29.3
Kentucky	3,661,433	153,856	409,853	29.1
Tennessee	4,590,750	199,794	517,524	30.1
Alabama	3,890,061	169,025	439,938	29.3
Mississippi	2,520,638	103,664	289,357	27.7
WEST SOUTH CENTRAL	23,743,134	934,102	2,463,352	28.5
Arkansas	2,285,513	110,278	312,331	30.6
Louisiana	4,203,972	161,682	403,939	27.4
Oklahoma	3,025,266	130,618	376,042	30.1
Texas	14,228,383	531,524	1,371,040	28.2

Source: Bureau of the Census. May 1981. 1980 Census of Population. Supplementary Report PC 80-SI-I.

area characterized by the in-migration of many people and businesses.

Demography of Aging in the Inclusive South

Table 4-1 shows the 1980 older population of the South for three census divisions: South Atlantic, East South Central, and West South Central, composed of sixteen states and the District of Columbia. In 1980 the South had an older population (65 years and older) of 8.5 million persons, who constituted 11 percent of the total population of the region. In absolute numbers, older people in the South constituted almost one-third of the country's total elderly population of 25.5 million people. This large number of the South's population is the collective result of the aging process. The proportion of the elderly in the South and in the country as a whole is certain to increase over the next several decades. This growth in the older population has implications for many aspects of social life and social structure: occupations, family structure, political processes, social programs, and public expenditures. The increase in the elderly population will slow somewhat during the 1990s. The most rapid growth is expected between the years 2010 and 2030 and when the "baby boom" generation reaches age 65. In 2030, it is expected there will be about sixty-five million older persons in the United States, who will constitute about 20 percent of the nation's population.

Table 4-1 also presents the median age for the region and its subdivisions. In 1980 the South had a median age of 29.7 years, compared to thirty years for the United States. There is considerable variation in the median age within the region, for six states and the District of Columbia had a median age above that of the nation. Florida had the highest median age of any state—34.7 years.

Table 4-2 presents comparative data of the older population for the four regions of the country and their divisions, and Table 4-3 provides a breakdown of the South into its three divisions and the states. The South had the largest number of elderly in 1970 and in 1980, and it also had the largest percent increase of elderly in two periods. As a region, the South has a large and growing older population and thus faces all of the challenges and public issues to be described later in this chapter.

Tables 4-2 and 4-3 also present the census data for the changes in

Table 4-2. Numbers (in thousands) and Percents of Change of the United States Elderly Population by Age, by Regions and Divisions, and by Dates, 1960-1980

Regions and Subdivisions	All Classes 65 and Over				Percent Increase 1960-1970	All Classes 75 and Over	
	Population 1980	1970	Percent Increase Amount	Percent Increase 1970-1980		Population 1980	Percent Increase 1970-1980
UNITED STATES	25,544	19,972	5,572	27.9	20.6	9,967	32.4
NORTHEAST	6,072	5,176	896	17.3	15.1	2,409	24.5
New England	1,520	1,264	256	20.3	12.7	625	25.1
Middle Atlantic	4,551	3,911	640	16.4	15.8	1,784	24.3
NORTH CENTRAL	6,691	5,703	989	17.3	12.3	2,735	21.5
East North Central	4,493	3,793	699	18.4	13.0	1,787	21.9
West North Central	2,199	1,909	289	15.2	11.0	948	20.7
WEST	4,298	3,080	1,217	39.5	28.3	1,649	39.5
Mountain	1,060	692	368	53.3	31.3	389	49.1
Pacific	3,237	2,389	849	35.5	27.5	1,260	36.9
SOUTH	8,484	6,014	2,470	41.1	31.2	3,174	46.8
South Atlantic	4,363	2,922	1,441	49.3	39.2	1,603	55.9
East South Central	1,657	1,263	393	31.1	20.1	626	34.9
West South Central	2,463	1,828	635	34.8	27.8	944	40.9

Source: Bureau of the Census. August 1984. "Demographic and Socioeconomic Aspects of Aging in the United States." Current Population Reports, Special Studies, Series P-23, No. 138, Table 4-1.

Table 4-3. Change in the Total Population (in thousands) 65 Years and Over, and 75 Years and Over, 1970-80 and 1960-70, for the South, the Divisions, and the States

The South, Divisions and the States	All Classes 65 and Over				Percent Increase 1960-1970	All Classes 75 and Over	
	Population 1980	Population 1970	Percent Increase Amount	Percent Increase 1970-1980		Population 1980	Percent Increase 1970-1980
UNITED STATES	25,544	19,972	5,572	27.9	20.6	9,967	32.4
THE SOUTH	8,484	6,014	2,470	41.1	31.2	3,174	46.8
SOUTH ATLANTIC	4,363	2,922	1,441	49.3	39.2	1,603	55.9
Delaware	59	44	16	35.8	21.2	23	37.4
Maryland	396	298	97	32.7	31.4	148	39.8
District of Columbia	74	70	4	5.5	1.9	28	10.1
Virginia	505	364	141	38.7	26.0	187	42.8
West Virginia	238	194	44	22.8	12.0	91	24.5
North Carolina	602	412	190	46.2	32.0	215	50.2
South Carolina	287	190	97	51.1	25.7	98	51.5
Georgia	517	365	151	41.5	25.5	186	42.8
Florida	1,685	985	700	71.0	78.2	627	85.5

Table 4-3. continued.

EAST SOUTH CENTRAL	1,657	1,263	393	31.1	20.1	626	34.9
Kentucky	410	336	74	22.0	15.0	161	25.0
Tennessee	518	382	136	35.5	23.6	195	39.3
Alabama	440	324	116	35.7	24.2	162	39.0
Mississippi	289	221	68	30.9	16.4	109	37.4
WEST SOUTH CENTRAL	2,463	1,828	635	34.8	27.8	944	40.9
Arkansas	312	237	76	32.0	22.0	120	33.3
Louisiana	404	305	99	32.4	26.0	149	42.0
Oklahoma	376	299	77	25.9	19.9	151	30.7
Texas	1,371	988	384	38.8	32.6	524	45.7

Sources: Bureau of the Census. August 1984. "Demographic and Socioeconomic Aspects of Aging in the United States." Current Population Reports, Special Studies, Series P-23, No. 138. Table 4-1.

the total population older than 65 years and older than 75 years for two census periods, 1970–80 and 1960–70. Among the four regions, the South had the largest percent increase (41.1) for the 1970–80 decade. The number of elderly persons 75 and older increased 46.8 percent. Within the South the population changes among those older than 65 years showed considerable variation. States with a large percentage increase from 1970–80 were Florida (with a 71.0 increase), South Carolina (with a 51.1 percent increase), and North Carolina (with a 46.2 percent increase). Those with the lowest increase were the District of Columbia (5.5 percent), Kentucky (22 percent), and West Virginia (22.8 percent). It also should be noted that the percent increase in those 75 and older from 1970–80 was larger for all the states than the percent increase for those 65 and older. The largest increase, 85.5 percent, occurred in Florida, and the smallest occurred in the District of Columbia and West Virginia.

When one compares the percent change in the elderly and in the total population, the census data show that in all the Southern states the elderly population grew faster than the total population. The large increase in the "over 75" category (the "old-old") is expected to continue and will constitute what Maddox (1982) has called the "geriatric imperative." The projection of an aging population is more than a vague expectation. Although there are always some risks in making population projections, and demographers have not always been on target, forecasting mortality trends has usually been viewed as a more accurate demographic exercise than forecasting the fertility trends. Aging is associated with the increasing risks of morbidity and functional impairments. The elderly, particularly the very old, will require medical resources and institutional care (Rosenwaike 1985).

Statistical Comparisons of the States

A comparative analysis of a variety of statistical measures on the eight Southern states under study that constitute the South (Garwood 1986) yields both similarities and differences. From 1970 to 1980, all of these eight states in the region grew in population at a rate that exceeded the national average. Nationally, Florida experienced the third largest percentage of population change in the census decade—an increase of 43.5 percent. The next highest increase in population was in South Carolina, with +20.5, followed by

Georgia, with an increase of 19.1 percent. The average population increase in the decade for the United States as a whole was 11.4 percent.

In terms of projected population, Florida, which has been seventh in rank order in the United States, is projected to be fourth by 1990; and by the year 2000, it is projected that Florida will be the country's third largest state, with a population of approximately 17,500,000 people.

Mississippi is the most rural of the eight states in the region, with 52.7 percent of their persons living in rural areas; it is followed by North Carolina, with 52.0 percent, and Kentucky, with 49.1 percent. The United States as a whole has 26.3 percent of the population living in rural areas, and Florida, reflecting its high degree of urbanization, has only 15.7 percent.

In terms of total migration in the decade from 1970 to 1980, Florida led all fifty states. Approximately 2.7 million persons migrated to the state of Florida (Longino and Biggar 1981). This compares with the second highest state, California, which was reported to have slightly more than 2,000,000 persons migrating into that state.

Florida also heads the list of states in terms of its median age. In 1980, the median age of Floridians was 34.7 years. This can be compared with the median of 30.0 years for the United States as a whole. In the Southern region, South Carolina had the youngest median age with 28.0 years.

Florida is different from its neighbors in that only 35 percent of its citizens were born in the state. This contrasts with Kentucky and Alabama, where more than 79 percent of the residents were born within the state.

The age of Florida's population is also reflected in its low birth rate. It ranks towards the bottom of the fifty states with a birth rate of only 13.5 per thousand. Mississippi has the highest rate in the region, with 19.0 per thousand.

On the other hand, Florida leads all of the states in its death rate—10.7 per thousand. The U.S. death rate is 8.7 per thousand, while South Carolina has the lowest death rate in the region, with 8.1 per thousand.

In terms of physicians per thousand, in 1981 Florida had the highest ratio of physicians to the population in the region, 1.76 per thousand, in contrast to Mississippi's 1.08 per thousand. Nevertheless, Florida's ratio of physicians is still below that of seventeen other states in the country and below the average of the United States as a whole.

Florida's high rate of in-migration is reflected in its school statistics. Several indicators present a favorable picture: in comparison with other states in the region, it had a lower percentage of persons with fewer than five years of schooling; it had a higher percentage of persons who had graduated from high school; and it had a larger number of persons who had completed four or more years of college.

The relative affluence of Florida is demonstrated by the higher median value of the owner-occupied dwellings in comparison with neighboring states. Similarly, Florida has a smaller percentage of persons below the poverty level than the other states in the region. In 1979, for example, Florida had 13.5 percent of persons below the poverty level as compared with Mississippi, which had 23.9 percent, and Alabama, with 18.9 percent. The relative affluence of Florida as compared with its neighbors is also shown in the ratio of Medicaid recipients to the total number of Social Security beneficiaries. Florida has approximately one-quarter of its elderly eligible for Medicaid as compared with Mississippi, which has almost three-quarters who are Medicaid recipients. Viewing the eight states in the region, we see that Florida is anomalous on a number of statistical measures.

Institutional Framework of Social Effects

The second major area for analyzing the South and its older people focuses upon institutional topics: the polity, the economy, the family, and religion. These institutions provide a structure of norms and expectations within which all age groups carry on their activities.

Political Economy

The political economy approach is employed by observers of many aspects of American society, including the elderly and their social circumstances. This approach is a form of functionalism that examines the connections among polity, economy, and society, and how they influence each other in a reciprocal manner, plus a critical or radical analysis of stratification and an emphasis on structural change. Writers in the field of aging (Estes 1979; Estes et al. 1982; Olson 1982) point out the shortcomings of the political and economic structures and highlight the basic contradictions of a monopoly-capitalist economic system. These writers argue that a democratic capitalistic state tends to promote the accumulation of profits and foster dependency of older people. Writers in this tradition also point out that any changes to meet the problems that are created by these contradictions merely enhance the dominant position of those who control the polity and the economy. The reintroduction of structural variables, economic and political, has enriched and enlivened the gerontological literature and sharpened policy debates concerning programs for the elderly. These writers in the political economy school have highlighted the limitations of other analysts who have neglected the linkages of the polity and the economy. The contemporary political economy approach heightens an awareness of the importance of structural factors and their roles in social change because much of the research in the sociology of aging has an individualistic bias. The focus of analysis has tended to be psychological or social-psychological.

Contemporary writers employing a structural political economy perspective often neglect two other institutions that are significant in the lives of all people, particularly the elderly—namely, family and religion. The inclusion of the institutions of religion and the family provides a more comprehensive perspective, particularly when one is studying the South and its elderly population.

The Changing Political and Government Context. The South, like the rest of the United States, has changed considerably since World War II. Havard (1972, 17) has offered a vivid description of the contemporary South: "Cotton has moved west, cattle have moved east, the farmer has moved to town, the city resident has moved to the suburbs, the Negro has moved north, and the Yankee has moved south." The political responses brought about by these changes are probably somewhat slower than the demographic shifts suggest, and their impact on government structure and programs obviously occurs after the political process has worked out its implications.

Earlier writers (Key 1949; Dauer 1972) have pointed to the slow emergence of a two-party South. These trends, which were noted as long as thirty years ago, have now come into being. The South now has Republican governors, Republican U.S. senators, Republican members of Congress, and voters who have switched party allegiance from the Democrats to the Republicans. The change of political affiliation occurs primarily because conservative Democrats now find themselves more comfortable with the platform, policies, and actions of the Republican Party than with those of the Democratic Party, which tends to be identified with a New Deal, liberal, pro-black orientation. This conservative drift is not only a Southern phenomenon, for in the last decade there has been a tendency for conservatism to become a political stance of the majority (see Chapter 11).

The changes in party affiliations are significant in their effect on political power and decision making as these bear on the operation of government programs for the elderly. Political climate determines whether the federal government takes the initiative in expanding or modifying programs and in the level of federal support for these programs. The fiscal crisis connected with Social Security indicates the dilemma faced by politicians from all sides of the political spectrum when they try to deal with a long-standing, well-established program. The continuation of benefits at existing levels became one of the major issues in the 1984 presidential campaign, so that both major candidates—Mondale and Reagan—pledged not to change benefit levels. Indeed, President Reagan's commitment to maintaining Social Security placed him in one of the major political dilemmas of his presidency, for the Republican senators were willing to make changes in benefit levels in order to deal with the federal deficit. At the last minute, however, the President refused to accede to any changes in the Social Security legislation. Such decisions at the national level have profound implications for the elderly in the South.

The Welfare State. The institution that has the greatest impact on the lives of most Southern elderly is the government of the United States through various programs that have been developed in the last fifty years.

The government or polity is of significance both in terms of the numbers of persons involved and the amount of dollars expended because of Social Security and Medicare, and the programs funded through the Older Americans Act. The importance of Social Security and other programs for the elderly can be analyzed sociologically by the concept of the welfare state. The writings of Van Heek (1974) and Gilbert (1983) provide a European and an American perspective on the welfare state as a sociological concept. These authors point out that the creation and development of a welfare state have to be viewed in terms of both the basic economic and political structures in which they are embedded. The welfare state is marked by a kind of dualism in which, on the one hand, what Gilbert calls the "social market" provides a package of goods and services based upon legal or ethical notions guaranteed by the state. The dualism arises because these rights or obligations or ethical concerns are implemented by decisions as to which goods or services will be produced by the private or profit-making sector. The profit sector operates with a price mechanism. There is bound to be a clash between the opposing principles of the welfare state or the social market and those of the economic or free enterprise market. Van Heek (1974, 10) has written: "The welfare state is less autonomous than is usually assumed. It works within a framework of institutions which themselves cause most of the problems which the welfare state is supposed to solve. . . . The nonautonomous character of the late-capitalist welfare state, which is essentially a compromise of pressure groups, causes tardy and post-facto reaction to problems whose significance is not directly manifest and whose solution is financially expensive."

In recent years a crisis of the welfare state has developed in the United States and in other western industrial societies (Chen 1983; Kingson 1983; Robertson 1981; Rosa 1982; Rose and Peters 1978). The major issue is whether a particular society has reached the limits of growth and support for the welfare state. This broad question, which affects not only the elderly but all age groups, can be stated bluntly: how much social welfare can and will a particular society afford? This question is answered by how much of a society's resources will be allocated through the social market via government-financed programs, in comparison to the amount allocated through the free enterprise market. In weighing the answer to this question, one must realize that although the welfare state is considered by advocates of the free market as nonproductive, some economists and sociologists argue that most social welfare programs are investments in human resources, which are conducive to the economic growth of the economy and the well-being of the society. There is recognition that the financial support of the social market is created and sustained by the economic surplus that is produced in the market economy and is allocated by taxation. This fact of economic dependence places a limit on the size of the welfare state. Gilbert (1983) points out that since the 1960s, the American welfare state has been approaching the limit of how much can be allocated to the social market. In fact, some persons assert that expenditures have long exceeded the economic limits of the welfare state to finance (Roberts 1986).

Social Security: The Heart of the Welfare State. It is useful in this connection to describe the political and adminstrative background of the Social Security law and indicate the South's involvement in this most important piece of legislation affecting the lives of millions of the elderly. The Social Security Act was one of the most far-reaching pieces of New Deal legislation passed in 1935 during the first administration of President Franklin D. Roosevelt. The Congress of the United States was then controlled to a considerable extent by representatives and senators from Southern states. The key committees in both the Senate and House were often chaired by representatives from the Southern states who, because of their seniority, held prime positions in the legislative process. Their power as chairs of committees and as key members of these committees enabled them to control the legislative agenda and the calendar, so that only legislation considered inimical to the interests of their constituents and the region would probably never reach the floor of the Congress.

The Social Security legislation illustrates this kind of legislative scenario. Passage of the legislation required the support of key Southern senators and representatives. In order to move the legislation forward to the floor and to have it placed before the President for his signature, it was necessary to include provisions that were in the interest of the Southern region. Two of these provisions, which excluded agricultural and domestic servants, are interesting for our understanding of the economic welfare of older Southerners today. At the time of the passage of the law in 1935, the South was predominantly an agricultural region. Many persons were engaged in agricultural employment, particularly in the eight states that are the focus of our description and analysis. Many of these agricultural workers were blacks, and in 1935 there was minimal interest by Southern legislators in providing pensions for the economic security of older black agricultural workers. Thus, when the original Social Security legislation was passed this category of employees was excluded from coverage. In addition, domestic servants in the South, who constituted a small proportion of the total labor force, were blacks, and it was not in the economic interest of their employers to include them in the Social Security program. Agricultural workers and domestic servants were included by a later amendment to the Social Security Act, as were members of the clergy, physicians, and other occupational categories.

This historical discussion of Social Security shows how leaders of the South shaped the welfare state during the crucial days of the New Deal. Down through the years the South has tended to be one of the more conservative sections of the country in moderating the development of the welfare state, although there have been notable exceptions at the local, state, and national level. The South's leaders have not been monolithic in opposition to the welfare state. Grantham (1983) has reviewed the history of the progressives in the South who were concerned with expanding traditional democratic principles. The leaders of the Southern Sociological Society and other professional societies (Havard and Dauer 1980) have been part of the impetus for incremental change. However, these reformers and progressives in politics, in government, and in professional organizations were not generally involved in the promotion of fundamental social change. There were Southern persons in and out of power who ridiculed reformers and accepted the label of Governor George Wallace, who described persons pressing for change as "pointy-headed intellectuals."

The Religious Factor and Old Age. The political economy perspective provides an understanding of U.S. institutions and how they affect the lives of older persons. This perspective also shows how difficult it is to produce change when structural alterations rather than reforms are required in the distribution of benefits and services through the health and welfare system.

Nevertheless, the political economy perspective does not take account of how two other institutions—religion and the family—are related to an older population. These are the two institutions that have traditionally been involved in the care and support of the elderly.

The South has been identified as a section of the country with great interest and participation in religious activities (Hill 1985). This strong emphasis on religion has a multifaceted effect on the region in general and various subgroups within it. For those who are members and actively participate in religious activities, there is social solidarity and psychological support. This may be a source of great comfort in times of illness, lowered income, loss of kin, family, and neighbors. The church is the center of the social activities for many Southern families, and after retirement may constitute an important part of their social and community linkages.

Religion and health have been studied by many researchers. Unfortunately, the approach is simplistic and atheoretical: a common approach is to study the correlates of religious attendance and health outcomes. It is claimed that religion is a protective variable with respect to health. These correlation studies do not take account of the multifaceted nature of religion and health. Levin and

Markides (1986) have employed a multivariate method to study attendance at religious services and its effect on subjective health by controlling alternately: religious attendance, social support, physical capacity, social class, and subjective religiosity. Among both older and younger women, zero-order correlations are explained away when the effects of physical capacity are removed. These authors conclude that religious attendance is a proxy factor for functional health, especially for older people.

The religious emphasis of the South is particularly important for blacks. It gives them a sense of personal identity, purpose, and group solidarity. Black churches and their leaders have been a source of political activism and an important force for societal change. Religious belief and participation have helped blacks to endure the indignities of prejudice, segregation, and discrimination.

Older blacks have shown an interesting racial mortality cross-over effect: after blacks reach an advanced age (75 years, for example), they have a more favorable mortality expectation than whites. The trend is particularly noted in older black women, and octogenarian black men have as favorable a life expectancy as do white women. Speculation as to the reaons for this phenomenon have been offered by various writers whose work Gibson (1986) has summarized. Psychological factors may be one set of causes that decrease the vulnerability of older blacks to illness and death. Genetic and social factors may also have an influence. It has been noted that long-lived people among blacks in the United States and in other cultures have similarities in the environment, diet, and activity levels that continue over a lifetime. Gibson (1986, 367) also points to "role constancy—a certain maintenance of positions of esteem within the family and social circle as age progresses."

Gibson also indicates that religion—particularly prayer—may be an important coping mechanism for older blacks. Her analysis of national surveys shows that some of the effective mechanisms that are sustaining older blacks may be a combination of religious factors and the kind of help-seeking that blacks employ in old age. Older black Americans use a more varied set of informal helpers than did their white counterparts. Gibson (1986, 368) concludes: "In spite of their economic and physical handicaps, the black elderly—the psychological survivors—may turn out to be part of the salvation of the black family of the future."

Religious organizations of all the major denominations have been foremost in providing excellent institutional care for older people

(Fahey and Lewis 1984; Kahana and Kahana 1984; Payne 1984). Care of members of the denominations has taken precedence in the founding of these institutions; but with the passage of time and public monies, these denominational organizations have opened their doors to nonmembers. In addition, some religious denominations have been among the leaders in developing new forms of care, such as the life care communities. The pioneering of religious organizations in the life care field has been picked up and adapted by profit-making groups in the last few years.

Although governmentally sponsored and financed programs may be much more important in offering actual services than are religious organizations, churches provide valuable informal and nonmaterial supports that make life meaningful for many older persons.

The strong religious emphasis of the South is associated, however, with other attitudes and behaviors that may have somewhat negative consequences for the elderly, such as less tolerance for the outgroup, more conservatism, more racism, more individualism, and so on. While some religious groups perform an important function in taking care of their own members, they may feel that the plight of other citizens is not their responsibility.

The Family and the Elderly in the South. Two contradictory themes are interwoven in this chapter—namely, the distinctive nature of the South as a region and the tendency of the region to become like other parts of the United States. These themes manifest themselves when one looks at the older family. A second important conceptual map is a life-course perspective, for it enables us to see how the contrasting themes manifest themselves at various stages of life as people age. It also provides a means to understand the family, intergenerational relations, and the changes that occur as people and families age.

The traditional Southern white family has been described by historians and by literary observers as having a special blend of Southern honor that is marked by feelings of pride, family loyalty, and solidarity (Wyatt-Brown 1982). Nevertheless, elements of ambivalence, instability, and conflict have also been described. Historians have given special attention to Southern honor as means of instilling a set of ethics and integrity, and have noted the transmission of these through a family hierarchy in upper-class families. This form of family honor is particularly powerful in small communities, where the reputation of family members and their behavior are under continued scrutiny.

Obviously, in earlier traditional times, the elderly were integrated into the life of the extended family. They had an extensive support system provided by family members, kinsmen, and servants. As the South has become industrialized and urbanized, this aspect of the Southern family, which focused on honor, solidarity, and social control, has lost some of its influence. However, the prevailing nature of the region suggests that residues of these important cultural patterns are still found in the "enduring South" among older, upper-class white families.

Viewing the region as a whole in the contemporary scene, we note that the South has the same kinds of families and living arrangements as are found in other regions of the United States. Most elderly people live in their own homes, where there are more widows than widowers. Family supports are particularly important for the frail elderly, and the daughter is the family member who most frequently provides care in old age. The importance to the elderly of family and kin ties is emphasized by the fact that only 5 percent of the elderly nationally live in institutions. Indeed, this emphasis on family and community care is receiving new attention because of the financial costs of health and institutional care for the older population. Thus, those whose family ties provide assistance in old age are in an advantaged group as compared with those whose families do not. When institutionalization is necessary, it is because there are no children, or because children do not live nearby or are unable to supply the services that are necessary.

One distinctive characteristic of the South as a region as it relates to old age and the family is the feeling of pride in the region and sense of belonging, which tend to motivate people to stay in the same areas where they have always lived. If they have moved to other areas because of employment demands, they often return to their early place of residence. Older Southerners do not migrate to Michigan or New Jersey.

Other regions of the country, on the other hand, have substantial numbers of older people who relocate to the South—for the climate, recreational opportunities, and life-style. The migrating elderly include the seasonal migrants ("snowbirds") and permanent residents. Although these migrants represent only a small percentage of older people in absolute numbers, they constitute a substantial proportion of older persons in the state of Florida. Retirement communities are also found in other states in the South and are now a growth sector of the housing industry.

The migrating elderly are an interesting topic for sociologists of the family because in many instances, the migrants have moved away from family and kin to establish a new residence and new life-style. Modern means of communication and transportation are very important in maintaining the social-psychological family bonds and sustaining feelings of family solidarity. Some indication of the way in which family ties become attenuated among new residents is revealed in a survey of a retirement community of 2,000 people in central Florida (Streib and Folts 1983). We found that 80 percent of the residents with living children did not have a child within 500 miles, and yet these people stated that they are in close contact with their children through frequent telephone contact and mutual vacation visiting.

Migrating elderly who move to age-dense communities are able to find many new neighbors and friends who have similar values and pursue a congenial life-style. Moreover, these communities—which vary in size, affluence, and class level—create neighborly networks that fulfill some of the basic functions of help and nurturance. Residents repeatedly mention the importance of their friends and neighbors in providing the kinds of support that family members give in other settings. There is some evidence that these communities become surrogate families for some residents. However, it must be added that kind and helpful neighbors, particularly when they are old themselves, have limits to their psychic, social, and economic resources in taking care of frail neighbors. Thus, there is still the problem in late life when the person becomes mentally or physically incapacitated. Viewing old age in a life-course perspective—which may mean chronic illness and functional incapacity for some—has stimulated an interest in continuing care communities that have multiple levels of living and service provisions.

Ethnic Variations and the Family. Like other regions, the South has many varieties of older families because of ethnicity, race, and class. Their number and distribution may vary in different regions and states, but the characteristic family patterns of behavior and support are similar. A life-course perspective is helpful in gaining insight on black families. Martin and Martin (1978) describe the roles of elderly women in strengthening the family's capabilities to meet crises and disabilities. However, other studies suggest that this pattern may be disappearing.

Nickens (1984), in a qualitative study in one Florida county, found that the rural elderly had very attenuated kin ties. Even when the

older black person had kin in very close proximity, they were sometimes dependent on neighbors and friends for support and services
such as transportation. Perhaps this situation verifies the observation of Scanzoni (1971, 315) who concludes: "Once economic re-
wards are taken out of the control of the kin and placed in the hands
of an impersonal formal organization, the focus of family organization shifts from the kin to the nuclear or conjugal unit. Since the
modern industrial setting promises not mere survival but also abundance and affluence, there is no compelling reason to maintain a
traditional type of extended kin structure."

Martin and Martin (1978, 98) concluded their study on the extended black family: "Industrialization called for a type of family
suited to its way of life. The extended family was not that type.
Whereas large families were an economic asset in an agricultural
setting, they spelled economic disaster in an urban industrial setting. Industrial society called for small, occupationally and geographically mobile families, not static kinship systems. The black
extended family was pressured to become consistent with the pattern of the industrial culture by forming the nuclear families which
were more compatible with it."

In some parts of the South, particularly Florida, there are large
minorities of Hispanic persons whose elderly are becoming a focus
of interest. The limited information we have on Hispanic elderly in
other regions suggested there is greater frequency of intergenerational contact among Mexican-Americans than among the Anglos.
Dowd and Bengtson (1978) reported this finding in their study in the
Los Angeles area—and their results would probably be confirmed in
Miami. Hispanic families are discussed by Frisbie in Chapter 6.

Another ethnic group that has a large concentration of population
in urban Florida are the Jewish elderly. The Jewish community has
been noted for both the traditional family ties between the generations and also the development of a rich array of social services and
institutions to support their elderly members. The upward mobility
of younger generations characteristic of both Jews and Gentiles has
important ramifications for older family life. Some older Jews live in
new types of gerontological ghettos in Northern cities; other elderly
Jews migrate to Sunbelt locations and also to retirement communities in southern New Jersey. This migration, which has taken
place in Florida for a generation, leads to the development of in-
stantly aged Jewish communities. Kahana and Kahana (1984) have
recently completed a study of two groups of Jews who undertook

long distance moves: one moved to Florida and another group to Israel. For some of these migratory Jews, the move represents continuation of a life-style of wandering. It also represents the continuation of a cultural life-style because these migrants join Jewish communities that already exist.

Kahana and Kahana (1984) summarize the contrast between the two groups: "An elderly person migrating from the United States to Israel represents an interesting case study illustrating the search of some Jewish older persons for challenge and environmental change. The typical Israel-bound emigrant undertakes a move for ideological, if not idealistic, reasons. In contrast to retirees emigrating to Israel, the Florida-bound Jewish migrant is motivated less by ideological reasons and more by a desire to spend retirement years in a warm, tranquil environment. He or she wants to leave behind the heterogeneous milieu of city life and opts for adult-age-segregated environment."

There are some noteworthy similarities among elderly Jews who relocate to Israel and Florida, state the researchers. Risk-taking is a common feature of both these groups. Kahana and Kahana (1984, 166) write: "They do not mind having to learn new behavior, adaptation, and life-styles. Both groups feel capable of emotionally investing themselves in their new environments and are willing to part with many of their life-long neighbors and friends as well as family."

Poverty and Programs for Older Americans

Poverty among older Americans—regardless of whether they live in the South or in other sections of the country—can be understood in relation to the sociological perspective employed in this essay: the institutional framework, including Social Security, patterns of social stratification, and the important variables of race and gender.

The elderly can be divided into three broad income strata (Streib 1984). Families headed by older persons with incomes above $20,000 are a pension elite (21 percent of the population). The middle mass (54 percent) have incomes from $8,000 to $20,000, and the poor (25 percent) have family incomes of less than $8,000. The poverty index, which was first developed by the Social Security Administration in 1959, is a standard measure of economic need. Since then, the index has gone through many revisions. It specifies a poverty index threshold that varies according to the size of the family, the age of persons in the household, and the number of children younger than 18. The index is also adjusted annually according to the Consumer Price Index. Because of these complex and sensitive variations, the index is useful for comparative descriptions of poverty.

In 1980 about four million persons 65 and older, or 16 percent of the elderly, had incomes below the official poverty line. Zopf (1986, 202) has emphasized that poverty must be understood comparatively and in life-course terms. He states: "No matter how the data are cross-classified, the levels of poverty tend to be very high for children, to decline steadily until later middle age, to rise somewhat after age 60 and to increase sharply after age 65. The problem is most severe for the nation's oldest people."

Rosenwaike (1985) has carried out a detailed study of those 85 and older—the fastest-growing segment of America's elderly population—and he found a very high percentage of low-income persons. Among the oldest-old, 43 percent of the men and 68 percent of the women had incomes of less than $4,000 per year.

Poverty among the elderly must be analyzed in relation to other important variables discussed earlier in this chapter, such as race and sex. Elderly blacks are roughly three times as likely to live in poverty as elderly whites. The poorest persons in American society are elderly black women. As Zopf has stated, (1986, 204): "The rates of poverty still tend to be higher among blacks who live in the South than in any other region in the nation, and also among those who reside in nonmetropolitan places rather than in SMSAs."

It is clear that the analysis of poverty requires attention to subgroups because of the heterogeneity of the elderly. Overall statistics may hide subgroup variations. For example, rural-urban differences may not be as large as the differences that are the consequence of race, sex, or living arrangements. Krout (1986, 43) has pointed out: "Finally, one other geographic variation is worthy of mention, namely, elderly living in the South, urban or rural, are more likely to be below the poverty levels than the elderly living in other regions of the nation."

The issue of poverty in old age must always be placed in juxtaposition to the rich array of programs established for older persons and the many public dollars involved. Most of these programs were planned for the poor, but they often miss their target. One of the major reasons for this situation is that the programs are actually based upon an age policy and not need. Two observers of the aged in our society summarized it clearly (Neugarten and Neugarten 1986,

44): "When all federal programs are considered together—the direct payments, the in-kind transfers, the tax benefits—it is evident that most of the benefits are going to those older people who are in the top third of the income distribution. Further, if these programs continue in their present direction, they will not only maintain the present inequalities, they will create even further disadvantage for those older persons who are poor." Furthermore, programs for the elderly designed to help the poor often miss the mark because there is a commitment to piecemeal change, and a general reluctance of policy makers to direct resources to those most in need.

Conclusions and Forecasts

In ending this chapter, I will focus on two topics: (1) whether the South will continue to be a distinctive region of the country, and (2) how the elderly in the South will fare in a changing society.

My studies of the elderly in the South lead me to conclude that John Reed (1974) is correct when he describes the South as enduring. At the same time, one must agree with the conclusions reached by McKinney and Bourque (1975) that the South is being incorporated into the nation. These two contrasting complex trends involve norms, behaviors, attitudes, and expectations. They establish the parameters for the sociological ambivalence of the region. Looking at the South in 1989 and into the future, one sees these two trends continuing. There will be a persistence of social and cultural patterns that have historical origins peculiar to the South, and there will also be an increasing homogenization of the region by its incorporation into the larger American society. The persistence of Southern customs, values, and behaviors is linked to the traditional parts of the region—namely, rural areas, small towns, and traditional religious groups and organizations. The elderly have a significant role to play in this preservation because they are the ones who are the bearers of traditions, and they are more likely to keep time-honored customs alive in rural areas and small towns.

The factors that work toward the incorporation of the region into the nation are industrialization and the accompanying process of urbanization, improvement in education at all levels, migration, and the influence of the mass media, particularly television. Some years ago, Fichter and Maddox (1965) pointed to religion as the factor that contributed to the persistence of the South as a special region. This generalization probably would be qualified today, but an emphasis on religion is undoubtedly one of the factors that give the South its special character.

Older people in the South are now similar to older people of their class, ethnic, and cultural background in other parts of the United States. Social Security and Medicare are two major ways in which the elderly are integrated into the larger system. For more than a half of the present cohort of older Americans Social Security is the only source of financial support. For another large sector, it is a major source, supplemented by other personal and pension resources. Only an elite of current pensioners have three sources of economic support, namely, Social Security, a pension from an employer, and some private income from savings and investments. The fact that millions of Americans receive Social Security checks gives them a degree of financial independence that is unprecedented in U.S. history. Thus the Southern elderly need no longer depend on the generosity of their children and kin. Social Security is particularly important for black families, for it is the first time that some persons have a dependable, predictable economic base. The elderly person who has a steady income may acquire new status and some power in the family. Instead of being recipients of financial support, older persons may contribute to the support of their children and grandchildren.

The monthly tide of Social Security checks is a significant economic contribution to many small towns that would otherwise have a limited economic base. The influence of retired citizens on Florida's economy, for example, is shown by the dollars that flow into the state from Social Security, pension funds, and other age-related income. According to the Florida Committee on Aging (1986) more than nineteen billion dollars came into the Florida economy in 1983 as a result of four programs: Social Security ($10.2 billion); railroad, federal, and state government retirement ($2.2 billion); military pensions ($2.5 billion); and Medicare transfer payments ($4.2 billion).

The linkages of the region and states to the national system of benefits for older persons are part of a complex administrative structure that permeates American society (Streib 1981). The national programs require that they be administered through state agencies, and the state organizations in turn have to deal with Area Agencies on Aging. These are adminstered by local officials who are familiar with the states and the localities. Thus, although the funds originate at the federal level, the final distribution and administration are carried out at the local level by people who determine the local priorities. The programs take on a local and a Southern coloration through this filtering down process. This means that local traditions and practices may be followed in the way a particular program is administered, whether it is through a voluntary organization or a health provider group or a local government agency. The decentralizing of programs and the distribution of resources may have some adverse results because powerful local interest groups are organized better than other groups—and decentralization often means that national goals and commitments may be supplanted.

As we look to the situation of the elderly at the turn of the century and beyond, what can we forecast concerning the possible outcomes of the present sociological ambivalence? Improvements in public health, a higher standard of living, and medical advances have been important factors in the graying of the population. In the future an important dilemma arising from this gerontological revolution will be the care of that 15 to 20 percent of the elderly designated as the "frail elderly." This group is a rapidly growing part of the population.

The traditional care of the frail elderly in the South (and elsewhere) has been the responsibility of women relatives, principally daughters, and in many instances, this pattern will continue. However, the number of female relatives who can and will assume caretaking roles has declined and will continue to do so. For those who do become caretakers, the responsibilities often become burdensome.

One of the results of modernization and the concomitant medical advances is that many older persons are able to live longer. For some persons, this means more years of active life—but for others, it means an extended period of dependence and supportive care. The South will experience the same problems in supplying and financing long-term care as the other sections of the country.

As I view the major direction of the South and the future of its elderly citizens, I am struck by the paradoxes in American and Southern culture. I note in the field of aging that the demand for collective solutions to social problems is juxtaposed to the increasing demand for individual free choice. Southerners have traditionally been fiercely independent and antagonistic to government interference. They are unwilling to be taxed heavily or invest in public expenditures. They do not like officials from the national government dictating programs and procedures.

The competing demands and sometimes conflicting requirements of collective solutions and individualism lay the groundwork for a series of issues. The juxtaposition of the welfare of all citizens and the freedom of the individual results in philosophical and social dilemmas that have perplexed many persons in the past and will continue to do so in the future. It is this very dialectic between the community's interests and the rights or wishes of individuals that is the core of much sociology and is integral to current political debate and policy discussion.

The central issue stems in many ways from the basic values or assumptions underlying American social structures and in the attitudes and beliefs of many persons. These assumptions and attitudes (which I label "individualism") should be specified further. In politics it is the principle of one person and one vote, of equal treatment under the law. In economics it involves a form of competitive capitalism. For consumers, it means the proliferation of goods and services so that each individual can choose anything he or she wishes—from consumer goods to life-style and health facilities.

What do these individualistic premises and values have to do with the roles of older citizens in contemporary America—and with their right, for example, to choose where they will live and what medical care they will receive? We observe that maximizing individual freedom to choose runs head-on into another desideratum—that private and governmental organizations should provide programs and services organized and paid for on a collective basis.

As to the elderly in the South, it is unrealistic to expect an individualistic society with a goal of maximum freedom of choice to shift suddenly to collective solutions. These require a long time to establish, and fast-track people are in a hurry. Collective solutions also require greater demands on tax funds. They must be enacted into law by legislative and executive actions. Even after the law is on the books, there may be long-drawn-out litigation in the courts, which may delay the carrying out of the public will. Or adequate funds may not be forthcoming to carry out the programs as mandated by law.

Those elderly who desire collective solutions do not realize that the benefits that may come in old age are sometimes the results of the acceptance of collective solutions established many years earlier, and certainly at the price of higher taxes. Collective benefits may have too high a price for some in the South and in the nation. Thus, as I look to the future, I predict that there will continue to be tension between the traditional individualism of the South and the desire of many of its elderly citizens for collective solutions. I hope that in the weighing of priorities there will continue to be persons in all strata of society who see the need for collective solutions to permit the elderly to live in comfort, dignity, and indepedence. In the balancing process there is a need for compassion, equity, and the reasoned application of knowledge.

Part II

Status Relations

The three chapters in this part explore and predict changing struggles between status minorities—women, Hispanics, and blacks—and the status dominants—men, Anglos, and whites—in the struggle for "equity," "structural assimilation," and the associated social and material resources. Although the three struggles are analogous, they differ in the characteristics of gender, native culture, and race. Women seek gender equality and equity in the political, economic, cultural, and social arenas. Hispanics, on the other hand, strive to join U.S. society without a penalty for having a different cultural heritage and language; this is called *structural assimilation.* Cubans, Mexicans, and Puerto Ricans differ significantly in the strategic approaches employed and the rate of progress. Though the ends and strategies of blacks resemble to some degree those of the other categories, the struggle is qualitatively different because of blacks' history as slaves. In the black community progress is most rapid in the middle-class sector and slowest in the underclasses. The differential analyses of these three similar struggles serve to illuminate the diversity of American life—and of human relations.

5

Southern-Style Gender: Trends in Relations between Men and Women

Patricia Yancey Martin,
Kenneth R. Wilson, and
Caroline Matheny Dillman

Are Southern men and women different than they were fifty years ago? Have relations between Southern men and women changed? If so, does this hold for all races, classes, and urban/rural locales? What accounts for the changes? Playwrights and novelists claim that Southern-style gendering is different from gendering in other regions (e.g., Mitchell 1936; Williams 1947; Welty 1970; Henley 1982)—but sociologists have paid little attention to this issue. Sociological research on gender has tended to ignore geographical regions (Cherlin and Walters 1981) or to study one region and speculate on differences between it and others. Because of this, Chapter 5 reviews historical analyses of Southern gender and compares gendering in the South with gendering in other U.S. regions. This allows us to anticipate future trends in Southern gender relations and in Southern conceptions of boy/man and girl/woman, as compared with those of other regions.

Gendering is the process and product of the social construction of roles, norms, perceptions, actions, beliefs, and explanations associated with biological sex (Lorber 1986). Grounded in a sociocultural, political-economic, and historical context, gendering involves practices that instruct and constrain biological males to be boys and men and biological females to be girls and women. Gendering is, in most societies, a fundamental basis for the structuring and constitution of social life on a daily and enduring basis.

We are concerned here with relations between Southern men and

103

women and with conceptions of Southern boy/man and Southern girl/woman as they are socially constructed and enacted. *Gender* and *age* are two characteristics around which social and cultural life are universally organized (Rossi 1980). (In the United States, especially when the South is involved, race must be considered also.)

The dearth of systematic or longitudinal research on gender in the South makes our task difficult. Despite fictional, journalistic, and even social science assertions, the empirical grounds are tenuous for specifying ways in which Southern-style gender is different today from what it was in earlier periods or from what it is in other regions. In view of this, we identify Southern gender issues contested in the literature and summarize available research findings. We also present and analyze selected data from national surveys, the U.S. Census, the Federal Bureau of Investigation, and other sources. Throughout we try to understand past and current developments that may portend the future of Southern gender relations and conceptions.

Southern Gender in Historical Perspective

Over the past two decades, historians of the South have focused on gender and gender-related issues. A recent bibliography lists twenty pages of historical publications (but only four pages of sociological publications) on Southern women (Center for Research on Women n.d.). Historians usually study Southern women or men without comparative data from other regions—thus claimed differences between regions are often undocumented (for an exception, see Fox-Genovese 1986). Additionally, historical works tend to concentrate on only one gender, race, or class (for example, white middle-class women or black slave women; see Clinton 1982). White women have been studied most, although a body of work on black women is accumulating (Dougherty 1978; Jones 1983; Jones 1985). The beginning work of feminist historians on women has stimulated interest in the history of men and maleness; nevertheless, studies of Southern men are scarce (see Wyatt-Brown 1982, and Breen 1980 on white men; Genovese 1974, and Ball and Robbins 1986 on black men).

Gender as socially constructed in the antebellum South has been studied by a number of historians (Spruill 1938; Clinton 1982; Scott 1970, 1983, 1984; Wyatt-Brown 1982; Jones 1985). Although Wyatt-Brown devotes eight chapters and 200 pages to "Family and Gender

Behavior," his analysis is limited to the antebellum era, and an attempt to incorporate race and class succeeds only partially. The lives of white and black girls and women and black men and boys are given considerably less attention than those of white men and boys. Wyatt-Brown's work is valuable, nonetheless, and similar research on women and black men could provide insights for sociologists regarding the economic, social, cultural, and structural conditions that set the stage for and continue to shape gendering in the South.

Patriarchy is a form of social organization where the father is the supreme head of the family (clan or tribe), where wives and children are legally dependent on the father, and where descent and inheritance are reckoned through the male line. Gender relations among whites were highly patriarchal in the antebellum South, particularly among the planter class (Scott 1984; Clinton 1982) and to only a somewhat lesser extent in the yeoman/common planter/small farmer and *poor white* classes (Wyatt-Brown 1982; Flynt 1985; Bellows 1985). Children belonged to the father (as did the wife's property) upon marriage. Married women had few rights under the law, and all legislators, juries, judges, and lawyers were male (Bynum 1984). Men were expected to *control their wives* yet had little interest in spending time with them. Women were viewed as property and sometimes wagered in horse races (Breen 1980) along with farms, cattle, and crops as prizes for the winner. White women were unable to inherit property, even when it had originally belonged to their fathers, unless their husbands specifically left it to them. Wives' family names were given as Christian names by fathers to sons to honor the males in their wives' family, not their wives *per se* (Wyatt-Brown 1982, 120). For numerous reasons, patriarchal control of white men over their wives, children, and slaves was essentially unchecked in the antebellum South.

Wyatt-Brown (1982, 17) asserts that little changed after the Civil War until the 1960s: ". . . in the South today devotion to family and country, restrictive views of women's place and role, attitudes about racial hierarchy, and the subordination of all to community values still remain in the popular mind to an extent not altogether duplicated in the rest of the land." Some historians claim that the Civil War produced major and permanent changes in gendering and gender relations in the South (Thomas 1979; Scott 1984), although other historians disagree (Escott 1983; Alexander 1983).

The intersection of patriarchy and slavery in the antebellum South fundamentally confounded gender and race relations in the region (Myrdal 1944; Hall 1984; Janiewski 1985; Friedman 1985; Burton 1985). Some planter class males described themselves as patriarchs with a wife, children, animals, farm, and bondmen and bondwomen (slaves) (Mullin 1976, 8). They referred to the slaves on their plantations as their *slave families* and took a personal interest in overseeing (or dictating) their lives. Catt and Schuler (1923), Morgan (1972), and Flexner (1959) argue that the South failed to ratify the 19th Amendment because of racist fears as well as misogyny. Predictions of doom if black women gained the vote were used by white (male) politicians to argue against female suffrage (Catt and Schuler 1923, 483–84). Patriarchy took different forms, persisted longer, and was more extreme in the South than in other regions, and its dialectical relationship to the domination of blacks under slavery, Reconstruction, and segregation is believed by many to have had a major influence on the character of Southern-style gendering (Jones 1983; Jones 1985; Dill 1983; Sterling 1984; Leslie 1986; Burton 1985).

Myrdal (1944, 1075) noted in the early 1940s that there was an "especially close relation in the South between the subordination of women and that of Negroes." W. E. B. DuBois argued in his 1903 ideological manifesto, *The Souls of Black Folk* (1961), for more rights for women as well as blacks. Some scholars argue that patriarchy, and its brother, paternalism, remained much stronger in the South than in other regions, continuing long after slavery and being particularly prevalent in the cotton and tobacco industries as the South industrialized (Grasmick 1973; Mullin 1976; Jones 1985; Frederickson 1982; Newman 1978; Janiewski 1983; Morgan 1972).

Major Influences on Southern-Style Gender

In many respects, the South is different from other regions. It is relatively less urban. Many citizens have comparatively low education, income, and occupational statuses, and the South's level of economic development is lower than that of other regions (Lee and Schultz 1982). The South has proportionately more Protestants than other regions, the highest proportion of church attenders, 50 percent of all Baptists, and 80 percent of all Southern Baptists (The Gallup Report 1985). Seventy-four percent of Southerners are Protestant and 16 percent are Catholic. Comparable figures for the East, Midwest, and West are, respectively, 40 and 44, 63 and 26, and 48 and 26. Almost 24 percent of the South's population is black, as compared with 6.4 percent in the West, 10.2 percent in the Midwest, and 11.4 percent in the East. More than 50 percent of all blacks reside in the South. White Southerners claim their ancestry as primarily English, Scottish, and Irish (Bureau of the Census 1983b). The historical lack of ethnic heterogeneity other than Anglo white and Afro-American black is given as one explanation for the region's distinctive character (Killian 1985; Stein and Hill 1977).

Reed (1983) reports that self-identified white Southerners are more likely than non-Southerners to be oriented to locale and family, to own guns and oppose gun control, to attend church frequently, and to hold fundamental religious beliefs. Historians claim that family, kin, and church have been the focus of life in the South more than in the North (Fox-Genovese and Genovese 1986). Data on murder and assault show the South to be a regional leader in interpersonal violence. Southerners are negatively stereotyped by non-Southerners. Killian (1985) suggests that Southerners' insistence on their regional distinctiveness may be a defense against outsiders' negative views.

Although many regional gender differences have been asserted, the degree, significance, and causes of them are disputed. Alleged causes of such differences include a unique historical and cultural legacy associated with slavery, a plantation versus urban/industrial economy, and loss of the Civil War—as well as the slower social, cultural, and economic development of an agrarian South. Possible influences on Southern gender are reviewed here in three categories: (1) Social/Political/Economic, (2) Cultural, and (3) Demographic/Geographic. These influences are highly interrelated and no claim of mutual exclusivity is intended. They are presented as a summary of themes in the literature and a guide for anticipating future trends.

Social/Political/Economic Influences

Social, political, and economic influences are noted in the work of historians and sociologists and refer primarily to the manner in which life in the antebellum and Reconstruction eras was organized. This included a plantation economy, the institution of slavery, and a political/legal code that denied white women and blacks equality before the law (Bynum 1984). The plantation way of life was based on an agrarian economy, with few urban centers, isolated farms at great distances from each other, and a low population density (Escott 1983). These circumstances fostered, some argue, a total and unchecked control over white women and blacks of both sexes by white male planters and other slave holders (Scott 1970; Jones 1985). Only 3 percent of antebellum households were planter class—with large acreage and twenty or more slaves—and only 25 percent of all white households owned any slaves, of which 60 percent had five or fewer (Thomas 1979). The social, political, and economic patterns established by slavery nevertheless affected all regional residents, not just slaves and slaveowners; and their legacies have persisted to the present (Litwak 1983).

Slavery hindered the development of common bonds or identity among white and black women (Clinton 1985) and prevented, in many cases, the ability of black men and women to maintain stable familial and sexual relations (Rose 1976; Jones 1985). Isolation and great distances hindered white women's abilities to develop same-sex networks and diminished alternatives to marriage for spinsters, widows, and divorced women (Friedman 1985). This led to extreme dependence of the white woman on her father and later her husband, brothers, and sons (Mullin 1976) and may have contributed to the emergence of the conception of the Southern lady as submissive, dependent, and passive (Scott 1984). Formal education was relatively unvalued, and many women and most slaves could not read or write. Some planter fathers refused to educate their sons as well (Wyatt-Brown 1982).

Slavery affected gendering not only among blacks but also between whites and blacks, as white men used black women as concubines and white women were forced to live with this, pretend not to see it, and somehow forgive and/or accept it (Smith 1949; Clinton 1982). Black men were, in this system of white paternalism, relegated to impotent bystanders with few rights to women of either race. Scott's (1984) analysis of the problems white women had in accepting their husbands' sexual errancy, particularly relevant to black women, may be important for understanding a claimed distrust of Southern white men by white women today (Abbot 1983; Daniell 1980). It is possible that legacies associated with an agrarian, rural South and an economic system built on the enslavement of blacks fostered a reliance on violence and force as ways of settling disagreements or disputes. Violence is certainly a part of men-to-men relations in the historical and modern South, both among and between whites (Cash 1941; Reed 1982) and blacks (Huff-Corzine, Corzine, and Moore 1986).

Southern white men's opposition to the 19th Amendment to the U.S. Constitution (the vote for women) was couched in racist language (The National American Woman Suffrage Association 1940; Catt and Schuler 1923); and the status of Southern white women appears to be structurally related to the fate of Southern blacks (Myrdal 1944; Janiewski 1985). This is more than a matter of heightened consciousness or organizing skills learned by white women in the abolitionist and Civil Rights movements. Rather, it reflects an edifice of paternalism, the twin pillars of which are patriarchy and racial oppression, culminating first in slavery, then segregation. When one pillar weakens, the entire edifice tilts. Southern white men's opposition to the 19th Amendment may have reflected an awareness of objective conditions. When one subordinate group gains status and partially escapes from paternalism, power over others weakens as well.

With passage of the 19th Amendment, many political, economic, and social forces were unleashed that affected gender relations in the South. Social legislation of the Depression years and the Civil Rights legislation of the 1960s improved the status of women in a variety of ways. As shown in Chapter 1, World War II and women's increased participation in the labor market brought other changes. After World War II, radical economic and social changes weakened antebellum traditions, enhanced the status of women, diminished the power and advantages of men, and in other ways altered gender relations and conceptions in the South.

Cultural Influences

Cultural explanations are popular with historians, sociologists, journalists, and the public. Claims that Southern men are the only (white) American men to have suffered defeat in war (prior to Viet Nam) imply that the Southern man's ego and self-confidence are fragile. Southern women are claimed to have responded to this by perceiving their men as weak and ineffectual (Abbott 1983) or by feeling they have to protect them (Middleton-Kern 1986). Roland (1960) credits Southern women with pushing young white men into the Civil War—by being more enthusiastic about it than the men were—and also with causing their defection when defeat seemed a certainty. Hostility over the loss of paternalistic rights to control blacks of both genders and their own families, white women especially, may also be a legacy (Thomas 1979; Scott 1983). Honor, shame, and community conformity were the primary norms that guided white men in the antebellum South. The South lagged for a hundred years or more in reaching the kinds of economic and social development that fostered emphasis on the human conscience, guilt, and economic individualism as guides to action (Wyatt-Brown 1982). This allowed Southern (white) men to cheat on and beat their wives, drink themselves to the grave, sexually exploit slave women, engage in duels, ignore the teachings of the church, yet still consider themselves "honorable" men (Smith 1961; Alexander 1983). "Southern males sometimes believed that a little home violence went a long way to ensure loyalty and inspire healthy respect. If it helps with blacks, it surely would help with meddlesome women. . . . [T]he Southern cultural emphasis upon total masculinity, total femininty encouraged male abuse and female submission that stimulated even worse violence" (Wyatt-Brown 1982, 283).

White men's exploitation of black women as concubines affected their relations with white women. Smith (1961, 121) claims: "The more trails the white man made to the back yard cabins, the higher he raised his white wife on her pedestal when he returned to the big house. The higher the pedestal, the less he enjoyed her whom he had put there." White men's desexualization of white women through illicit sexual relations with black women is confirmed by Clinton (1982)—and, according to Abbott (1983, 101), persists today: "Even in the South today, the old lie persists that white girls are pure, and black girls are dirty, and that a youth in search of sexual training will be better off in the arms of a black woman." Antebellum apologists for slavery claimed that black women concubines allowed for the preservation of white women's *purity* (Leslie 1986, 39). Ironically, black men today, according to Staples (1982), believe white women are sexier, freer, and less inhibited than black women.

Among whites, church and religion were the province primarily of women in the antebellum South and are claimed to have shaped not only standards of right and wrong but women's self-images and aspirations (Scott 1970; 1984). Fundamentalist/evangelical religion in the South reinforces traditional relations between men and women, particularly for whites (Martin et al. 1980; Abbott 1983). Scott (1970, 7, 13) claims that submissiveness in (white) women was reinforced by evangelical theology and that "religion confirmed what society told [the Southern white woman]—namely that she was inferior to men." The church provided wider opportunities for black women, although men held official leadership roles. Black women used the church to offer needed social welfare services to other blacks, and women leaders in this effort came from all social classes (Berkeley 1985). Pious, older black women who knew about natural healing were held in high esteem by the black community; and mature black church women across the South were the staunchest supporters of Martin Luther King, Jr., during the Civil Rights Movement of the 1950s and 1960s (Jones 1985).

White Southerners, particularly in the planter class, were inclined to pretensions of aristocratic origins (Escott 1983; Wyatt-Brown 1982). This culminated in an emphasis on family, kin, and ancestry that persists today in Southern fiction (Alther 1975; Welty 1970) and reality (Friedman 1985). Most Southerners can name their first, second, and third cousins, something that non-Southerners are less able to do.

Pretense and fiction also characterize Southerners' use of alcohol. Heavy alcohol use in the South's frontier and antebellum days is said to have come to an end after the Civil War (Taylor 1982). In the late 1960s, two-thirds of Southern Protestants said they were teetotalers, and one-half favored restoring national prohibition (Taylor 1982). Although many Southern counties remain *dry* in the 1980s, wet counties are often overrun with customers from nearby dry counties (Jaynes 1983). Recent research indicates that Southerners, men and women, report that they drink less than people in other regions, particularly in the West (Wilson and Martin 1988b).

The post-World War II influx to the South of residents from the East and Midwest, the South's rapid urbanization, and the spread and impact of national television led to the intrusion of "mass culture" into the South. Reed (Chapter 8 in this volume) shows that this new mass culture, expressing the views and ways of outsiders, differed dramatically from the traditional culture of the Old South. One likely effect of these influences was to homogenize gender conceptions and relations in the South, making them more similar to those in other regions.

Demographic/Geographic Influences

Whites who originally settled in the South differed from those who remained in the East or migrated to the Midwest and West (Killian 1985; Walsh 1985). As noted earlier, white Southerners are primarily British in origin, and black Southerners were brought from

Africa against their will to perform slave labor in an agricultural, plantation-based economy. As European immigrants came to America in the nineteenth and early twentieth centuries, most remained in the East or migrated West. The ethnic homogeneity and geographic isolation of the South contributed to a way of life that differed from the rest of the nation and culminated in a claimed unique folk (Potter 1964) or regional subculture (Thomas 1979; Scott 1984). The institution of slavery, that *peculiar institution* (Thomas 1979), left its indelible stamp on the South, a stamp that affected not only white-black relations but those between men and women as well.

Early settlers in the South were said to have been politically conservative, uneducated, lower-class, indentured servants, mostly male and single (Escott 1983). They settled less frequently in villages and more often on isolated farms and plantations, particularly as compared to New England (Queen et al. 1985, 288). Chesapeake women had fairly high status early in the eighteenth century because there were few of them. High death rates made marriage and remarriage easy (Walsh 1985). As life expectancy rates lengthened and the number of available women increased, patriarchal practices strengthened—and the quality of life for women, white and black, declined. Without the modernizing effects of education and urbanization, the South changed little from the Revolution to the Civil War. After the War and Reconstruction, a similar pattern occurred again until the Civil Rights Movement of the 1960s (Wyatt-Brown 1982). Rough and tough, rural and farming types contributed to a culture of violence not only between men and women but also among men of both races. Private action was a preferred way of preserving honor or settling scraps (Russell n.d.). Lack of education, absence of urban living or sophistication, and an agrarian life-style points, as suggested earlier, to a *traditional* orientation and way of life. As argued by Grasmick (1973), traditionalism entails aspects of paternalism, patriarchy, and racism. In this view, the South's greater reliance on physical violence springs from a traditional way of life and the latter stems from the types of inhabitants who settled in the region.

Throughout the nineteenth and twentieth centuries, both birth and death rates were high. Immigration was limited and the South's population grew slowly. After World War II, however, in-migration increased rapidly, and cities grew dramatically in number and size (see Chapters 2 and 3). The South's population shifted from rural to urban and became increasingly elderly. These demographic trends doubtlessly affected gender and gender relations in the South, mitigating antebellum legacies and making the South more similar to other regions.

Gender and Race in the South

Fiction, film, and the media perpetuate images of Southerners such as the Southern lady and gentleman; the redneck, cracker, or good-old boy; no-good poor white trash; the woman on a pedestal; the manipulative bitch; the hillbilly, rube, or nitwit; the mammy, matriarch, or concubine; and the loafer, rapist, or stud. Stereotypes associated with these characterizations are objects of social science research and persist in the public's mind. In this section, we summarize research on four race/gender categories (white men, white women, black men, and black women).

Southern White Men

Until recently, Southern history was a history of white men. A focus on the public domain of politics, the military, war, law, trade, and economic issues, which by custom and law were dominated by white men, led to an equation of historical and contemporary research with the white man's viewpoint. This viewpoint is now recognized as only one perspective. Wyatt-Brown (1982), in focusing on white men in the antebellum period, depicts the planter-class man as a rather lazy, hard-drinking (an average of 7.1 gallons annually vs. 2.5 gallons in 1970), idle creature who valued honor above all. He was careful to avoid the appearance of either liking his wife too much or spending time in the company of women. He used black women as concubines, particularly during adolescence, and was capable of affection toward children and cruelty toward anyone who violated the codes of the day. The Southerner's code of honor is not to be confused with gentlemanliness. When James Foster of Natchez, Mississippi, beat his wife to death in 1830, he was in a drunken stupor and could not remember what he had done (Wyatt-Brown 1982).

Both planter- and yeoman-class men valued "masculine virtues such as independence, self-reliance, physical strength, courage, endurance, personal honor, racism, and individualism" (Escott 1983,

24). Mary Chesnut's Civil War diary showed disdain for her planter-class husband who lacked ambition and spunk. She longed for the advantages of travel, authority, and career that her husband took for granted (Woodward and Muhlenfeld 1984). Chesnut wrote that planter-class wives felt their husbands' character was besmirched by illicit sexual relations with black slave women.

With some exceptions, Southern white men are described as dishonest and/or uncomfortable with women. Daniell (1980, 155) claims that Southern men are chronic liars "about personal intentions, marital status, genealogy, money and achievement." Carter (1950, 77) writes that "the otherwise heroic Southern male is abjectly afraid of erudite females." Abbott (1983) says Southern men are intolerant of nonconformity in their women, and Darden (1986, 113), in an analysis of fiction by Southern women writers, says the South is uncomfortable with intellectuals of either sex. An intellectual Southern man, she concludes, has "to be crazy or alcoholic to survive." English (1985, 104) in contrast, romanticizes the Southern gentleman as having good character, excellent manners, a sense of responsibility for those dependent on him, and being a defender of traditions "in the service of frail feminine virtue."

Research on Southern working-class men is rare. Boles and Tatro (1979) compared Southern blue-collar white men (N = 123) with a national sample of men and found that Southern men hold more conservative views of women on core gender issues and contribute less time to household chores. Their national sample included all social classes, however; thus, differences between non-Southern and Southern working-class men were untested. Chandler, Chalfant, and Chalfant (1984, 134), in an analysis of country music, found the themes before World War II to depict men and women traditionally and "dwelt primarily upon love, home, family, and church" (also Vander Mey and Bryant 1985). In the 1980s, sexual content, primarily marital infidelity or cheating, is a major theme, and women cheaters are about 75 percent as frequent as men. Current music, they suggest, reflects actual conditions of increased adultery and divorce. Alcohol consumption or *boozing* is celebrated as a positive value for men (but not women) in country-western music lyrics (Chandler, Chalfant, and Chalfant 1984, 142).

Contradictory images of the Southern working-class white man as hell-raiser, redneck, sexist, and racist but also sweet, a pussy-cat, and easily controlled by a smart woman are reported by Abbott (1983). The claimed conservatism and backwardness of Southern working-class men may reflect a traditional life-style associated with rural residence and low socioeconomic status rather than misogynist views of women's status and roles.

Southern White Women

Although historical and sociological research on Southern white women has burgeoned recently, its findings are inconsistent, often contradictory. A special issue of *Sociological Spectrum* (Dillman 1986) was devoted to Southern white women, and several conferences with this focus have been held in Southern states. Historical research on the antebellum Southern white woman by Scott (1984), Clinton (1982), and Woodward (1981) indicates that the image of the Southern lady as helpless, submissive, empty-headed, and a woman of leisure was largely untrue. Clinton (1982) describes a plantation mistress as playing hostess for her husband's dinner guests in the evening—and the next day, laboring at tending vegetable gardens and domesticated animals, supervising children and house slaves, making clothes for family members and slaves, making soap, drying and storing food and vegetables, caring for the sick, and overseeing the entire plantation in her husband's absence.

Atkinson and Boles (1985) report that white upper-class Southern women are aware of the myth of the Southern lady (and belle) but fail to live up to it. Contrary to their hypothesis, their respondents said a Southern lady was rugged (versus delicate), strong (versus weak), deep (versus shallow), poor (versus rich), and intellectual (versus nonintellectual). In related research, Boles and Atkinson (1986) compare upper-middle-class Northwestern and Southern women on their conceptions of an *ideal lady*. Northwestern women said ideal ladies perform few stereotypical behaviors but reported their behavior as consistent with the ideal. Southern women, in contrast, believed that the ideal Southern lady has many stereotypical qualities (eleven versus six for the Northwestern women) but perceived little similarity between the ideal and themselves. Southern women said they engaged *less* than Northwestern women in traditional wife/mother behaviors such as teaching children family traditions, writing letters to their relatives, entertaining their families, managing the household, keeping in touch with their husbands' families by phone, and keeping in touch with their families by phone. Boles and Atkinson concluded that Southern women believe they fail, while Northwestern women believe they succeed, in being ideal ladies. It is also possible, however, that Southern women see the ideal Southern lady as a myth or legend rather than a model for behavior. Findings from two national surveys call into question claims of marked differences between Southern and non-Southern women on gender preferences or ideals (Johnson and Stokes 1984; Courage 1987; also see Table 5-1).

Jones (1983, 92) says the Southern white middle-class and upper-class woman does not have a creative core. "She has been seen and given a voice—a soft, low voice. . . . [S]he struggles to survive in the margin." Brabant (1986), in a sociological analysis of her personal biography, reports that Southern upper-class women live by three values: survival, survival with dignity, and responsibility for those who are dependent on them, particularly children. The sense of duty to family that she describes is similar to English's (1985) description of Southern gentlemen's views on women and family.

Rural Southern women are disadvantaged by poor labor market conditions. Economic development in the South has failed to benefit them (Southeast Women's Employment Coalition 1986). Banes (1981) says Southern white working-class women are hard-working, faithful, honest, simple, and strong, and view family as more important than career. Middleton-Kern's (1986, 104) comparison of working-class women from the South and Northwest found that Southern blue-collar women were much more likely to say that to be fulfilled, "a woman needs a home, husband, children, and a job if necessary." More Southern than Northwestern women (50 versus 9 percent) said they would like to be full-time homemakers. They also expected men to treat them chivalrously (89 versus 9 percent). These women are not necessarily compliant, however. Some Southern respondents said their marriages failed because they wanted to work and their husbands objected. One commented that she lets her husband believe he is in charge "although I am really the dominant one" (p. 96).

Middleton-Kern claims there is "cultural hegemony among contemporary Southern plain folk of a stereotypic gender role ideology" (p. 104). If this is true, we ask why. The women in her sample from the South (N = 28) and the Northwest (N = 42) are in similar occupations, but the labor markets of the two regions are not identical. Differences between women in the two areas may reflect economic and market conditions rather than a hegemonic folk culture. Kanter (1977) notes that ambition in women follows opportunity, not vice versa. When the local labor markets of Southern working women are highly restricted, the desire to work and have a lifelong career under-standably may be low. This interpretation is consistent with Johnson and Stokes (1984), who found only minor differences on gender norms between Southern and non-Southern women in a na-tional survey of married women (N=3404). They conclude that the slightly greater traditionalism of Southern women on gender con-ceptions results from education and labor market conditions rather than a regional subculture. Courage (1987) found that Southern women are *less* traditional on gender issues than women in the East and Midwest.

Southern women are depicted in fictional and nonfictional liter-ature as having many contradictory qualities and a wariness of Southern men (McKern 1979). Florence King says that a Southern white woman "is expected to be frigid, passionate, sweet, bitchy, and scatter-brained all at once. Her problems spring from the fact she succeeds" (1975, 32). Darden (1986) reports that white Southern women are depicted in literature as both strong and spineless, sane and crazy, pure and evil. She concludes that they are "strong with a gritty strength of the farm woman who made it scratching through the dirt of the Civil War to scratching through the dirt of the depres-sion" (p. 113). Abbott says Southern girls are taught at an early age that honesty with men is a tactical error and "of all the skills a Southern woman is supposed to master, managing men is the most important" (1983, 106). Myths and beliefs about Southern white women need to be studied to separate fiction from fact.

Southern Black Men

Southern black men are reported on rarely in the sociological lit-erature. Genovese (1974) and Jones (1985) claim that the pre-eman-cipation black family was father-centered, and the majority of black children were reared before and after the Civil War in two-parent households. Scott (1983) and White (1985) question the father-centered slave household. According to Burton (1985) and Sterling (1984), slaveowners encouraged masculinity among black men and tried to shore up the slave nuclear family by encouraging a tradi-tional division of labor between the sexes. Black men often super-vised the work of slave women; they hunted for game to feed their families (adding to what the master supplied); and they refused to engage in *women's work* (e.g., weaving, cooking, child care). Black men's struggle to become and remain men under slavery may have "included some unattractive manifestations of male aggression" and resulted in a view of wives as "property, virtual slaves, helpless children who had to be taught everything" (Genovese 1974, 180). However, freedmen in the South demanded sufficient wages to allow their wives to stay home and care for the family after slavery's end, suggesting, among other things, a desire to protect their women from further exploitation at the hands of white men (Jones 1985).

The spate of lynchings in the late nineteenth and early twentieth centuries is an important part of the Southern black man's story—as is his fate under slavery, where he was bred and sold for strength, forbidden control over his own amorous and family relations, and denied work opportunities and full inclusion in Southern society for a century after emancipation (Bowers 1984; Genovese 1974; Rose 1976; Mullin 1976). Myths of the black man as superstud and seducer of white women were used to inflame the ire of antebellum plantation owners, to justify lynch mobs in the early 1900s, and to influence jury decisions on rape, murder, and so forth in Southern states (Wyatt-Brown 1982; Bowers 1984).

Hawkins (1986) concludes, ironically, that relations between black and white men may be *better* in the South than in other regions. Reviewing 1980 imprisonment data by state, he found that blacks were nine times more likely to be imprisoned than whites outside the South, compared with five times more likely in the South. Imprisonment was more a function of arrest rates in the South than outside the South. Hawkins surmises that there may be (1) less social distance between whites and blacks in the South, (2) less fear of blacks by whites in the South, and (3) greater imprisonment of whites in the South.

Rural, married North Florida black men are *less* satisfied with life than unmarried men are regardless of age, socioeconomic status, health, or social participation—although 70 percent report high satisfaction with their parental role (Ball and Robbins 1984). Total family income is the best predictor of overall family life satisfaction for married black men (Ball and Robbins 1986). Married black men's lower satisfaction contradicts most prior research on marriage and life satisfaction for men, black and white, and for black women (Zollar and Williams 1986). This may help to explain the comparatively low marriage rate of black men, irrespective of region. In 1980, 43.7 percent of black men versus 63 percent of white men (and 35.6 percent of black women and 57.8 percent of white women), nationally, were married (see Table 5-3 below).

Southern black men are more likely than Southern black women or Midwestern white men and women to engage in premarital coitus. This holds regardless of church attendance or commitment to a relationship (Johnson 1978). Johnson suggests that heterosexual activity is normative at an earlier age for Southern black males. Black men nationally have high death rates from homicide, suicide, and drug/alcohol abuse (Staples 1982; Huff-Corzine, Corzine, and Moore 1986). Staples attributes self-destructive patterns of black male youth to systematic exclusion from legitimate opportunity structures such as education, jobs, and housing. Whatever the cause, black males' high death rate contributes to a skewed sex ratio among blacks. Proportionately fewer black men than women are alive by age 19, and the imbalance worsens with each successive year (Bureau of the Census 1984a, Table 311).

As shown above, the literature is contradictory on the status of black men during and for many years following the Civil War. Some historians depict them as lacking a clear family role, whereas others claim they played relatively predictable roles in stable, monogamous slave and freed families. Developments in the South following World War II—primarily the expansion of the regional economy, slowly improving education, a growing self-consciousness, assimilation into protest movements, and federal social legislation— changed the life circumstances of Southern black men. Whether they were influenced to become more or less involved in normative family roles, to conceive of or play out their gender in unique ways, or to behave differently towards women is unclear. Answers to these questions await additional research.

Southern Black Women

Stereotypes of the black woman depict her as sexually promiscuous, a domineering matriarch, and rearer and nurturer of white children. Research by historians and sociologists contradicts these depictions. Jones (1985) characterizes the American black woman as a courageous, feisty team player who tried to protect her children, family, and home against the destructive forces of slavery, Reconstruction, and segregation. Research indicates that most slave women had their children by one father (Steckel 1980; Genovese 1974; Jones 1985), that they worked in the fields beside the men as much or more than they worked "in the big house" (Jones 1985), and that they cooperated among themselves to preserve their families and a quality of life that ensured safety and nurturance (Sterling 1984; White 1983, 1985).

Research recounts the role of black women in collective struggles in the South throughout American history (Janiewski 1983; Frederickson 1982). Black women played important roles in the Abolitionist and Woman Suffrage Movements (e.g., Sojourner Truth). White male union leaders credit the success of a 1943 strike against the R. J. Reynolds Tobacco Company in Winston-Salem to the commitment and courage of black women workers (Jones 1985, Chapter 7). Rosa Parks sparked the Civil Rights Movement of the mid-twentieth century by refusing to relinquish her seat on a Montgomery, Alabama, bus in 1955.

Black women have long enjoyed high status in the black church (Jones 1985). Although seldom formal leaders (i.e., ministers), they helped make the church the most important social institution in the black community besides family and home. Between the end of the Civil War and the early twentieth century, black women established church-based mutual aid societies that provided material and financial assistance to thousands of needy blacks (Berkeley 1985). Leaders of these groups came from all social classes, and those who held leadership positions for the greatest length of time came from the *least skilled* occupations (Berkeley 1985, 194). Myrdal (1944) claims the church has always afforded Southern black women more opportunity for leadership and equality than it has white women. Jones (1985) claims that the primary supporters of Martin Luther King, Jr.,—and the backbone of the Civil Rights Movement—were respected older women who were influential in the black church.

In a study of poor black Southerners who migrated to Chicago in the 1950s and 1960s, Stack (1974) found a complex pattern of reciprocity and sharing, or swapping, where people exchanged household objects (e.g., cooking utensils), Food Stamps, money, child-minding, clothes, and more. Privacy had little value—or chance—in an intricately linked communal system of family and kin. Kin-based relations were stronger than those between husbands and wives, and members of both genders found the securest support in their own kin group. "Mothers generally regard their children's fathers as friends of the family—people they can recruit for help—rather than as fathers failing in their parental duties" (1974, 119). Men's unemployment had a particularly negative influence on relations between women and men. Stack's subjects had been away from the South for some time when they were studied—some for as many as twenty years—yet she believes that their mutual support and kin-based networks were survival mechanisms transported from the rural South.

Dougherty (1978) studied rural black girls who were becoming women in north central Florida by focusing on adult bonding, sexual relations, and motherhood. Similar to others (e.g., White 1983), Dougherty found they had determination and a special ability to survive. Research on older black women in a segregated South found that family and community in combination with work and mutual aid sustained them in difficult times (Wilson 1973). More black than white women of all ages and classes are employed outside the home for pay, and proportionately more black than white women are heads of households inside and outside the South (Bureau of the Census 1984b, Table 318; also see Table 5-5 below).

Scholarship and fiction depict the Southern black woman as spirited, strong, stable, and a survivor. Mention is often made of a special quality, an irrepressible optimism and hope in the face of seemingly insurmountable odds. Jones (1983, 92) describes this as a "sustaining core of creativity, born of the effects of cultural invisibility and oppression . . . a spring of creativity." She claims that white Southern women do not have a similar sense of who and what they are. Alice Walker's (1982) *The Color Purple* and Zora Neale Hurston's (1937) *Their Eyes Were Watching God* are fictional accounts of the indomitable spirit that Southern black women are said to have.

Southern-Style Gender: Trends and Conditions

This section presents four types of data relative to Southern-style gender. Census Bureau data enable us to compare marriage, family, employment, and occupational statuses by gender, region, and race for twenty years, 1960–80. We also analyze selected 1980 data for the four national regions. Besides Census data, we review: (1) national public opinion poll data on women's rights; (2) data on legislative action by the fifty states on women's rights (the vote and equal rights); and (3) FBI data on violent crimes against persons. These data allow us to describe various aspects of Southern-style gender and to anticipate changes that the next fifty years may bring. Minimal regional differences are revealed in some tables, and the reader is reminded that the U.S. Census definition of the South includes some states and Washington, D.C., that are not viewed usually as Southern. To compensate for this, we examine some results for the Old South as well (Killian 1985). Both models of the South are described in Chapter 1.

Opinions on Women's Rights

Table 5-1 reports data from a 1982 Gallup poll of a national sample of 26,000 adult Americans (The Gallup Report 1982). Items are shown by region with states grouped according to Census Bureau boundaries (see Table 5-2). Results indicate minor regional differences in attitudes toward women's rights. Southern respondents are somewhat more likely than respondents in other regions to believe that women have job opportunities equal to those of men—48 percent versus 41 or 42 percent in other regions (Item 1)—and are only slightly less likely to endorse the opinion that women *should* have such opportunities. More than 8 of 10 Southerners favor equal job opportunities for women, whereas 9 of 10 Westerners do (Item 2). Southerners' beliefs that a competent woman's chances for rising to company executive are as good as a man's differ only from those of Westerners. Easterners and Midwesterners' views resemble those of Southerners (see Item 3). Eighty-five to 95 percent of all respondents have heard of the Equal Rights Amendment (ERA), with the South having the lowest percent (see Item 4). Among those who knew about the ERA (Item 5), Southerners and Midwesterners were least supportive (51 and 52 percent), with Easterners most favorable (67 percent). Similar results held for whether the ERA should be re-offered to the states for ratification (Item 6).

When asked about preferences for a boss's gender, Southern respondents were only slightly more favorable toward a man and equally likely to prefer a woman (Item 7). When asked about an ideal life-style—with options ranging from "married with children and a full-time job" to "unmarried with a full-time job" (Item 8)—Southern women are similar to women in other regions and, in fact, are slightly *less desirous* of a traditional, full-time homemaker role. Southern women are least likely to prefer "marriage with children and no fulltime job" and most likely to prefer a "full-time job without marriage." (These results contradict Middleton-Kern 1986, and confirm Johnson and Stokes 1984 and Courage 1987.) Differences are small, however, and without controls for race, social class, and urban/rural residence, conclusions are tentative. The failure of

Southern women to endorse home and family over paid work *more* than women in other regions is nevertheless noteworthy.

Data in Table 5-1 suggest that Southerners are slightly more conservative on women's rights than Westerners and Easterners but are similar to Midwesterners. The differences are modest, however, and Southerners and non-Southerners alike favor equal rights for women. Recent research by Courage (1987) extends and clarifies our findings. Analysis by gender, race, and region of a 1985 sample of 4,000 adults shows that Southern women, black and white, are less traditional than Southern men and, more significantly, less traditional than women in the Northeast and Midwest in their views of women's normative family and work roles. Only Western women hold views of women's family-work roles that are as nontraditional as Southern women's. Courage concludes that Southern men are conservative on gender but Southern women are not. Her research shows, furthermore, a wider *gender gap* on conceptions of women's family and work roles among Southerners—blacks even more than whites—than among adults in other regions.

Women's Legal and Political Status

Most Southern states failed to ratify the 19th Amendment early in the twentieth century and the Equal Rights Amendment more recently. Data in Table 5-2 show how consistent this trend has been. Dates of ratification or enactment are shown for four types of legislation: state legislation that gave women the right to vote in Presidential (and some state and local) elections prior to the 19th Amendment; ratification action on the 19th Amendment that gave women the right to vote in all governmental elections; ratification action on the Equal Rights Amendment that would have added an article to the U.S. Constitution giving equal rights under the law to all regardless of sex; and state action on state Equal Rights legislation relative to sex.

Regions that gave women the vote prior to the 19th Amendment were the Midwest and West. All states in both regions (with the exception of New Mexico in the West) passed such legislation. In contrast, only three of nine Eastern and five of sixteen Southern states did so. The East's reluctance was overcome, however, when the 19th Amendment was offered for ratification and every state in the union (except Southern ones) ratified. With the exceptions of

Table 5-1. Attitudes Toward Women's Rights (in June 1982) among Adults by Region

Survey Questions Asked	East[a]	Percent Yes Mid-West	South	West
1) Do women have equal job opportunities with men?	42	41	48	41
2) Should women have equal job opportunities with men?	85	86	83	92
3) If a woman has the same ability as a man, does she have as good a chance to become the executive of a company?	46	42	45	33
4) Have you heard or read about the Equal Rights Amendment?	87	94	85	95
Asked only to those who have heard of ERA:				
5) Do you favor the ERA	67	52	51	56
6) Should ERA be re-offered to the states to ratify?	62	54	52	57

Table 5-1 continued.

7) In taking a new job, would you
prefer a man or woman as a boss?

Prefer man	44	46	49	45
Prefer woman	10	11	13	14
No difference	40	39	35	38
No opinion	6	4	3	3

Asked of women only:

8) Which would be the ideal life-style
for you?

Married, children, fulltime job	44	35	38	43
Married, no children, fulltime job	4	7	4	5
Married, children, no fulltime job	.41	39	37	40
Married, no children, no fulltime job	-	3	3	1
Unmarried, fulltime job	5	3	8	7
No opinion	6	13	10	4

Source: The Gallup Report. 1982. "Women." Report No. 203 (August), pp. 23-29.

[a]U.S. Census Groupings, see Table 5-2.

Table 5-2. Some Political Status-Raising Actions on Behalf of American Women, by Dates and by Geographic Areas

Geographic Areas	The Vote before 1919[a]	Ratify 19th Amendment[b]	Ratify ERA[c]	State Equal Rights Amendment[d]
New England (6 states)	1917-1919 (2 states)	1919-1921 (6 states)	1972-1974 (6 states)	1974-1976 (3 states)
Mid-Atlantic (3 states)	1917 (1 state)	1919-1920 (3 states)	1972 (3 states)	1971 (1 state)
East North Central (5 states)	1913-1919 (5 states)	1919-1920 (5 states)	1972-1977 (4 states)	1970 (1 state)
West North Central (7 states)	1912-1919 (7 states)	1919 (7 states)	1972-1975 (6 states)	
South Atlantic (8 states)		1920, 1941-1971 (7 states)	1972 (3 states)	1971-1972 (2 states)
East South Central (4 states)	1919-1920 (2 states)	1920-1953 (3 states)	1972* (2 states)	
West South Central (4 states)	1917-1918 (3 states)	1919-1970 (4 states)	1972* (1 state)	1972 (1 state)

Mountain West (8 states)	1890-1896 (4 states) 1912-1914 (3 states)	1919-1920 (8 states)	1972-1974 (5 states)	1890 (1 state) 1973-1977 (2 states)
Pacific West (5 states)	1910-1913 (4 states)	1919-1920 (3 states)	1972-1973 (5 states)	1972 (3 states)

Sources:

[a]The National American Women Suffrage Association. 1940. Victory: How Women Won It. A Centennial Symposium 1840-1940. New York: H. W. Wilson.

[b]Morgan, David. 1972. Suffragists and Democrats: The Politics of Woman Suffrage in America. Lansing: Michigan State University Press.

[c]Boles, Janet, and Charlotte Tatro. 1979. The Politics of the Equal Rights Amendment: Conflict and the Decision Process. New York: Longman.

[d]Dean, Virginia, Patti Roberts, and Carroll Boone. 1984. "Comparable Worth under various Federal and State Laws." Pp. 238-266 in Helen Remick, ed., Comparable Worth and Wage Discrimination. Philadelphia: Temple University Press.

*State rescinded or attempted to rescind Equal Rights Amendment.

Mississippi and Delaware, which have never ratified, all remaining states finally did so by 1971. At the time it was offered, only six Census-South states ratified the 19th Amendment: Arkansas, Oklahoma, Texas, Tennessee, Kentucky, and West Virginia. This pattern was replicated closely half a century later on the ERA.

The East is the only region that ratified the ERA 100 percent (Table 5-2, Column 3). Two of twelve Midwestern states, Illinois and Missouri, failed to ratify, as did three Western states, Arizona, Utah, and Nevada. The South again stood out. Six states ratified—including Delaware, Maryland, West Virginia, Kentucky, Tennessee, and Texas—and ten did not. If Old South states are examined, only two ratified the ERA (Tennessee and Kentucky), and the legislatures of both tried later to rescind. Only fourteen states (Column 4) have state ERAs, and three of these are in the Census-South: Maryland, Virginia, and Texas.

Eight of eleven Old South states failed to ratify the 19th Amendment, and nine of eleven failed on the ERA. Swain (1983) notes that popular opinion in the South favored the ERA but state legislators did not approve it. With the exception of belated ratification of the 19th Amendment (by six of the seven), seven states have never passed any legislation giving women equal rights—and all seven are Old South: Alabama, Florida, Georgia, Louisiana, Mississippi, North Carolina, and South Carolina. Mississippi has done nothing at all. The low status of women in Mississippi, compared with other Southern states, is confirmed by statistics on women who have been appointed or elected to public office.

Southern women have made progress since 1970 in gaining elective and appointive political office. Five of fifty states in 1981 had women in at least 20 percent of appointed cabinet posts, and three of these were Southern: Alabama 21 percent, Arkansas 20 percent, and North Carolina 22 percent (Swain 1983, 48). In contrast, Georgia had 3 percent, Mississippi 6 percent, and Texas and South Carolina none. Four of five female Supreme Court justices in the nation in 1981 were Southern: North Carolina, Alabama, Mississippi, and Texas. (Florida has named one recently.) The decade of the 1970s showed an increase in women elected to the state legislature. The proportion of female state legislators increased in the South from 2.5 percent in 1971 to 7.6 percent in 1981, compared with a non-South increase from 7.0 to 14.1 percent (Main, Gryski, and Schapiro 1984). The South lags behind the national mean of 12.1 percent, but if the 1970 rate of increase holds in the 1980s, the gap could close by 1991 (Swain 1983, 49).

Women's electoral success for state legislative office is affected by rurality and incumbency. Southern women candidates are more likely to be elected in urban than rural areas and in contests not involving incumbents (Fowlkes 1984). Of 121 women in Southern state legislatures in 1981, 17 (or 14 percent) were black (Swain 1983). Virginia and Mississippi are the only Southern states that have never elected a black woman to the state legislature. Southern black women have won more local than state offices. In 1973, one-third of all black women in elective office were in the Confederate states, and most of them were on school boards (Swain 1983). The South is similar to the nation on women's representation on county governing boards (5 percent are women versus the national mean of 6 percent), although Kentucky led all fifty states in 1980 with 45 percent women. Mississippi, in contrast, had only 1 percent (Swain 1983, 48). Mississippi and Louisiana were lowest in the nation in 1980 on proportion of women state legislators (1.1 percent and 1.4 percent, respectively).

Marriage and Family/Household Status and Changes

Americans are marrying later and having fewer children than before, and the proportion of family households with only one parent has increased substantially since 1970 (Bureau of the Census 1985). To determine if the South has mirrored these national trends, data in Table 5-3 report the marital status of adults in 1960, 1970, and 1980 by race and gender, for the United States as a whole and for the South separately.

Data in Table 5-3 show that Southerners are similar to non-Southerners on marital status. Southerners are somewhat more likely than adults nationally to be married, and this is true for men and women of both races. Somewhat fewer Southern whites than blacks are single. Marriage is the modal marital status for all four race/gender groups, but the proportion married, in the South and elsewhere, is considerably higher for whites than blacks. Between 1960 and 1980, black women, Southern and otherwise, have experienced the greatest increase in single status and the greatest decrease in marriage. Divorce has increased 150 percent or more since 1960 for all four race/gender groups inside and outside of the South. The proportional rise in divorce was greatest for Southern black men, who were, nevertheless, slightly less likely than all black men to be divorced in 1980.

Table 5-3. National and Southern Percents of Persons by Race, Gender, and Marital Status and Ratio of Southern to National Changes by Dates, 1960-1980

Race, Gender, and Marital Status	Year					
	1960[a]			1970		
	Nation	South	Ratio	Nation	South	Ratio
White Men						
Single	24.5	24.1	0.98	27.6	26.0	0.94
Married	68.9	69.8	1.01	65.8	67.8	1.03
Separated	1.0	1.1	1.10	1.1	1.1	1.00
Widowed	3.5	2.9	0.83	2.8	2.4	0.86
Divorced	2.1	2.0	0.95	2.7	2.7	1.00
White Women						
Single	18.7	17.4	0.93	21.6	19.1	0.88
Married	65.2	66.7	1.02	60.8	63.2	1.04
Separated	1.3	1.3	1.00	1.5	1.4	.93
Widowed	12.0	11.9	0.99	12.3	12.4	1.01
Divorced	2.7	2.7	1.00	3.8	3.8	1.00
Black Men						
Single	30.5	31.4	1.03	35.8	36.7	1.03
Married	56.5	56.1	0.99	50.8	50.6	1.00
Separated	5.6	5.4	0.96	5.6	5.2	0.93
Widowed	4.9	5.3	1.08	4.3	4.8	1.12
Divorced	2.4	1.9	0.79	3.3	2.7	0.82
Black Women						
Single	22.3	23.4	1.05	28.5	29.2	1.02
Married	51.8	56.1	1.08	43.6	43.8	1.00
Separated	8.3	7.6	0.92	9.3	7.9	0.85
Widowed	14.0	15.5	1.11	13.4	15.0	1.12
Divorced	3.6	2.8	0.78	5.2	4.1	0.79

[a]The 1960 figures for blacks include all nonwhites. The figures for 1960 and 1970 include adults 14 years and older while the figures for 1980 include adults 15 years and older.

	Year				
	1980			Percent Change 1960 to 1980	
Nation	South	Ratio		Nation	South
28.0	25.2	0.90		14.3	4.6
63.0	65.9	1.05		-8.6	-5.6
1.4	1.4	1.00		40.0	27.3
2.4	2.2	0.92		-31.4	-24.1
5.2	5.3	1.02		148.0	165.0
21.2	18.1	0.85		13.4	4.0
57.8	60.6	1.05		-11.3	-9.1
1.7	1.7	1.00		30.8	30.8
12.5	12.7	1.02		4.2	6.7
6.8	6.8	1.00		151.9	151.9
40.6	39.8	0.98		33.1	26.8
43.7	45.4	1.04		-22.7	-19.1
5.8	5.5	0.95		3.6	1.9
3.6	3.9	1.08		-26.5	-26.4
6.3	5.4	0.86		162.5	184.2
34.1	33.0	0.97		52.9	41.0
35.6	37.6	1.06		-31.3	-33.0
8.6	7.8	0.91		3.6	2.6
12.6	13.9	1.10		-10.0	-10.3
9.1	7.7	0.85		152.8	175.0

Sources: Bureau of the Census: 1964, 1960 Census
of Population: Characteristics of the
Population, Vol. 1, Tables 48 and 53;
1973, 1970 Census of Population:
Characteristics of Population, Vol. 1,
Tables 54 and 58.
1984, 1980 Census of Population: Characteristics of Population, Vol. 1, "Chapter D: Detailed
Population Characteristics." Tables 264 and 317.

From Table 5-3, we conclude that gendering as reflected in marital and family arrangements has changed in the South since 1960, and these changes parallel national trends. This is confirmed by data in Table 5-4 on the proportion of families that contain married couples and married couples with children younger than 18 in the household. Among whites, Southern and national, more than 85 percent of families contain married couples. This proportion has decreased since 1960 but by less than 5 percent. The proportion of married-couple homes with children younger than 18 decreased substantially over the twenty-year period, by 21 percent nationally and 27 percent in the South, so that by 1980, the percentage of such families in the South and nation was almost identical (42.4 and 42.6 percent). Among blacks in this period, the percentage of married-couple families decreased much more. Southern blacks, nevertheless, changed more slowly. Decreases since 1960 in married-couple black families, and married-couple black families with dependent children, were somewhat less in the South than in the nation as a whole.

Overall, Southerners' marital and family statuses in 1960, 1970, and 1980 are very similar to non-Southerners', and the changes that have occurred mostly follow national trends. This suggests that Southern trends over the next fifty years, with minor exceptions, will replicate national trends. It is impossible to know whether Americans will continue to marry later and have fewer children and whether marriage will continue to decrease among blacks. Almost as many blacks in 1980 were single as were married. This reflects, in part, a dearth of eligible black men for black women to marry (Bureau of the Census 1984a) and the economic hardships that blacks—men and women, Southern and non-Southern—experience in trying to support their families (Wilson 1987b).

Labor Force Participation, Education, Earnings, and Occupation

Employment and socioeconomic data provide information on changes in Southern gendering. Are Southern women working for pay more often today than previously, as women nationally are? Are more Southern mothers with small children employed? Are fewer Southern men employed today? The answers to these questions are yes. Data in Table 5-5 show that labor market participation rates of

Southern men and women are similar to national rates, as are increases in women's employment and decreases in men's employment since 1960. Increases in employment among Southern white women with children younger than age 6 were 10 to 12 percent less than women's nationally because, in part, more Southern white women were employed in 1970. These results show that Southern women and men, white and black, are engaged in paid employment at rates the same as or higher than non-Southerners. If recent trends continue, more Southern women will become employed over the next fifty years. As this occurs, Southern fertility rates, at least among white women, will probably continue to decline. Data not shown indicate that *employed* Southern black women have higher fertility rates than unemployed Southern and non-Southern black and white women (Bureau of the Census 1984b, 1145–1238).

Education. Are Southern men and women completing high school more than in the past? Do they increasingly resemble non-Southerners on educational achievement? Again, the answer is yes. Data in Table 5-6 show that white Southerners, like most Americans, had a median of twelve-plus years of education in 1980, an increase from 1960 of 16 percent for women and 25 percent for men. Southern blacks' education increased even more, with women increasing by 52 percent and men, 76 percent. Continuation of these trends, which are dramatic for a twenty-year period, may soon erase Southern blacks' deficiency on educational achievement. As Southerners gain more education, this will presumably translate into higher earnings in the labor market. An education gap between black and white Southerners persists in 1980, however, with blacks completing about one year less of schooling.

Earnings. Data in Table 5-7 show that earnings of employed Southerners increased substantially between 1960 and 1980. Southern black women, like black women nationally, earned more than 100 percent more in 1980 than in 1960, and Southern black men earned 71 percent more. Southern white women's earnings increased by 61 percent, almost 20 percent more than white women's nationally. Southern white men benefited also, with a 36 percent increase, compared with a national increase of 19 percent. These data show an improved standard of living for Southerners and probably reflect the South's development from agrarian and rural to industrial and urban. Southern black women's earnings in 1980 were only 85 percent of the national median for black women and black men's, 89 percent of the black men's median. Southern black men's earn-

Table 5-4. National and Southern Percents, Ratios of South to Nation, and Percent Change of Nation and South of Married Couples with and without Children under 18, by Race and by Years 1960-1980

| | Whites | | Blacks[a] | |
| | Percent of Families | | | |
Year	Married Couples	Married Couples with children	Married Couples	Married Couples with children
1960				
Nation	89.2	53.7	78.3	45.2
South	89.4	58.0	74.2	44.7
Ratio	1.00	1.08	0.95	0.99
1970				
Nation	88.5	48.9	67.5	40.5
South	88.9	48.6	68.4	40.8
Ratio	1.00	0.99	1.01	1.01

1980				
Nation	86.2	42.4	57.1	33.3
South	87.2	42.6	59.7	35.1
Ratio	1.01	1.00	1.05	1.05
Percent Change 1960 to 1980				
Nation	-3.4	-21.0	-27.1	-26.3
South	-2.5	-26.6	-19.5	-21.5

Sources: Bureau of the Census:

1964. 1960 Census of Population: Characteristics of the Population. Vol. 1. Tables 79 and 102.
1973. 1970 Census of Population: Characteristics of the Population. Vol. 1. Tables 54 and 58.
1983. 1980 Census of Population: Characteristics of the Population. Vol. 1. Tables 121 and 205.

[a]1960 figures are based on data for all nonwhites.

Table 5-5. Rates, Percent Change and Ratio South to Nation of Labor
          Force Participation, United States and the South, by Race,
          Gender, and Year; and for Women Only, by Race, Family
          Composition, and Year: 1960-1980

Race and Gender	1960			1970		
	Nation	South	Ratio	Nation	South	Ratio
White Men	80.9	79.6	0.98	77.4	76.3	0.99
White Women	34.8	33.0	0.95	40.6	39.5	0.97
Women/Men Ratio	0.43	0.41		0.52	0.52	
Black Men	75.7	73.8	0.97	69.8	68.1	0.98
Black Women	43.7	42.8	0.98	47.5	46.7	0.98
Women/Men Ratio	0.58	0.58		0.68	0.69	

White Women Only						
With at least one child under 6	NA	NA		28.4	32.3	1.14
With husband present and child under 6	NA	NA		26.1	29.9	1.15

Black Women Only						
With at least one child under 6	NA	NA		47.6	51.8	1.09
With husband present and child under 6	NA	NA		48.1	50.8	1.06

Sources: Bureau of the Census: 1964, <u>1960 Census of Population:
         Characteristics of the Population, Vol. 1</u>, Table 144; 1973,
         <u>1970 Census of Population: Characteristics of Population,
         Vol. 1</u>, Table 132.

Year					
	1980			Percent Change 1960 to 1980	
Nation	South	Ratio		Nation	South
76.1	75.2	0.99		-5.9	-5.5
49.4	48.1	0.97		42.0	45.8
0.65	0.64				
66.7	66.6	1.00		-11.9	-9.8
53.3	53.1	1.00		22.0	24.1
0.80	0.80				
White Women Only					
43.6	46.3	1.06		53.5	43.3
41.7	44.0	1.06		59.7	47.2
Black Women Only					
58.3	63.2	1.08		22.5	22.0
65.1	67.6	1.04		35.3	33.1

Sources: 1983, <u>1980 Census of Population:</u>
<u>Characteristics of Population. Vol. 1,</u> "Chapter
C: General Social and Economic Characteristics,"
Tables 86, 87, 206, and 228.

Table 5-6. Median Years of School Completed, Percent Change, and Ratio South to Nation, by Race, Gender, and Year, 1960-1980

Year	Race and Gender					
	White Men	White Women	Women/Men Ratio	Black Men	Black Women	Women/Men Ratio
1960						
Nation	10.7	11.2	1.05	7.7	8.4	1.09
South	10.0	10.7	1.07	6.3	7.5	1.19
Ratio	0.93	0.96		0.82	0.89	
1970						
Nation	12.1	12.1	1.00	9.4	10.1	1.07
South	11.8	11.9	1.01	8.2	9.0	1.10
Ratio	0.98	0.98		0.87	0.89	
1980						
Nation	12.6	12.5	0.99	12.0	12.0	1.00
South	12.5	12.4	0.99	11.1	11.4	1.03
Ratio	0.99	0.99		0.93	0.95	
Percent Change 1960 to 1980						
Nation	17.8	11.6		55.8	42.9	
South	25.0	15.9		76.2	52.0	

Source: Bureau of the Census. 1983. 1980 Census of Population: Characteristics of the Population. Vol. 1, Chapter C: "General Social and Economic Characteristics," Table 83.

ings disadvantage decreased linearly from 1960 to 1980; but Southern black women were worse off in 1970 than in 1960, and their improvement, relative to black women nationally, was minimal by 1980. Additionally, Southern black men and women earned considerably less in 1980 than Southern white men and women. In 1980, Southern black women earned 85 percent of the median earnings of black women nationally, 75 percent of Southern white women's earnings, and 33 percent of Southern white men's. Southern black men in 1980 earned 89 percent of all black men's median earnings, 59 percent of Southern white men's, and 54 percent of all white men's.

Occupation. Since comparable data on occupational statuses for the three time periods are unavailable, 1980 data are reviewed by region. Table 5-8 shows that occupational differences are greater between genders and races than between regions. Nevertheless, regional differences do involve the South, primarily for blacks. Southern black men, along with Midwestern black men, are considerably more likely to be laborers. Southern black women, compared to Southern white women and other black women, particularly Western, hold fewer support (secretarial, clerical, sales) jobs. Southern black men are somewhat less successful than other black men (and than Southern black women) in securing managerial or professional jobs. Blacks of both sexes are more advantaged on occupational status in the West. The data suggest that labor market opportunities for Southern blacks are highly restricted (Horan and Tolbert 1984). It is nevertheless probable that Southern blacks' occupational statuses have improved since 1960 and will continue to do so. They are likely, however, to lag behind those of Southern (and non-Southern) whites, slowly approaching those of blacks in other regions.

Southern Gender and Violence

Reed (1986) asserted that interpersonal violence is a long-standing Southern tradition, and a good deal of evidence supports his claim. Some scholars claim that Southern men are prone to employ violence in their relations with both women and men (Wyatt-Brown 1982), but others argue that Southern violence is primarily a masculine, man-to-man, phenomenon (Huff-Corzine, Corzine, and Moore 1986). In the latter view, Southern women are sheltered and protected from violence by Southern men (Russell n.d.).

Table 5-7. Median Income,[a] Percent Change, and Ratio South to Nation, by Race, Gender, and Year, 1960-1980[b]

			Race and Gender			
Year	White Men	White Women	Women/Men Ratio	Black Men	Black Women	Women/Men Ratio
1960						
Nation	10,799	3,760	0.35	5,613	2,254	0.40
South	8,776	3,280	0.37	4,092	1,823	0.45
Ratio	0.81	0.87		0.73	0.81	
1970						
Nation	13,408	4,700	0.35	8,053	3,964	0.49
South	11,506	4,518	0.39	6,417	3,069	0.48
Ratio	0.86	0.96		0.80	0.77	

	(1)	(2)	(3)	(4)	(5)	(6)
1980						
Nation	12,881	5,356	0.42	7,827	4,674	0.60
South	11,916	5,292	0.44	6,988	3,984	0.57
Ratio	0.93	0.99		0.89	0.85	
Percent Change 1960 to 1980						
Nation	19.3	42.4	20.0	39.4	107.4	50.0
South	35.8	61.3	18.9	70.8	118.5	26.7

Source: Bureau of the Census. 1964. 1960 Census of Population: Characteristics of the Population. Vol. 1, Table 219.

1972. 1970 Census of Population. "General Social and Economic Characteristics." United States Summary. PC (1)-1C.

1983. 1980 Census of Population: Characteristics of the Population. Vol. 1, "Chapter C: General Social and Economic Characteristics," Table 95.

[a] in 1979 dollars.

[b] Figures of 1960 and 1970 are based on persons aged 14 years and older; 1980 figures are for persons aged 15 years and older.

Table 5-8. Numbers and Percents of Workers by Occupation, by Race, by Gender, and by Region

Race, Gender, Region	Managers, Professionals	Support Occupations	Service Occupations	Farming	Precision Production	Laborers
White Men						
East	26.3	20.0	9.4	2.1	20.2	22.0
Midwest	21.7	17.1	7.9	5.8	21.2	26.3
South	23.5	19.5	7.1	4.1	23.7	22.0
West	26.9	20.0	8.9	4.3	21.3	18.7
White Women						
East	22.9	47.3	14.8	0.5	2.1	12.5
Midwest	20.3	45.6	18.8	1.1	2.3	12.0
South	22.5	47.7	14.1	0.8	2.4	12.4
West	24.0	48.3	16.8	1.0	2.5	7.3

Table 5-8 continued.

Black Men						
East	13.8	19.8	19.2	0.8	14.5	31.8
Midwest	11.4	15.0	16.6	0.8	14.4	41.7
South	9.5	12.0	15.2	5.4	16.5	41.2
West	16.1	21.3	18.1	1.9	15.8	26.6
Black Women						
East	17.2	41.4	25.7	0.1	2.0	13.5
Midwest	16.7	39.7	24.3	0.1	2.1	17.1
South	15.6	29.2	31.8	1.0	2.6	19.9
West	20.0	47.3	22.1	0.3	2.6	8.8

Source: Bureau of the Census. 1984. 1980 Census of Population: Characteristics of the Population. Vol. 1, Chapter D: "Detailed Population Characteristics," Table 325.

Note: The experienced labor force is composed of:

	East	Midwest	South	West
White Men	11,315,520	14,256,593	15,401,017	9,559,116
White Women	8,088,075	9,775,616	10,615,218	6,660,048
Black Men	884,473	981,971	2,575,164	452,941
Black Women	890,263	924,067	2,467,910	409,478

To address these issues, we pose two questions: Are Southern men particularly violent toward Southern women, and are Southern men particularly violent toward each other, as compared to the other U.S. regions? Has this issue changed over time? Data from the Federal Bureau of Investigation (that are not reported here) suggest that the answer to the question on greater Southern inter-gender violence is "No." Southern men are not particularly violent toward Southern women. In regards to forcible rape, for example, the eleven Old South states have a rape incidence-rate in 1984 (Department of Justice 1985, 44–51) that is no different from that in the Midwest, only slightly higher than that in the East, and considerably lower than that in the West. Additionally, Wilson and Martin (1988b), in reporting on data from a national sample of married adults, find that Southern husbands and wives report less wife beating than do husbands and wives in other regions. The incidence of reported rapes increased by 318 percent in the nation as a whole between 1960 and 1980. The increase for the Census South (16 states plus Washington, D.C.) during this time was 352 percent. Because the South began the twenty-year period with a lower (reported) incidence rate, its greater increase brought it into line with the rest of the nation by 1980. Whether these results indicate a growing incidence of forcible rape (and thus a deteriorating quality of inter-gender relations in both the South and other U.S. regions) or an increase in willingness to report the crime, or both, is unknown.

On the issue of male-to-male violence, the South does appear to be violence prone. Most murders are by and of men, and murder rates for the Census South states, and the Old South states, were somewhat higher than in other regions in 1984. The West was most similar to the South with an index of 8.4 compared to the Census South's 10.0 and the Old South's 9.2. The West led the nation on aggravated assaults in the mid-1980s (330 vs 318 for the South, 260 for the East, and 249 for the Midwest), suggesting that the South's status as the most violence-prone region is changing. Reasons for this change are not a decline in murder and aggravated assault rates in the South but a rise in these crimes in other regions. For the United States as a whole, the murder rate increased by 100 percent between 1960 and 1980 but by only 37 percent in the South while the aggravated assault rate increased by 300 percent nationwide and 207 percent in the South (Department of Justice 1961, 1971, 1981).

Looking to the Future

Questions posed at the beginning of Chapter 5 can now be addressed. Have Southern gender relations and conceptions changed in fifty years? Is Southern gendering different from gendering in other regions? The answer to the first question is yes; to the second, possibly. Southern women, white and black, are less oppressed and restricted in their normative roles than before. They lag behind women in the rest of the nation in election to political office, but increases over the past two decades show they may be catching up. Data on legislation for women such as the 19th Amendment, ERA ratification, and, more recently, comparable worth or pay equity (Godbey 1987) show that the South lags behind the nation in granting women the same legal rights that men have. Southern women are employed for pay, even with small children, and this has increased dramatically in just twenty years. Southern men and women, and their relations to each other, have very likely changed as their educational achievement, earnings, and occupational statuses have risen, their experience of divorce has increased, their age at marriage has risen, and their family size has decreased.

In anticipating the future, we return to the three categories of influence (1) social/political/economic, (2) cultural, and (3) geographic/demographic. Speculations assume an absence of catyclismic social, economic, or political changes such as takeover by another nation-state, severe economic depression, and nuclear warfare. National and international influences will continue to affect the South in the next fifty years as they have since World War II. Because their objective status lags behind that of non-Southern women, Southern women have "further to go" than women in other regions, thus changes in their life circumstances and roles are likely to be great. As their lives change, so will Southern men's. We have argued that gendering is intertwined with material and ideological conditions— thus, as the South develops economically and becomes more urban, its ideological and behavioral character, including gender conceptions and relations, will change. The South's historical ethnic mix of Anglo-white and Afro-black may condition these changes, however; so, while Southern gendering is likely to resemble gendering in the rest of the nation in fifty years, some distinctiveness may remain.

(1) *Social/Political/Economic Influences.* As the South becomes

more urbanized and as population continues to migrate to large urban areas away from small towns and farms, Southerners' gender conceptions and practices may become less traditional. Urban women work for pay more than suburban and rural women do, and urbanites' conceptions of women's paid work and home responsibilities are less traditional. Southerners' conceptions of gender and gendering may become similar to those of men and women in other regions where dense, urban living is already modal. At the same time, economic development may contribute to an increase in divorce among Southerners. As women become more independent economically, escape from unsavory domestic situations is more feasible. The South's higher proportion of married couples and higher rates of child-bearing in 1980 may disappear as economic development and urbanization increase.

The movement of American business and industry into the South, in search of low taxes, cheap labor, and mild climate, should lead to an improved labor market for Southern workers, male and female. Economic development will increase men's earnings more than women's—thus the economic gap between men and women will widen. This may contribute to increased marital breakups and an overall lowering of women's standard of living as more women become single heads of households after divorce. Some information about corporate salaries indicates that female corporate officers in the South are paid one-half of their female peers in other regions, whereas Southern male officers are paid the same as non-Southern men. Moreover, Southern women executives are more likely than non-Southern women to have had children and to be divorced heads of households. Expectations that women will marry and have children, regardless of what else they do, are strong in the South. Greater similarity to the rest of the nation on economic development and urbanization could lead to a decline of this norm.

As urbanization and industrialization increase, Southern women's success at election to public office will improve. The increases of the 1970s and 1980s will continue into the 1990s and thereafter, since starting points in the South, prior to then, were so low. On the other hand, the South may continue to lag behind the nation on affirmative legal action for women. The confounding of gender and race and the Southerner's political conservatism and suspicion of change will retard changes in the legal/political sphere until sufficient numbers of women, blacks, and urban/liberal male commissioners, legislators, and governors are elected to public office.

Southern women are unlikely to enjoy a legal/political status equal to that of women in other regions for years to come.

An increase in economic prosperity in the South should lead to lower murder rates. Southern white men's murder rates are a function of poverty (Huff-Corzine, Corzine, and Moore 1986). Improved economic conditions could contribute to a reduction of such murder rates. Prosperity should affect black men also. Blacks' economic well-being will improve more slowly and less fully than whites', however, and the murder of Southern black men by each other may remain prevalent into the twenty-first century.

(2) *Cultural Influences.* The South's cultural distinctiveness is perhaps clearest in regards to organized religion. Its citizens are not only more Protestant than those in other regions, but more of them are affiliated with fundamentalist denominations that tend to hold traditional conceptions of men and women. Membership trends show that fundamentalist denominations are gaining members while mainstream churches are losing. Membership in the Southern Baptist church grew by 15 percent in the 1970s (The Gallup Report 1985). If fundamentalist religion contributes to traditional conceptions and practices of gendering, church-going Southerners may cling to conservative views on women's roles and place well into the next century.

Sexual assault of women by men occurs in the South less than in the West and only slightly more than in the East. Southern men's traditional conceptions of women's rights and place (Courage 1987) appear not to engender hostility that culminates in a higher incidence of violence or abuse. Wife battering is no more prevalent in the South than elsewhere (Wilson and Martin 1988a), and no evidence suggests that this will change.

Available research is unable to confirm or reject claims that Southerners' gender conceptions and practices are more traditional or stereotyped than those of non-Southerners. Even more in doubt are the causes of difference. Although historians (such as Wyatt-Brown) claim that Southerners are more traditional, recent survey research casts doubt on this, particularly for women (Courage 1987; Johnson and Stokes 1984). Regional differences, if any, may result from culture and ideology or from economic development, urbanization, or political and material conditions. If Southern culture—language, vocabulary, idioms, ways of speaking, thinking, and doing—loses its distinctiveness, does this mean that distinctive gender conceptions will disappear? The intrusion of national television, newspapers, and other media into its most rural reaches has no doubt affected the South (and non-South). Southerners increasingly imitate non-Southern trends, adopt non-Southern vocabularies and speech, imitate outsiders' behavior (sexual practices, drug and alcohol use, fashions), and so on. Cultural change in the South may be toward greater similarity to the rest of the nation, with the result that gendering will become more similar as well.

(3) *Demographic/Geographic Influences.* Contrary to trends of prior decades and even centuries, many outsiders moved to the South in the recent past. They flocked to large, urban areas where industries and corporations are located, but they also moved to small towns and medium-sized cities. These "new Southerners," often well-educated and skilled, arrived with good paying jobs and high expectations for educational, cultural, and social affairs. They neither knew nor cared about distinctive Southern ways. If such immigration continues, differences in gender conceptions between Southerners and non-Southerners will erode. Outsiders will come to view themselves as "Southern" but will lack identification with Southern ancestors, the Civil War, or myths about family, slavery, and a Southern uniqueness that ties them to a "Southern" view of the world, including conceptions of and relations between women and men.

With the recent immigration of Hispanics and Asians to the South (see Chapter 6), the ethnic homogeneity of the Old South is disappearing. Greater ethnic diversity will dilute normative constraints on Southern men and women, boys and girls, black and white, as they venture into new realms, social positions, and relationships. With the influx of outsiders into the region, a distinctive Southern-style of gendering, if it now exists, may disappear.

6

Trends in Ethnic Relations: Hispanics and Anglos

W. Parker Frisbie

Defining the Issues

This analysis assesses trends and current conditions in relationships of Hispanics and Anglos (non-Hispanic whites) in the South in an effort to anticipate what intergroup relations may be like over the next fifty years. The present effort will take the figure of fifty years seriously, but not literally. That is, my concern is with what Hispanic-Anglo relations may be like in the medium-to-long-run and not in any specific date.

The aspects of Hispanic-Anglo relations of primary interest are those that indicate the degree to which Hispanics have acquired the socioeconomic and political characteristics of the general population. The focus will be on what Frisbie and Bean (1978) have referred to as "structural assimilation" (or on what McLemore [1980] terms "secondary structural assimilation"). As employed by Frisbie and Bean, the concept is quite different from that defined by Gordon (1964) and is more closely akin (but is not identical) to van den Berghe's (1967) view of social (structural) pluralism as distinguished from cultural pluralism. Specifically, I will be interested in evaluating the potential for Hispanics to achieve equal access to, and full participation in, the social, economic, and political structures of American society over the next several decades. It is my assumption that, although cultural assimilation (acculturation) may be related

149

to structural assimilation, it is not a requisite for the achievement of the latter.

In order to carry out this undertaking, it will be necessary (1) to assess briefly the current position of Hispanics in American society, (2) to bring to bear salient information on past trends, and (3) to identify and analyze a set of determinants that can be expected to influence future trends in structural assimilation as defined above.

These three tasks dictate the organization of this chapter. But before proceeding, it warrants mention that the various Hispanic or Latino groups are far too diverse to allow treatment of them as if they formed a single, homogeneous entity. A highly generalized consideration of Hispanic-Anglo relations conceals more than it reveals. The data must at least be decomposed into separate, but not unrelated, analyses of the largest Hispanic minority populations—Mexican Americans, Cubans, and Puerto Ricans.

Ethnic Status and Minority Status

The relationship between minority and majority populations is a complex amalgam of the historical conditions of contact, the current ecnomic context (both local and national), and the social and cultural differences separating the groups. Understanding these relationships becomes even more complicated when minority and ethnic status coincide to some degree. It should be obvious that an ethnic group may or may not be a minority. The term *minority* may be reasonably taken to refer to a group "whose members experience a wide range of treatment and frequently are relegated to positions relatively low in the status structure of a society" (Gittler 1956, vi; quoted in Yetman and Steele 1975, 1–2). An ethnic group, on the other hand, may be defined as a "collectivity within a larger society having real and putative common ancestry, memories of a shared historical past, and a cultural focus on one or more symbolic elements defined as the epitome of their peoplehood" (Schermerhorn 1970, 12). To illustrate, at an earlier point in the history of the United States, "the Irish were clearly both an ethnic group and a minority, but currently they would not seem to constitute a minority . . ." (Frisbie and Bean 1978, 5).

Although all Hispanics, to some degree, share a common cultural heritage (Padilla 1984), the extent of overlap between ethnic and minority group status varies across the several Hispanic subpopulations—and, for any particular group, the applicability of the term *minority* has varied over time.

Hispanic Populations

Over the years, the Census Bureau has employed several operational strategies in an attempt to define the Hispanic population in as complete and reliable a manner as possible. The only identifiers consistently available over more than the past two enumerations are those that identify persons of "foreign stock" and persons of Spanish surname. The former definition excludes all persons except those of foreign birth or foreign parentage. That is, no third- and later-generation individuals are picked up by this item. The Spanish surname designation, as determined by a post-censal classification, is available from 1950 to 1980, but its coverage has been limited to only the five states of the Southwest (Arizona, California, Colorado, New Mexico, and Texas). Since 1970, the census has relied heavily on self-identification by respondents, a procedure that seems to provide the most appropriate operational definition (Hernandez et al. 1973). Based on items of this sort, individuals may identify themselves as being of Mexican, Puerto Rican, Cuban—or, for that matter, of any Spanish origin.

Despite the changing methods of identification employed by the Census, for the three largest Hispanic groups, it is possible to draw consistent comparisons and trace trends back to 1960 and, in some cases, to 1950. Spanish surname primarily identifies Mexican Americans, for close to 90 percent of this group continued to reside in the Southwest in 1960 (87 percent in 1970; see Grebler et al. 1970), and the vast majority of the Spanish surname population in the Southwest is of Mexican origin. As to Puerto Ricans and Cubans, the limitation to the foreign stock items is, fortunately, not a serious one. Even as late as 1970, more than 80 percent of all Cubans in the United States were foreign born and most of the remainder were of Cuban parentage, and more than 97 percent of all Puerto Ricans were either Puerto Rican born or of Puerto Rican parentage (U.S. Bureau of the Census 1973b; 1973c; 1973d). Thus, before 1970, one may rely on surname (in the case of Mexican Americans) and foreign stock items (in the case of Puerto Ricans and Cubans), and from 1970 onward one may employ the preferred self-identification indicator with the expectation of a high degree of reliability in defining the major Hispanic populations.

Another issue is how to refer to the groups whose origins trace back to Spain and its influence on the New World. For the entire population, one may choose among the terms *Hispanic, Spanish origin,* and *Latino.* For some of the subpopulations (e.g., Cubans and Puerto Ricans), there seems to be only one rubric in common use. However, the list of terms used both within and outside the group to designate persons of Mexican origin includes: *Mexican American, Chicano, Latin American, Hispano, Mexicano,* and *La Raza.* As McLemore and Romo (1985) suggest, each of these rubrics has both advocates and opponents, and popularity of nomenclature is partly a function of region of residence. Here, the choice is *Mexican American* or *Mexican origin,* since these terms appear to be the most generally used and accepted.

Interregional Scope of the Analysis

In addressing the question of Hispanic-Anglo relations in the South, it is necessary to recognize the non-Southern regional concentrations of various Hispanic groups. Of the three largest Hispanic populations, Mexican Americans, Cubans, and Puerto Ricans, only the first two reside in substantial numbers in the South. The census of 1980 enumerated about 8.7 million persons of Mexican origin of whom roughly 3.1 million (or 35.5 percent) lived in the South—primarily in Texas—while 4.7 million (54.1 percent) were found in the Western United States, with about 3.6 million in California alone (Table 6-1). On the other hand, Table 6-1 shows that nearly 64 percent of the 800,000 Cubans in the United States were in the South in 1980, including approximately 470,000 in Florida. By contrast, only 9 percent of Puerto Ricans and less than 25 percent of all other Spanish origin groups combined were residents of the South in 1980. The latter, consisting of persons from a large number of Central and South American countries (as well as from Spain itself), show some preference for the West, while the vast majority of Puerto Ricans in the United States are found in the Northeast, especially in the New York City area.

These regional concentrations are nothing new. For example, from the earliest large wave of immigration following the ascent to power of Fidel Castro to the present, Cubans have settled primarily in Flor-

Table 6-1. Regional Distribution of the Hispanic Population in the United States, 1980

	Region					Percent of Total
	Northeast	North Central	West	South	Total	
Total Spanish						
Number	2,608,074	1,269,994	6,257,167	4,468,448	14,603,683	100.0
Percent	17.9	8.7	42.8	30.6	100.0	
Mexican American						
Number	90,431	809,540	4,699,332	3,079,329	8,678,632	59.4
Percent	1.0	9.3	54.1	35.5	99.9	
Puerto Rican						
Number	1,479,554	208,076	135,690	181,641	2,004,961	13.8
Percent	73.8	10.4	6.8	9.1	100.1	
Cuban						
Number	183,544	32,874	74,353	515,452	806,223	5.5
Percent	22.8	4.1	9.2	63.9	100.0	
Other Spanish						
Number	854,545	219,504	1,347,792	692,026	3,113,867	21.3
Percent	27.4	7.0	43.3	22.2	99.9	

Source: Bureau of the Census. 1980. General Social and Economic Characteristics, United States Summary PC80-1-C1 (December 1983), Table 233.

ida in and around the Miami area (Davis et al. 1983). And while there are fast-growing Mexican American populations in certain Midwestern states (Illinois and Michigan), the historical concentration of Mexican Americans in the five Southwestern states has very largely persisted. About 83 percent remained there in 1980 (Davis et al. 1983, 13; U.S. Bureau of the Census 1982c). These relative numbers denoting geographical concentration are not greatly different from those based on counts and estimates of Mexican Americans in the Southwest that stretch back to the period of the Mexican Revolution (i.e., to 1910; see Grebler et al. 1970, Chapter 6).

Obviously, then, an examination of Hispanic-Anglo relations that is limited to the Southern region would yield important—but incomplete—results. Expanding our horizons to take into account populations in other regions, especially the Southwest, will perhaps not take us too far afield from the orienting theme of this book, particularly since the trend in Hispanic population redistribution is in the direction of the Sun Belt. Bean and Tienda (1987) document a strong migration trend toward the South for the three Hispanic subpopulations between 1975 and 1980. Whether one focuses on the net change in numbers of migrants or on the net migration rate, the South ranks ahead of all other regions in gains of Mexican American, Puerto Rican, and Cuban populations. In fact, only the South and West show net migration gains for Hispanic populations between 1975 and 1980 (Bean and Tienda 1987, Table 5.10). Should this trend continue, it is obvious that Hispanics will become increasingly important in the social, economic, and political life of the South.

Past Trends and Current Conditions

Population Size and Growth

One of the features that distinguishes sharply among Hispanic groups is the length of time each group has been in this country in significant numbers. Persons of Mexican origin, of course, preceded Anglos as residents of what is now the southwestern United States, and it may be argued that the Mexican Americans, as an ethnic group, emerged with the acquisition of Texas and other border territories by the United States in the mid-nineteenth century. It was not until the early twentieth century that a large population of

Mexican origin began to reside north of the U.S.-Mexico border (McLemore and Romo 1985).

In any event, the history of Mexican Americans in this country is long when contrasted with that of Puerto Ricans (few of whom left the island for residence on the mainland before World War II) and that of Cubans (for whom immigration was minimal before the rise to power of Fidel Castro in 1959). The small size of the latter two groups prior to 1960 imposes the usual limitations on collection and dissemination of official statistics. However, as Table 6-2 shows, by 1970 all three of these groups had attained sufficient size for most analytical purposes, and each of the three was growing at a rate far in excess of the total population.

The total Spanish origin population grew about six times faster than the total population between 1970 and 1980. The fastest growth, by far, is observed in the *near doubling* of the number of Mexican Americans counted in the 1980 census as compared with the 1970 enumeration. Some fraction of this increased count of Mexican Americans is no doubt a result of the Census Bureau's concerted effort to enumerate undocumented aliens in 1980. Since current research indicates that approximately 1.1 million undocumented immigrants from Mexico were counted in that year (cf. Passel and Woodrow 1984), and since there is no reason to believe that large numbers of *indocumentados* were included in earlier censuses, part of the increased count must be the result of improved coverage. Nevertheless, the largest part of the increase was obviously owing to real growth, especially through natural increase (Browning and Cullen 1983). Among Cubans, immigration is the largest single source of growth. Nearly 300,000 Cubans immigrated to the United States between 1970 and 1979 (see Davis et al. 1983, 22). Although Puerto Ricans are citizens of the United States (due to Commonwealth status of the island) and therefore, technically, cannot be immigrants, it may be noted that movement from the island to the mainland has slowed considerably in recent decades (Davis et al. 1983).

Initial Contact and Minority-Majority Relationships

Because of the data limitations described above, this analysis is restricted primarily to contrasting the social structural conditions and trends that have characterized the three Hispanic groups over

Table 6-2. Population by Race/Ethnicity in the United States, 1970-1980

Race/Ethnicity	1970		1980		Change 1970-1980
	Number	Percent[a]	Number	Percent[a]	Percent
Total	203,210,158	100.0	226,545,805	100.0	11.5
White	178,119,221	87.7	189,035,012	83.4	6.1
Black	22,549,815	11.1	26,482,349	11.7	17.4
Total Spanish Origin	9,072,602	4.5	14,603,683	6.4	61.0
Mexican American	4,532,435	2.2	8,678,632	3.8	91.5
Puerto Rican	1,429,396	0.7	2,004,961	0.9	40.3
Cuban	544,600	0.3	806,223	0.4	48.0
Other Spanish	2,566,171	1.3	3,113,867	1.4	21.3

Sources: Bureau of the Census. 1970. "Persons of Spanish Origin." <u>Subject Reports</u> PC(2)-1C (June 1973), Table 1.

Bureau of the Census. 1970. "Negro Population." <u>Subject Reports</u> PC(2)-1B (May 1973), Table 1.

Bureau of the Census. 1970. "General Social and Economic Characteristics." <u>United States Summary</u> PC(1)-C1 (June 1972), Table 68.

Bureau of the Census. 1980. "Persons of Spanish Origin by State." <u>Supplementary Report</u> PC80-S1-7 (August 1982), p. 2.

Bureau of the Census. 1980. "General Social and Economic Characteristics." <u>United States Summary</u> PC80-1-C1 (December 1983), Tables 72, 74, 75.

[a]Percentages do not sum to 100 percent since persons of Spanish origin may be of any race. However, well over 90 percent of Hispanics are white by conventional census definitions.

the past two decades. Yet it is evident that (1) minority structural assimilation (as the term is defined herein) will be affected by the response of the majority, and (2) current minority-majority relationships cannot be understood without some reference to the conditions of initial contact and the very different historical experiences of Mexicans, Puerto Ricans, and Cubans in the United States.

The presence of Cubans in significant numbers is a recent phenomenon. Although Cuban settlement in the United States dates at least to the nineteenth century, prior to 1959 this country had fewer than 50,000 Cuban residents (Davis et al. 1983, 8; Perez 1986). The first large wave of immigrants came from the upper and middle classes and, as escapees from the Castro regime, these people were viewed as deserving a warm and supportive welcome. As later tabular presentations indicate, Cubans have gone some considerable distance toward structural assimilation.

Puerto Rico became a U.S. territory in 1898 as a result of the Spanish-American War. But even though Puerto Ricans have been American citizens with free access to the United States since the passage of the Jones Act in 1917, the census of 1940 enumerated fewer than 70,000 Puerto Ricans on the mainland (Davis et al. 1983, 7–8). Things began to change dramatically in the late 1940s, as thousands of Puerto Ricans migrated to the East Coast of the United States, especially to the New York City area, in search of jobs. These newcomers were more than a little reminiscent of earlier European immigrants. They were leaving a location where industrialization was supplanting a formerly agrarian-based economy and where population was in excess relative to economic opportunities. Their destination was the large metropolitan areas, and the niches they found often took the form of entry-level manufacturing jobs (Ortiz n.d., 2–3). The influx was so rapid that, in the 1950s, nearly half a million Puerto Ricans left the island for the mainland and made up more than half of all Hispanic migrants to America. Since that time, movement to and from Puerto Rico has ebbed and flowed with changes in economic conditions, but the overall volume of Puerto Rican migration has declined substantially. In fact, only a little more than 40,000 Puerto Ricans migrated to the mainland in the 1970s (Davis et al. 1983, 22). Decreases in labor force participation among Puerto Rican household heads (Table 6-5, discussed below) mirror diminishing opportunities in blue-collar employment in the Northeast and help explain the decline in movement from the island.

   Immediately after Mexico achieved independence from Spain in
1821, permission was granted for limited settlement of Anglo-Amer-
ican immigrants in Texas. Within less than two decades, a revolt was
mounted that led to the independence of Texas. Unfortunately, the
fact that many native Mexicans joined forces with Anglos in the
latter conflict did not prevent strong antagonisms between the two
groups from emerging, a situation that deteriorated even further
with the annexation of Texas by the United States and the war with
Mexico that followed (McLemore 1980). Although the territory
ceded to the United States by Mexico under the terms of the Treaty
of Guadalupe Hidalgo was vast, "the entire Mexican population of
the Southwest in 1848 may have been no more than 80,000"
(McLemore and Romo 1985, 12). On the other hand, movement back
and forth across the border was frequent and relatively unrestricted,
and the borderlands were the scene of violent conflict between the
Anglo and Mexican-origin populations (McLemore and Romo 1985).
By the 1890s, the land and labor policies of the Mexican government
forced millions of persons from the land, thereby setting the stage
for large-scale emigration to the United States during the early part
of the twentieth century. Spurred partly by chaotic conditions resulting from the 1910 revolution, more than 600,000 legal immigrants from Mexico were reported for the 1910–1930 interval, who,
along with an unknown number of undocumented immigrants, contributed heavily to a more than sixfold increase in the Mexican
origin population (Cardoso 1980, 52–53, 94). Although sharply diminished during the Great Depression, the volume of Mexican immigration again surged during and following World War II. This new
immigration was supplemented by workers who came under the
Bracero Program—a 1942 executive agreement between Mexico and
the United States whereby Mexican workers came to this country to
work temporarily under government-controlled conditions. However, as an attempt to create an orderly and regulated movement of
Mexican labor, the *Bracero Program* was a distinct failure—and
large numbers of undocumented workers continued to enter the
United States. Legislation passed in 1952 and 1965 did little to in-
hibit the northward surge. It remains to be seen whether the recently enacted Immigration Reform and Control Act of 1986, which
for the first time imposes stiff legal sanctions on persons who knowingly employ undocumented aliens, will substantially reduce the
flow of undocumented workers.
   During World War II, Mexican Americans began a rapid transfor-

mation from a population more heavily concentrated in rural areas and in agricultural occupations than the general population to a distinctly urban group with only a small fraction of workers remaining in the extractive sector (Grebler et al. 1970; Davis et al. 1983). Despite the highly conflictual nature of the early contact between Anglos and the Mexican-origin population, the latter have made remarkable socioeconomic progress in the years since World War II. Nevertheless, a number of studies have shown that Mexican Americans continue to experience both prejudice and discrimination (Frisbie and Neidert 1977; Poston and Alvirez 1973; vander Zanden 1972, 100–02; Verdugo and Verdugo 1984).

Although few studies exist that allow specific comparisons of the degree of discrimination encountered by the three Hispanic groups, Mexican Americans clearly seem to have encountered greater opposition from the majority to their efforts to enter the social, economic, and political mainstream than have Cubans or Puerto Ricans. The data presented below demonstrate that inequalities continue to separate Hispanic groups from the majority population and from each other. Of course, inequality does not necessarily denote discrimination, since human capital resources and numerous other factors may be responsible for socioeconomic disparities. Thus, in a later section, socioeconomic returns to education, labor force experience, and other such factors are considered in more detail.

Socioeconomic Conditions and Trends

In the discussion that follows, comparisons are drawn sometimes with the total population and other times with the Anglo population, depending on data availability and comparability over time. Since Anglos constitute such a large proportion of the total, it is not surprising that where both types of comparisons are possible, conclusions reached are exactly the same. As is to be expected, the differentials are slightly greater when the contrast is with respect to Anglos as opposed to the total population. For some tabular entries, census data do not distinguish non-Hispanic blacks from blacks of Hispanic origin (e.g., U.S. Bureau of the Census 1973a).

(1) *Education*. Education is a key socioeconomic attribute in assessing the ease and degree of participation of any group in American society. In the first place, education serves as a mechanism of

acculturation. Although cultural assimilation does not necessarily give rise to structural assimilation, the knowledge and skills acquired through formal education obviously play a major part in determining opportunities for obtaining higher status in general, and more highly rewarded occupations in particular.

The various Hispanic populations have lower levels of education as compared with the total population. Mexican Americans and Puerto Ricans have by far the lowest levels of educational achievement. For example, Table 6-3 shows that, in 1980, only about 40 percent of Mexican Americans and Puerto Ricans aged twenty-five years and older had completed high school, and, on the average, education for these two groups was terminated after only a year or two of schooling beyond the elementary grades. The figures for 1980 represent a substantial improvement over 1970 levels; nonetheless, Mexican Americans and Puerto Ricans lag well behind the general population. The trend for Cubans was also upward in the 1970s, so that by 1980, a majority (55.3 percent) aged twenty-five or older had completed high school (Table 6-3). Furthermore, median level of education for Cubans stood at 12.2 years in 1980, only a little below the average for the general population and slightly above the black median. The fact that Cubans have higher levels of education than Mexican Americans and Puerto Ricans and on average lag only slightly behind Anglos is not surprising, since the major influx of Cubans fleeing the Castro regime came from the middle and upper classes, while migrants from Mexico and Puerto Rico were more apt to emerge from groups farther down the socioeconomic hierarchy (Jaffe et al. 1980; Davis et al. 1983). Later waves of Cuban immigrants have not been selected so heavily from among the better educated, and the most recent large migration from Cuba, which occurred via the Mariel boatlift, arrived after the completion of the 1980 census.

(2) *Labor Force Participation.* Since large proportions of each of the Hispanic groups are migrants to the United States—and since in modern times, migration has been largely a movement of labor (Portes 1978; Portes and Bach 1985)—labor force participation should be a useful indicator of the reception encountered by recent immigrants, as well as of the subsequent accessibility of the American economic system to them and their offspring. Of course, factors other than the structure of majority-minority group relations will impinge on labor force trends. Economic decline may reduce the number of available jobs, and the rapid growth in the number and

Table 6-3. Level of Educational Attainment in the United States by Type of Spanish Origin, Race, and Dates, 1970 and 1980

Groups	Percent High School Graduates (Persons 25+)		Median Years of School Completed	
	1970	1980	1970	1980
Mexican American	24.2	37.6	8.1	9.6
Puerto Rican	23.4	40.1	8.7	10.5
Cuban	43.9	55.3	10.3	12.2
Black[a]	31.4	51.2	9.8	12.0
Total Persons	52.3	66.5	12.1	12.5

Source: Bureau of the Census. 1970. "Persons of Spanish Origin." Subject Reports PC(2)-1C (June 1973), Table 4.

Bureau of the Census. 1970. "General Social and Economic Characteristics." United States Summary PC(1)-C1 (June 1972), Table 88.

Bureau of the Census. 1980. "General Social and Economic Characteristics." United States Summary (December 1983), Table 166.

[a]All blacks in 1970; blacks not of Spanish origin in 1980.

proportion of female workers may directly or indirectly produce a decline in male participation rates. Despite these complications, substantial variation in labor force participation by ethnicity would certainly indicate differences in the degree of structural assimilation.

At least three important conclusions are suggested by the data on labor force participation rates in Table 6-4. First, except for a small increase among Mexican Americans, male workers in all groups showed a decline in labor force participation in the 1970–80 interval. In sharp contrast, participation of women in the work force grew substantially between 1970 and 1980. The increase is particularly marked among Mexican American women, who recorded the only double-digit (12.6 percent) increment. Third, race or ethnicity per se does not seem either to stimulate greatly or stifle seriously this participation. Mexican American and Cuban males have the highest rates at both points in time, and the same is true for black and Cuban females. Thus, except for the gains among Mexican Americans and the overall comparatively low rates among black males, no major racial/ethnic differentials emerge from Table 6-4.

However, there is evidence of more substantial ethnic variation (and especially a deteriorating situation for Puerto Ricans), if one tracks labor force data from 1960 onward (Cooney and Warren 1979; Ortiz n.d.), and particularly if one focuses attention on workers who are household heads (Frisbie et al. 1985, Chapter 5). In Table 6-5 are data on labor force participation by race/ethnicity for two types of household heads between 1960 and 1980. The two household types, female-headed and intact (never disrupted) male-headed households are important because, in a very real sense, they represent the range of economic characteristics related to household and family structure. Households containing a head and spouse with no history of marital disruption and with children present have typically been found to be better off economically than "non-couple households" (Bianchi 1981; Frisbie et al. 1985). In addition, if there is such a thing as an ideal or traditional household type in the United States, it would likely be one composed of a married couple, neither of whom has ever experienced marital dissolution, who are residing with their child or children. Although such a traditional arrangement has become less and less normative over time, it remains the modal type for all the racial/ethnic groups (except for blacks) included in this analysis (see Frisbie et al. 1985, Chapter 4). Thus, household heads in this category would seem to be a logical baseline against which to draw comparisons.

Table 6-4. Civilian Labor Force Participation Rates of Persons Aged 16 and Older in the United States, by Spanish Origin, Race, Sex, and Dates, 1970[1] and 1980[2]

Groups	Males			Females		
	1970	1980	Change 1970-80	1970	1980	Change 1970-80
Mexican American	77.4	79.7	2.3	36.4	49.0	12.6
Puerto Rican	76.1	71.4	-4.7	32.3	40.1	7.8
Cuban	83.7	78.0	-5.7	51.0	55.4	4.4
Black[a]	69.8	66.7	-3.1	47.5	53.3	5.8
Total Persons	76.6	75.1	-1.5	41.4	49.9	8.5

[1]Source: Bureau of the Census. 1970. "Persons of Spanish Origin." Subject Reports. June, 1973 Table 7.
Bureau of the Census. 1970. "General Social and Economic Characteristics." United States Summary, PCC1-C1, June, 1972. Table 90.

[2]Source: Bureau of the Census. 1980. "General Social and Economic Characteristics." United States Summary, PC80-1-C1, December, 1983. Table 168.

[a]All blacks in 1970; blacks not of Spanish origin in 1980.

One of the most salient of other comparisons involves female-headed households, which in the past two decades have grown several times faster than the number of households with both spouses present (Ross and Sawhill 1975; Glick 1984). Second, female-headed households constitute such a growing and disproportionately large share of low-income households that many observers have begun to speak of the "feminization of poverty" (Auletta 1982). In addition to the importance of these two household types for analytical and policy-related purposes, their comparison makes clear the case for marital status as a predictor of progress toward structural assimilation by Hispanics over the next several decades.

As can be seen in Table 6-5, allowing for illness and disability, participation in the labor force is virtually universal among male heads of intact families where children are present. (Other research [Bianchi 1981, 89] suggests that it may be more the presence of children per se, rather than number of children, that is associated with stable participation in the labor force among male heads.) The one exception, alluded to above, is in regard to Puerto Ricans, among whom rates for male heads of traditional families are relatively low compared with those of their counterparts in the other racial/ethnic groups.

The low levels of labor force participation among female heads contrast markedly with those of married male heads. Again, with the exception of Puerto Ricans, female heads in all racial/ethnic groups recorded minor (0.2 percent among blacks) to large (13.9 percent among Mexican Americans) increases in rates. Puerto Rican females who head households experienced a sharp decline over the twenty-year period, so that by 1980 the rate was only about half that for the other groups of female heads. One explanation for this diminution of attachment to the labor force probably lies in the decline of employment opportunities (especially in manufacturing) in the Northeast, where Puerto Ricans continue to be rather concentrated (Ortiz n.d., 19). Also important appear to be shifts in labor demand by education (or skill) level (Cooney and Warren 1979). Likewise, the propensity of Mexican Americans to settle in the Southwest, which has figured prominently in the Sun Belt economic boom (reported in Chapters 1 and 3) may partially explain the overall improvement in labor force participation (Table 6-4), including the major rise in rates among female heads (Table 6-5).

Neither the rapid increase in rates among Mexican American females—nor the large declines among Puerto Rican women—can

Table 6-5.   Labor Force Participation Rates of Household Heads in the United States by Household Type, Spanish Origin, Race, and Dates, 1960-1980

	HOUSEHOLD TYPE							
	Never Disrupted with Spouse and Children				Female Headed			
Groups	1960	1970	1980	Change 1960-80	1960	1970	1980	Change 1960-80
Mexican American[a]	97.8	95.3	95.5	-2.3	50.7	55.6	64.6	13.9
Puerto Rican[b]	93.1	90.3	89.0	-4.1	52.1	32.1	35.3	-16.8
Cuban[b]	98.3	96.0	96.1	-2.2	69.8	74.3	73.7	3.9
Black[c]	95.5	93.7	93.5	-2.0	63.9	60.7	64.1	0.2
Anglo[d]	98.2	97.6	97.0	-1.2	68.8	72.9	76.5	7.7

Source: Frisbie, W. Parker et al. 1985. Household and Family Demography of Hispanics, Blacks, and Anglos. Final NICHD Report. Austin: University of Texas Population Research Center, Table 5-3.

[a] In 1960, Mexican Americans are identified as whites of Spanish surname. In 1970 and 1980, Mexican Americans are defined as those who self-identify as of Mexican origin.
[b] In 1960, Puerto Ricans and Cubans are identified in terms of foreign birth and foreign parentage. In 1970 and 1980, Puerto Ricans and Cubans are those who self-identify as of Puerto Rican and Cuban origin, respectively.
[c] Non-Hispanic blacks.
[d] Non-Hispanic whites.

continue indefinitely. Nevertheless, one is forced toward the conclusion that obtaining a desirable economic niche in the U.S. economy is a much brighter hope for Mexican Americans and Cubans
than it is for Puerto Ricans. However, if the explanation of the down-
turn among Puerto Ricans offered above is correct, a reversal might
be achieved in relatively short order by a greater dispersal of Puerto
Ricans out of the Northeast coupled with training that would facilitate the acquisition of jobs requiring higher skill levels (Ortiz n.d.,
20).

(3) *Income.* Income data yield much the same conclusions in regard to the economic position of Hispanics in American society as
does information on other socioeconomic characteristics. Both in
hourly wages and median income, Cuban males most nearly approach the level of Anglo males (Bean et al. 1985). By contrast, the
income of Puerto Rican and Mexican American males is lower and
more nearly approximates that of blacks (Table 6-6). Female hourly
wages are comparatively low, especially among Mexican Americans.
It is interesting to note that, while Puerto Rican hourly wages tend
to exceed Mexican American wages, median income is higher for
the latter group. A similar finding holds when black and Mexican
American males are compared. A plausible explanation of this
seeming anomaly is that Mexican Americans, who are concentrated
in a region where wages are relatively low, simply work more hours
than Puerto Ricans or blacks.

Table 6-7 presents trends in occupational and income distributions by type of household headship. The table indicates that, in the
case of both husband-wife and female-headed households, the proportion employed in white-collar jobs has increased faster in each of
the three largest Hispanic populations than in the Anglo population.
On the other hand, comparisons such as the latter mask the fact that
minorities may be concentrated in lower-paying jobs within the
broader occupational categories (McLemore 1980, 238). Thus, for
most comparisons, the income (in constant dollars) of Hispanic
household heads, relative to their Anglo counterparts, did not rise
appreciably in the twenty years between 1960 and 1980—and in
some cases the Hispanic/Anglo ratios actually declined.

While female heads are more apt to have obtained white-collar
jobs than are male heads of families, on the average they earn much
less. This may be the result of (1) the concentration of females in the
lower ranks of white-collar employment, (2) gender differentials in
seniority, full-time employment, and wage levels, and/or (3) discrim-

Table 6-6.   Average Hourly Wage and Median Annual Income by
              Sex, Race, and Hispanic Group[1]

Groups	Average Hourly Wage, 1975[a]	Median Annual Income, 1979[b]
Mexican American		
Males	$4.31	$8,858
Females	2.88	4,556
Puerto Rican		
Males	4.52	8,519
Females	3.36	4,473
Cuban		
Males	5.33	10,249
Females	3.47	5,307
Black		
Males	4.65	7,835
Females	3.46	4,676
White		
Males	5.97	13,029
Females	3.67	5,378

[1]Sources: National Commission for Employment Policy. 1982.
              Hispanics and Jobs: Barriers to Progress, Washington:
              National Commission for Employment Policy, Table 8.

              Bureau of the Census. 1980. "U.S. Census of Population and
              Housing: General Social Economic Characteristics" (U.S.
              Summary), Table 170.

              Bean, Frank D., et al. 1985. "The Mexican Origin
              Population in the United States: A Demographic
              Overview," in Rodolfo O. de la Garza et al., eds.,
              The Mexican American Experience: An Interdiscipli-
              nary Anthology. Austin: The University of Texas
              Press, pp. 57-75.

[a]Persons 14 years and older, working for a wage or salary.
[b]Persons 15 years or older with income.

ination. Our interest here is not primarily in gender stratification, but it should be noted that, whatever the reasons for the differences, the trend for all workers over the twenty-year interval was in the direction of growing gender inequality (see Chapters 5 and 9 for confirmation). Except among Mexican Americans, income growth (in constant 1960 dollars) between 1960 and 1980 was greater for male heads than for female heads.

Returning to our focus on ethnic differentials, the income data in Table 6-7 tell a familiar story. Once again, Cubans surpass all other Hispanic groups, as well as blacks, in their level of economic achievement, followed at some distance by Mexican Americans and Puerto Ricans. Although characterized by lower levels of education than other Hispanics. Mexican American male heads of intact households have higher mean income than Puerto Rican heads at each of the three points in time covered in Table 6-7.

One interesting contrast within categories of headship is that the ratio of black to Anglo income increased substantially. Income improvements of blacks in these years is a result in part of the Civil Rights Movement and intervention of the government (see Chapter 9). Among female heads, the ratio for blacks and Mexican Americans also increased, while both Puerto Rican and Cuban ratios dropped rather sharply. The result is that the income advantage that Puerto Rican and Cuban female heads enjoyed over Mexican American and black women in 1960 had narrowed substantially (or disappeared) by 1980, while the overall advantage of Anglo women was preserved in absolute dollar terms.

Political Conditions and Trends

In 1980, at the national level there were five Hispanic members of the House of Representatives. However, "one Hispanic was appointed to the House in 1980 and three more were elected in 1982"—but only one of these was from outside the Southwest (Welch and Hibbing 1984, 328). There are, of course, many more Hispanics who are politically active at the state and local level, as is evidenced by the fact that, as of the date of this writing, three major United States cities (Denver, Miami, and San Antonio) have had Hispanic mayors.

It is also true that, in certain regions of the country, it may be a mistake to view as discrete the political activities of the various

Table 6-7. Economic Characteristics of Household Heads in the United States by Household Type, Spanish Origin, Race, and Dates, 1960-1980

HOUSEHOLD TYPE

Groups	Never Disrupted with Spouse and Children			Female Headed		
	Percent White Collar	Mean Personal Income[e]	Ratio to Anglo Income	Percent White Collar	Mean Personal Income[e]	Ratio to Anglo Income
Mexican American[a]						
1960	18.3	$4,126	.68	27.6	$1,444	.63
1970	18.5	5,009	.64	28.7	1,955	.64
1980	21.2	4,886	.66	44.8	2,360	.73
Change 1960-80	2.9	760		17.2	916	
Puerto Rican[b]						
1960	20.3	$3,386	.55	14.9	$1,677	.73
1970	21.0	4,527	.58	29.3	2,176	.71
1980	27.2	4,341	.58	47.5	2,008	.62
Change 1960-80	6.9	955		32.6	331	
Cuban[b]						
1960	33.6	$4,954	.81	30.2	$2,173	.95
1970	36.8	5,638	.72	39.8	2,596	.85
1980	45.7	6,311	.85	54.8	2,602	.80
Change 1960-80	12.1	1,357		24.6	429	

Table 6-7. continued.

	Percent White Collar	Mean Personal Income[e]	Ratio to Anglo Income	Percent White Collar	Mean Personal Income[e]	Ratio to Anglo Income
Black[c]						
1960	12.6	$3,040	.50	12.8	$1,232	.54
1970	19.6	4,499	.57	27.0	1,791	.59
1980	27.7	4,865	.65	45.7	2,373	.73
Change 1960-80	15.1	1,825		32.9	1,141	
Anglo[d]						
1960	41.0	$6,108	1.00	58.9	$2,293	1.00
1970	46.1	7,847	1.00	62.9	3,058	1.00
1980	46.5	7,451	1.00	69.4	3,254	1.00
Change 1960-80	5.5	1,343		10.5	961	

Source: Frisbie, W. Parker et al. 1985. Household and Family Demography of Hispanics, Blacks and Anglos. Final NICHD Report. Austin: University of Texas Population Research Center, Table 5-4.

[a]In 1960, Mexican Americans are identified as whites of Spanish surname. In 1970 and 1980, Mexican Americans are defined as those who self-identify as of Mexican origin.
[b]In 1960, Puerto Ricans and Cubans are identified in terms of foreign birth and foreign parentage. In 1970 and 1980, Puerto Ricans and Cubans are those who self-identify.
[c]Non-Hispanic blacks.
[d]Non-Hispanic whites.
[e]In 1960 dollars.

Hispanic groups. As Padilla (1984) has pointed out (based on his study of Mexican Americans and Puerto Ricans in Chicago), somewhat similar experiences of inequality have given rise to the conscious adoption of a Latino ethnic identity that at least partially cuts across any differences that separate Hispanic groups. According to Padilla, the concept of *Latinismo* "is based on the premise that particular circumstances and social conditions determine when this type of group identity and consciousness is appropriate for social action and mobilization" (1984, 651). Although each of the three largest Hispanic groups has achieved some degree of success in U.S. politics, Mexican Americans have exerted the most prominent influence (de la Garza and Vaughn 1984; McLemore and Romo 1985).

The reasons for the greater political prominence of Mexican Americans are not hard to determine. They are by far the largest and most geographically dispersed of the major Hispanic populations. Also they have been present in large numbers for generations— whereas up to 1960, Puerto Ricans and Cubans formed no more than a tiny fraction of the U.S. population.

The Future of Hispanic and Anglo Relations

To this point, the intent has been to survey the earlier trends and current conditions that characterize the three largest Hispanic populations as a basis for informed speculation on the future course of Hispanic-Anglo relations, with special emphasis on the potential for achieving full participation in the socioeconomic and political structures of our society. The most powerful predictor of a given variable at some future point in time is usually the state or level of that variable at an earlier point in time. Thus, we can draw on past trends with respect to Hispanic education, occupation, income, and political influence that have been documented in earlier sections as one useful means of projecting future conditions and trends. Also important is the degree to which attempts by Hispanics to enter the socioeconomic and political mainstream are supported or resisted by the majority population. In addition, there are other determinants, including demographic, social, and cultural conditions that, theoretically and empirically, have been shown to affect majority-minority relations and the pace at which structural assimilation is achieved.

Size and Growth of the Minority

One of the most widely investigated hypotheses bearing on majority-minority relations focuses on a basic demographic variable, size of the minority. In his classic commentary, Allport (1954) suggests that the larger the size of the minority, the greater the likelihood of conflict with, and discrimination by, the majority. The most systematic development of this notion is found in the work of Blalock (1956, 1957, 1967), who proposes that there will be an inverse relationship between the relative size of a minority and that group's economic position and political power. The rationale is that the larger the minority population relative to the majority, the greater the perception of threat by the majority, which in turn leads to more intense discrimination. Various empirical investigations have adduced support for this hypothesis with respect to income inequality experienced by blacks (Blalock 1956, 1957, 1967; Dowdall 1974; Glenn 1963, 1964, 1966). A similar (but less voluminous) set of findings suggests the viability of this hypothesis in the case of Mexican Americans (Frisbie and Neidert 1977). The results with respect to occupational inequality are more mixed in that the presence of a relatively large minority population may relate positively to minority occupational status due to a spillover of better jobs or to the development of a "semi-separate economy" (Dowdall 1974; Frisbie and Neidert 1977; Glenn 1966). In the political realm, Matthews and Prothro (1963) discovered a strong negative association between percent of blacks and black voter registration in the South. However, these results pertain to a period before the emergence of a strong civil rights movement. Given the political gains made by all minorities (including Hispanics) in recent decades, as well as the growth of support for and court implementation of the one-man-one-vote concept, it is not to be expected that political representation will diminish as minority percentages increase. In fact, some evidence of a reversal of the pattern found by Matthews and Prothro has been uncovered in the 1970s (Black 1978, 436–37).

It may be that *absolute* size of a minority imposes certain structural constraints on rapid improvement of the economic position of the group. In developing the concept of "demographic opportunity," Schoen suggests: "In ethnically stratified societies, some lower socioeconomic status groups have an opportunity to move into a middle niche while others do not, and groups that can and do move up will have predictably different economic and demographic patterns from other groups that do not" (1978, 468–69). For example, Schoen argues that one reason Japanese Americans have been able to ascend the socioeconomic ladder much more rapidly than Mexican Americans is simply that the former are a much smaller group. That is, the number of middle and higher level economc niches needed to accommodate upward mobility of Japanese Americans is much smaller than the number that would be required for Mexican Americans to enjoy a proportionately equivalent degree of mobility. "For Mexican-Americans to have achieved the same degree of rapid social mobility would thus have involved profound social and economic changes for the larger society" (Schoen 1978, 478)—changes of such magnitude that they are difficult to envisage except over a long period of time.

To the extent that the notion of demographic opportunity is viable, the implication is that the larger size and rapid growth of the Mexican American population may act as a partial constraint on the ability of the group to achieve full access to the economic resources of U.S. society. Other Hispanic populations, especially Cubans, may find the road to upward mobility a bit smoother as a result of their smaller numbers. On the other hand, there is clearly not a simple one-to-one relationship between minority size and economic opportunity. The nature and strength of the association between minority size and discrimination and between discriminatory practices and life chances are not easily determined—and, in any event, these relationships may vary over both time and space (Wilcox and Roof 1978).

Spatial Concentration

One of the arguments for attempting to reduce segregation by race or ethnicity is that inequality is inherent in separateness. One often-expressed concern is that concentraton of blacks in inner-city neighborhoods shuts them off from equal access to better schools and job opportunities. By contrast, residential segregation of Hispanics from non-Hispanic whites has been consistently quite low, compared with black-white and black-Hispanic segregation. Furthermore, much of the segregation of Hispanics appears to be accounted for in terms of socioeconomic differentials (Massey 1979). But as is the case with blacks, Puerto Ricans at all socioeconomic levels are highly segregated (Massey 1979; Massey and Bitterman 1985). Except for Puerto Ricans, then, the residential patterns of Hispanic groups do not appear to pose a major obstacle to their structural assimilation.

An interesting complexity is added to the consideration of possible effects of residential segregation by the finding that, in some instances, residence in ethnic enclaves may be turned into a benefit instead of a liability. Such a result can come about if a minority is able to develop a semiseparate economy in which businesses owned and operated by ethnic group members provide jobs, as well as goods and services, for other members of the group. Cubans, for example, appear to have been able to achieve a successful ethnically based enclave economy (Wilson and Portes 1980; Portes and Bach 1985). There is some preliminary evidence that foreign-born Mexican Americans may also experience positive increments in socioeconomic achievement from residence in ethnic enclaves, although the opposite effect appears to hold for Puerto Ricans (Tienda and Neidert 1984).

However, there are other forms of concentration besides residential segregation. As mentioned earlier, each of the three Hispanic populations is heavily concentrated in different regions: Mexican Americans in the Southwest, Puerto Ricans in the Northeast (especially in the New York City area), and Cubans in the Miami/Dade County area of Florida. Whether such lack of geographic dispersion will have beneficial or deleterious effects depends, among other things, on regional variation in economic conditions. To the extent that the Sun Belt continues to experience growth in employment opportunities (see Kasarda 1980 and Chapter 3 above), Mexican Americans and Cubans may well share in the expansion, while Puerto Ricans may suffer to the degree that employment chances remain less abundant in the Northeast (Ortiz n.d.). Happily, some areas of the latter region are currently enjoying a substantially improved economic climate.

Another form of concentration is seen in the decidedly urban settlement pattern of Hispanics. "Fully 88 percent live in metropolitan areas, according to the 1980 census, compared to 75 percent of the general population and 81 percent of blacks. Moreover, 50 percent of United States Hispanics live in the central cities of metropolitan areas. This is far more than the 30 percent of the general population living in central cities" (Davis et al. 1983, 13). Note that prior to World War II, Mexican Americans were a predominantly rural, agricultural population, but by 1950, their proportionate representation in urban areas had begun to approximate that of Anglos and non-whites (Grebler et al. 1970, 112–13). Puerto Ricans and Cubans in the United States, from the time of their presence in appreciable numbers, have been largely urban populations (Bean and Tienda 1987; Davis et al. 1983).

Disproportionate representation in the urban core does not bode well for the economic chances of any group, given the fiscal crisis, deterioration of the housing and industrial facilities, and residence/job location mismatch that appear to characterize many central cities (Kasarda 1980, 1985). On a more hopeful note, Bean and Tienda (1987) show that Hispanics participated in the general suburbanization trend over the 1960–80 interval. Deconcentration was especially pronounced for Cubans. By 1980, only 45 percent of the Cuban metropolitan population resided in central cities, but about 65 percent of Mexican Americans and 81 percent of Puerto Ricans living in metropolitan areas were central-ciy residents. Apparently, redistribution in the direction of the suburbs has proceeded much more slowly for Mexican Americans and Puerto Ricans (Bean and Tienda 1987, Table 5.6).

Household and Family Structure

It has been well documented that households in which both husband and wife are present fare better economically than other types (Bianchi 1981; Frisbie et al. 1985). That this difference is not merely a function of the number of earners is evident from Table 6-7 in which only the personal income of heads of households is compared. In particular, female-headed households constitute a disproportionate share of households living in poverty (Auletta 1982; McEaddy 1976).

There is no single, unambiguous explanation of why traditional families tend to be more financially secure. A complete understanding of the issue would involve multiple determinants, including the overall disruptive effects of marital dissolution, constraints on the earning power of women as related to gender inequalities, and difficulties associated with attempts to pursue a career while maintaining sole responsibility for rearing children. Whatever the case, it appears necessary to take into account trends in household structure and marital status in assessing the future chances of Hispanics for socioeconomic advance.

Size, as well as stability, of households is an important consideration. Large household size that arises from high fertility may create
an obstacle to socioeconomic achievement, since time and mone-
tary resources that might otherwise be used for the advancement of
careers and business enterprise must be diverted to the support of
dependent children. The fertility literature is replete with references
to the fact that, as satisfying and fulfilling as bearing and raising
children may be, in the modern world, children tend to be economic
liabilities. To illustrate, Preston (1974) has demonstrated the negative impact of high fertility on chances of intergenerational upward
mobility for blacks, and there is no apparent reason that the effects
should be substantially different in the case of Hispanics.

Table 6-8 shows that Hispanics have both advantages and disad-
vantages in regard to household size and structure. As is to be expected based on the high fertility of these groups (Bradshaw and
Bean 1973; Sweet 1978), Mexican Americans and Puerto Ricans
were characterized by much larger than average household size in
1960, 1970, and 1980. In fact, in 1980, the mean household size
among Mexican Americans (3.8) was a full half-person larger than
was the case for all households two decades earlier (Frisbie et al.
1985).

Turning to marital status, it can be seen that all of the racial/
ethnic groups included in Table 6-8 followed the national pattern of
marital dissolution between 1960 and 1980. Nevertheless, even
though the prevalence of marital disruption increased from 1960 to
1980, and the proportion of never-disrupted families declined across
the board, Mexican Americans and Cubans continue to have a majority of households with no history of marital dissolution. (The
never-disrupted category in Table 6-8 refers to households in which
neither spouse has previously been married.) Currently, about one-
fifth of Mexican American households are headed by a person whose
spouse is absent because of divorce, separation, or widowhood. This
compares to about 25 percent of Anglos and Cubans, 33 percent of
Puerto Ricans, and 40 percent of blacks in the disrupted status in
1980. Research taking individuals as the units of analysis—and
focusing only on the dissolution of marriage because of divorce or
separation—has produced similar findings for the five groups, net of
controls for age at marriage, education, and current age (Frisbie
1986).

The conclusion is that, to the extent that household structure and
marital status influence the quest of Hispanics for full participation
in the socioeconomic system of the United States, Mexican Amer-

Table 6-8. Household and Family Structure by Race/Ethnicity and by Dates, 1960-1980

Household Structure	Total			Anglo			Black		
	1960	1970	1980	1960	1970	1980	1960	1970	1980
Mean Household Size	3.3	3.1	2.8	3.2	3.0	2.7	3.8	3.5	3.1
Mean Number of Adults Per Household	2.1	2.0	2.0	2.1	2.0	1.9	2.2	2.0	1.9
Current Marital Status									
Percent Never Married	6.1	7.6	12.2	6.0	7.4	11.3	6.2	9.7	17.9
Percent Never Disrupted	60.2	55.1	47.1	62.1	57.0	49.0	41.7	37.7	30.1
Percent Disrupted	19.2	23.4	27.0	17.8	21.8	25.4	32.8	37.8	40.6
Percent Remarried	14.6	13.9	13.8	14.1	13.8	14.3	19.4	14.7	11.4

Table 6-8 continued.

Household Structure	Mexican American[a]			Puerto Rican[a]			Cuban[a]		
	1960	1970	1980	1960	1970	1980	1960	1970	1980
Mean Household Size	4.4	4.2	3.8	4.0	3.8	3.3	3.2	3.5	3.0
Mean Number of Adults Per Household	2.2	2.2	2.2	2.2	2.0	1.9	2.2	2.3	2.2
Current Marital Status									
Percent Never Married	4.8	7.0	10.5	7.7	9.0	18.5	11.0	7.0	10.2
Percent Never Disrupted	61.4	58.3	54.9	57.8	52.1	39.0	57.6	61.0	52.5
Percent Disrupted	18.8	21.1	22.6	20.9	28.7	32.8	17.8	18.5	24.0
Percent Remarried	15.0	13.6	12.0	13.6	10.2	9.8	13.7	13.5	13.2

Source: Frisbie, W. Parker et al. 1985. Household and Family Demography of Hispanics, Blacks and Anglos. Final NICHD Report. Austin: University of Texas Population Research Center, Table 4-1.

[a] The Mexican American population is defined in terms of the white Spanish surname identifier in 1960 and in terms of the self-identification item in 1970 and 1980. Puerto Ricans and Cubans are defined in terms of the foreign stock items in 1960 and in terms of the self-identification item in 1970 and 1980.

icans and Cubans can be expected to move forward at a somewhat faster pace than Puerto Ricans. The potential for Mexican Americans may be even greater than the figures in Table 6-8 suggest, as the mean number of children per household declined more sharply between 1970 and 1980 among Mexican Americans than among any of the other four racial/ethnic groups under consideration (Frisbie et al. 1985, Table 4-2).

Acculturation/Language Use

Acculturation, or cultural assimilation, might be conceived as a determinant of an ethnic minority's ability to become structurally assimilated. It seems indisputable that cultural assimilation does not ensure structural assimilation (van den Berghe 1967), but it is possible that certain features of a minority group's culture may impede easy entry into majority-dominated economic and political spheres. To a large extent, the issue with respect to Hispanics comes down to the concern by a number of scholars and policy-makers that retention of Spanish may negatively affect structural integration.

It has been noted that the "One issue unique to Hispanics . . . is that they share a common language" (Davis et al. 1983, 21), and Grenier suggests that, "Although Hispanics are not a homogeneous group of people, they have some characteristics in common, the most important one being their language . . ." (1984, 537). While it is clear that Spanish-use is a prominent manifestation of Hispanic cultural heritage, this observation, in itself, certainly does not constitute evidence of a detrimental effect. To the contrary, fluency in more than one language is an asset, not a liability. What, then, might be the problem?

Mirowsky and Ross, in their investigation of Spanish language networks among Mexican Americans, suggest one possibility. These authors posit that, to a rather large extent, individuals depend on others for information and resources needed for advancement. Specifically, "Language carries the vast majority of this information, and is itself information about social origins and social position. When one language group is economically dominant, as is the case with English-speaking whites in the United States, then having friends, family, and acquaintances who speak the language provides the information, common experiences, and social contacts that facilitate upward mobility. In order to move into the middle classes in the United States, it helps a great deal to speak English and to be embedded in an English-speaking network (Fishman et al. 1966; Olmedo 1979; Lopez 1978)" [Mirowsky and Ross 1984, 552].

If retention of Spanish has, in the past, impeded social mobility because of its channeling of Hispanics away from English-speaking networks, the problem appears to be of declining significance. Data from the 1976 Survey of Income and Education show that, among those who spoke Spanish as a child, only 48 percent of Mexican Americans have retained Spanish as their primary language of communication, compared to about 57 percent of Puerto Ricans and 68 percent of Cubans (Grenier 1984, 541–42). Moreover, these figures indirectly give rise to a counterargument. Cubans have the highest level of Spanish retention, yet they "outpace other Hispanics in high school achievement tests and college entrance" (Davis et al. 1983, 33). Cubans also lead the way in occupational and income attainment. Since a large number of Cuban immigrants came from the better educated and more affluent strata of Cuban society, it is entirely likely that it is lack of English proficiency and other class-related phenomena, rather than Spanish-use per se, that impedes structural assimilation. Mirowsky and Ross reach a somewhat similar conclusion regarding the class-related basis of the current status of Mexican Americans (1984, 561–62).

Substantial support for this interpretation emerges from the Tienda and Neidert study (1984) of Mexican, Puerto Rican, Central/South American, and other Spanish-origin males. These authors conclude that "retention of Spanish does not hinder the socioeconomic achievements of Hispanic origin groups, provided that a reasonable level of proficiency in English is acquired" (1984, 533). An exception to this general conclusion is the case of immigrants from Mexico, "for whom Spanish bilingualism and monolingualism exert independent negative effects on the occupational achievement of adult men" (1984, 533).

Finally, there is evidence that Mexican Americans (and presumably other Hispanics) take advantage of opportunities to become fluent in English, and that, as would be expected, English proficiency varies by immigrant generation and increases over time. For example, fully 90 percent of Mexican Americans born in the United States speak English well, although only about 30 percent use English exclusively. Among recent Mexican immigrants (arrived in 1975 or later), about 70 percent speak English poorly or not at all (Bean et al. 1984).

Discussion and Summary

If one takes current indicators of structural assimilation as a basis for projecting future conditions, one would have to say that Cubans (at least those who arrived before 1980) are beginning to approach full access to the economic resources of American society. Their progress over the past two or three decades makes the achievement of full structural assimilation during the next fifty years seem quite likely. Available data suggest that the position of Puerto Ricans has deteriorated somewhat vis à vis the other two large Hispanic populations. For example, Mexican Americans now surpass Puerto Ricans in terms of labor force participation and median income. Some additional ambiguity must be acknowledged here because of the uncertain impact of the recent changes in the immigration statutes, which will, of course, affect Mexican Americans to a much larger extent than Puerto Ricans (who are already citizens) or Cubans (among whom the number of undocumented immigrants is negligible).

One of the major changes included in the Immigration Reform and Control Act of 1986 is the provision for legal sanctions against employers who knowingly hire undocumented workers. Another is the granting of amnesty (i.e., adjustment to legal status) of illegal aliens who have maintained continuous residence in the United States since January 1, 1982. It is much too early to say to what degree the former provision will be enforceable or to what extent the second will be taken advantage of. The pressures that have given rise to large-scale immigration (legal or illegal) of Mexicans show no signs of immediate abatement (Bouvier and Gardner 1986).

Simply removing the illegality of status may strengthen the position of Mexican immigrants in terms of labor market opportunities and ability to gain access to social services. On the other hand, a number of groups voiced oposition to the new law on the grounds that employer sanctions might lead to resistance to hiring Hispanics either as an excuse for discrimination or out of an understandable desire to avoid any risk of possible penalties (Bouvier and Gardner 1986). In any event, it is by no means certain that the effect of Hispanic immigrants to the United States is negative, even in terms of the earnings of groups with whom they might be expected to compete. In fact, there is growing evidence that undocumented Hispanic immigrants tend to perform complementary functions, rather than acting as substitutes, for native-born workers (Bean et al. 1986; King et al. 1986).

As mentioned earlier, there are few studies of yields to human capital that include the three largest Hispanic populations—thus, it is not possible to specify precisely the differentials in the degree of discrimination each has encountered. Nevertheless, some relevant evidence can be adduced. For example, an analysis of mean earnings among white, black, and Mexican American male workers shows that, overall, whites "were better able to use their human capital than were minorities." However, "Mexican Americans realized greater returns to experience than either whites or blacks" (Verdugo and Verdugo 1984, 421). The rates of income returns to occupational status were higher among Mexican Americans than among blacks, but the reverse was true for education, with non-Hispanic whites receiving the highest rates of return (Verdugo and Verdugo 1984).

The situation is even more complex when differentials by nativity and gender are considered. For example, a college education has a strong positive effect on the occupational achievement of Hispanic males regardless of whether they were born in the United States, but completion of high school has a smaller impact and one that "seems confined to the native-born" (Tienda and Neidert 1984, 530–31).

In the case of immigrants, "Mexicans have a more favorable 'conversion' of resources into prestige, but a lower level of resources to convert. The 'conversion' factors for Mexican males, however, are more favorable than those for Mexican females." On the other hand, "Cuban females (and males) have a particular advantage in converting citizenship into occupational prestige. . . . For Cuban women naturalization is associated with structural assimilation to a much greater degree than it is for Mexican women" (Sullivan 1984, 1057). The implications of rapid growth for structural assimilation are multiple and complex. Large size could give impetus to the growing political influence of Hispanics, but this result is not automatic. "Only 30 percent of Hispanics of voting age cast ballots in the 1980 Presidential election, compared to the national figure of 59 percent—down from 38 percent in 1972" (Davis et al. 1983, 40). Geographic concentration of large numbers of Hispanics can be beneficial in economic terms, if enclave economies of the sort described earlier are successful, but so far, only Cubans have profited significantly from a "semi-separate" economy. Also, as noted earlier, large size and rapid growth may impede a general improvement in socioeconomic status for a minority.

It is possible that the redistribution of Hispanic populations may begin to rival growth itself as an influence on Hispanic-Anglo relations in the South. At present, Hispanics remain regionally concentrated, but an examination of internal migration patterns between 1975 and 1980 shows that Hispanic groups have followed the national trend of movement in the direction of the South and West, with the South emerging as the most prominent destination point (Bean and Tienda 1987). The gains by the South are most striking in the case of Cubans (for whom the South was the destination chosen by significantly more than 80 percent of all migrants regardless of region of origin), followed in general by Mexican Americans and Puerto Ricans. In fact, Bean and Tienda (1987, Table 5.11) show that, with the single exception of Mexican American migrants from the Northeast, the South was the principal destination for each of the three Hispanic groups on which our attention has been focused. Although relative comparisons can be misleading because of the very different sizes of Hispanic populations by region, should present trends continue, one would anticipate greatly increased Hispanic presence in the South over the next several decades.

By way of summary, several generalizations may be offered. Currently, Cubans have moved farthest in the direction of structural assimilation. They arrived in the United States with more resources, as individuals and as a group, than other Hispanics. They have been successful in improving their access to the social and economic benefits of U.S. residence by taking advantage of an enclave-based form of organization. Their human capital resources apparently exceed those of other Hispanic groups. Full structural assimilation seems well within their grasp.

In comparison to Cubans, Mexican Americans have fewer resources to draw upon, at least on a relative, per capita basis. On the other hand, the research reviewed above indicates that persons of Mexican origin are at times able to convert their resources into occupational and income gains at a higher rate than that observed among other groups. Mexican Americans, like Cubans, are characterized by a household-family structure (especially with respect to marital status) that appears to be associated with socioeconomic advance. And, like Cubans, they are concentrated in areas where the economy has been expanding. (Of course, the vitality of regional economies is subject to rapid fluctuations.) Furthermore, Mexican Americans have the most extensive political organization of any Hispanic group. On the negative side, the larger size and rapid growth of the Mexican origin population may impede structural assimilation. The tendency for Mexican immigrants to be slow to become naturalized and the persistence of the educational gap are other obstacles. In sum, one might expect a movement of Mexican Americans toward structural assimilation at a pace slower than that projected for Cubans, but it does not seem unreasonable to expect the process to be more or less complete within the next fifty years.

The situation with respect to Puerto Ricans seems to warrant less optimism. As American citizens, Puerto Rican migrants to the mainland should face fewer obstacles to assimilation than Cuban or Mexican immigrants. However, the relatively large number of female-headed households and the decline in labor force participation may limit their ability to carve out a larger share of the social, economic, and political pie. The sharp decline in labor force participation of female heads of Puerto Rican origin is a particular cause of concern. In the 1970s, movement from the island to the U.S. mainland dropped dramatically. Whether this trend signals a retreat from efforts to structurally assimilate or simply reflects the relative attractiveness of opportunities in Puerto Rico in recent times is not clear. Whatever the case, full structural assimilation for this group seems farther from realization than for their Mexican American and Cuban counterparts.

Acknowledgments

The author gratefully acknowledges the support provided for portions of this research by NICHD Grant #HD19321 and NICHD Contract #HD12812.

7

Trends in Race Relations: Blacks and Whites

John J. Moland, Jr.

Over the past five decades, the issue of civil rights as related to blacks in the United States—the South in particular—has been greatly impacted by a series of executive, judicial, and legislative actions of the federal government. During the 1940s, the civil rights of blacks became increasingly difficult to ignore as blacks themselves became more vocal in pursuit of their rights and as the racial issues raised in World War II drew the attention of a widening world audience. Mounting legal and vocal pressures from the NAACP, followed by other civil rights groups and individuals, set the stage for action by the executive branch of the federal government (Berry 1971; Williams and Jaynes 1989, 64–65).

The Supreme Court decisions of 1883 and 1896 upheld state-imposed segregation, thereby sealing the fate of civil rights for blacks for many decades to come. Consequently, segregation, enforced by court laws in the South, was in effect in all institutional areas and relationships involving blacks and whites. Blacks were segregated in neighborhoods, workplaces, schools, public accommodations, and transportation. The legalization of segregation supported the practices of discrimination in employment, income, education, housing, public accommodations, and social services. The right to vote was denied by such tactics and/or requirements as the Grandfather Clause, literacy tests, the poll tax, and white primaries (Woodward 1966). In addition, threats, intimidation, and violence were used by whites to maintain segregation and discriminatory practices to keep blacks in "their place" (Williams and Jaynes 1989, 58–64).

The 1954 Supreme Court Decision in effect removed the legal barriers to desegregation in these areas, and the decision opened the way for more federal intervention and enforcement of civil rights for blacks in cases of discrimination and violence by whites. Such intervention and enforcement of civil rights measures by the federal government were necessary given the resistance in the South by state and local governments. Given these actions and others, the general concern of this chapter is with ascertaining through a comparative analysis the trends in black/white relations over the past four decades or more, with emphasis on the South.

In 1941, President Roosevelt, under pressure from black leadership and A. Phillip Randolph's threat of a march on Washington, issued an executive order creating a Fair Employment Practices Committee (Fleming 1965, 373). In 1946, President Truman created the Committee on Civil Rights, and in 1948 he asked Congress to establish a permanent Fair Employment Practices Committee. He issued an executive order in 1948 declaring equality of treatment and opportunity for all men in the armed services regardless of race, color, religion, or national origin (Emerson and Kilson 1965). In addition, President Truman urged Congress to enact anti-lynching, anti-poll tax, and fair employment laws (Berry 1971). Thus, the Truman Administration provided the executive leadership for bringing into national focus and attention the wide range of civil rights guaranteed to all by the Constitution but denied blacks by the states, particularly the Southern states. Decisions handed down by the Supreme Court during the Roosevelt-Truman Administrations upheld the desegregation of interstate travel, the rights of blacks to vote in the Southern Democratic primaries, and their right to enroll in publicly supported institutions of higher learning. However, it was not until 1954 that the Supreme Court handed down its landmark decision, which set the stage for eliminating all forms of state-supported segregation and discrimination (Fleming 1965).

Federal legislative actions in support of civil rights for blacks were slow to come. Congress passed the Civil Rights Act of 1957, the first civil rights legislation since 1875. It provided limited injunctive powers in voting rights disputes (Berry 1971). It was not, however, until the mid-sixties that the landmark legislative actions occurred with the passage of the Civil Rights Act (1964) and the Voting Rights Act (1965). The very nature of these executive, judicial, and legislative actions validated the underlying struggle of blacks to gain and maintain equal rights in the face of opposition and violence exercised by whites in order to maintain the status quo. These actions by the federal government removed the legal barriers to black pursuit of equal rights under the law. Still, institutional racism prevailed as a means of continuing to deprive blacks of economic, educational, political, and legal rights. Consequently, blacks were forced to pursue a case-by-case struggle to obtain the rights that were theirs by law and the Constitution of the United States.

Following the Supreme Court decision of 1954, blacks, led by Dr. Martin L. King, sought relief from the institutionalized racism of the South through nonviolent confrontation and actions involving demonstrations in the form of sit-ins, marches, freedom rides, and so forth, which focused national and international attention upon the injustices and violence perpetrated upon them (Van Der Slik 1970). Resistance to desegregating public schools and institutions of higher learning brought federal intervention in the form of military enforcement during the Eisenhower and Kennedy administrations (Berry 1971). In this regard, an essential stage in the civil rights movement was that of direct confrontation (Himes 1966), which involved entering and attending public educational institutions (Little Rock, Arkansas; University of Alabama; etc.); sit-ins (Greensboro, Atlanta, Tallahassee, etc.); marches; and freedom rides (Alabama, Mississippi, etc.). To ensure obedience to the law and the protection of blacks, both President Eisenhower and President Kennedy ordered military troops into service (Berry 1971).

Given the nature of conflict in black-white relations in the South in 1963, President Kennedy delivered a nationwide television address in support of the passage of his civil rights bill. He was assassinated in November of that year, and President Johnson championed his bill through Congress, thereby providing the landmark Civil Rights Act of 1964. In addition, President Johnson persuaded Congress to pass the 1965 Voting Rights Act.

In support of the Civil Rights Act of 1964 and the Voting Rights Act of 1965, the federal government established a policy of "affirmative action" aimed at breaking the patterns of institutional racism that served to exclude blacks from equal access and opportunity. In the 1970s, federal policies and actions mandated affirmative action programs designed to ensure minority representation in public programs, employment, and education. The decades of segregation and oppression had severely impacted blacks and produced significant gaps between them and whites in education, occupation, income, housing, health, and other indicators of social well-being.

Affirmative action programs addressed the need to close these gaps.

When power passed to Republicans in the 1980s, however, the executive branch of the federal government was opposed to many civil rights measures, especially affirmative action, extension of the Voting Rights Act, and basic support programs for the disadvantaged and working poor. Thus, recent efforts by the executive branch are directed toward removing the mechanisms by which blacks are afforded the means to pursue equal access to political, educational, economic, and other opportunities (Carter 1985). The expressed opposition and positions taken by the executive branch are that blacks have made substantial progress toward achieving parity with whites and that the gaps in education, occupation, income, and so on have been substantially closed. This line of reasoning implicitly assumes that blacks will be able to pursue and achieve equal access to all opportunities unobstructed by institutional racism.

It should be recognized, however, that the removal of legal barriers to black pursuit of equal rights did not eliminate the operation of racism on the individual and institutional levels. Individual racism includes individual attitudes and actions that are recognized as prejudging a person's behavior and discriminating on the basis of race. Institutional racism is embedded in policies, social structures, and demographic patterns, which operate on a more or less subtle and impersonal level (Jorgensen 1978). Consequently, the struggle for equality must be an ongoing process for blacks.

The focus of research in this chapter can be stated in the following questions regarding trends in black-white relations in the South and their implications for the 2030s: (1) To what extent have blacks achieved parity with whites in the political, educational, and economic arenas over the past three decades or so? (2) In these areas, what implications for the future can be drawn from trends of the past decades? (3) Will changes in policy by the federal government alter these trends? As mentioned before, this chapter will address these questions by focusing on trends in black/white relations from the perspective of a comparative analysis of demographic and institutional data by region over the past four decades or more with emphasis on the South. Changes in the circumstances of blacks over time must be viewed in relation to changes in the same areas for whites. Consequently, trends in the political, economic, educational, and related conditions of blacks in the South will be examined in light of the changes in these same areas for whites.

Trends in Race Relations in the Recent Past

Political Trends: Elected Officials

Trends in black-white relations will be increasingly affected as blacks gain the political power to influence decision making and the enforcement of laws. The Voting Rights Act of 1965 supported political rights for blacks by empowering the Justice Department to send federal examiners to counties where low registration indicated persistent discrimination (Berry 1971, 204). This major achievement opened the political arena to blacks as voters and as elected officials (those elected by popular vote to public office in a governmental capacity).

There were only 103 black elected officials in the Nation in 1965, 21 in the South. By January 1985, there were 5,764 in the nation, not including the District of Columbia, with 3,549 in the South, 62 percent of the total (Joint Center for Political Studies (JCPS) 1985). Grenier (1985) reports (in his study of the black electorate in Louisiana) that the passage of the 1965 Voting Rights Act produced a dramatic impact on the black registration rates in the state. The registration of eligible blacks in Louisiana nearly doubled from 1964 to 1968—rising from 33.8 percent to 62.8 percent—and it reached a high of 73 percent during 1970 (Grenier 1985). In a similar fashion, blacks made significant advances in voter registration in other Southern states. In 1985, the four states with the largest number of black elected officials were in the deep South: Louisiana, 475; Mississippi, 444; Alabama, 375; and Georgia, 340 (JCPS 1985). Although the number of black elected officials increased considerably over the twenty-year period, black representation remains below their proportion in the voting age population in each census region as well as the nation as a whole.

The extent to which blacks are underrepresented among elected officials by region is shown in Table 7-1. In 1985 blacks constituted 16.3 percent of the voting age population in the South but only 3.5 percent of the elected officials. Conversely, though whites constituted 83.7 percent of the voting age population, they had 96.5 percent of the elected officials. Black underrepresentation relative to their proportion in the voting age population in 1985 was -78.7 percent. Given the present proportion of black elected officials in the South and the rate of increase relative to the proportion of blacks

Table 7-1. Blacks as a Percentage of Voting Age Population, Black Elected Officials as Percentage of All Elected Officials, and Underrepresentation of Blacks in Government by Regions (Excluding the District of Columbia) and by Dates

Region and Year	Voting Age Population	Percent Black	All Elected Officials	Number Black	Percent Black	Black Representation Indexes
1969						
South	40,426,812	16.0	101,797	480	0.47	-97.1
Northeast	33,014,905	7.9	112,753	281	0.25	-96.8
North Central	35,916,019	7.2	247,107	291	0.12	-98.3
West	21,291,059	4.6	60,636	101	0.17	-96.3
All	130,648,795	9.7	522,293	1,153	0.22	-97.7
1981						
South	40,323,500	16.0	102,124	2,817	2.76	-82.8
Northeast	32,957,084	7.9	102,309	572	0.56	-92.9
North Central	36,665,400	7.2	224,545	1,070	0.48	-93.9
West	22,822,500	4.3	61,453	302	0.49	-88.6
All	132,768,484	9.5	490,431	4,761	0.97	-89.8
1985						
South	58,671,000	16.3	102,132	3,549	3.47	-78.7
Northeast	37,494,000	9.3	102,302	694	0.68	-92.7
North Central	43,063,000	8.4	224,478	1,150	0.51	-93.9
West	34,254,000	5.2	61,488	371	0.60	-88.5
All	173,482,000	10.6	490,400	5,764	1.18	-88.9

Source: Adapted from Joint Center for Political Studies, Black Elected Officials, 1969, 1981, and 1985.

in the voting age population over the past twenty years, fifty years from now blacks would achieve only about 70 percent parity with whites. However, black underrepresentation as elected officials relative to their proportion in the voting age population is greater in other regions of the country than in the South. By region the range is from −88.5 to −94 percent underrepresentation relative to their proportions in the voting age populations. In all regions combined, black elected officials hold less than 1.5 percent of all elective offices while they make up approximately 11 percent of the voting age population in the Nation (U.S. Bureau of Census 1979; JCPS 1979 and 1985).

State Legislators

Political power at the state level rests upon representation in the state legislatures. The state legislature makes laws and appropriates funds for governmental agencies of the state. When the Voting Rights Act was passed in 1965, only 94 blacks held positions as state legislators and executives in the United States—16 in the South (U.S. Bureau of Census 1979). Consequently, blacks had little or no influence on the law-making process and the deliberations concerning the appropriation of state funds.

Table 7-2 presents the number and percentage of state legislators by race and region for the years 1974, 1979, and 1984. Ten years after the passage of the Civil Rights Act, there were 236 black state legislators in the four regions as compared to 94 in 1964. By 1979 the number of black state legislators had increased to 294 and by January 1985 the number had reached 384. Although some progress has been made, this number is only 5.2 percent of all state legislators, even though blacks constitute 10.6 percent of America's voting age population. Over this twenty-year period the greatest increase in total black state legislators occurred in the South, where the number of legislators grew from 16 in 1964 to 211 in 1985. This number represents 8.6 percent of all legislators in the South, although blacks constitute 16.3 percent of the voting age population in the region. The difference between the two percentages divided by the black percent of the voting age population yields an underrepresentation ratio of −47.2 (see Table 7-3). Other regions have experienced only slight gains in the number of black state legislators,

Table 7-2. Number of Black State Legislators as a Percentage of all Legislators by Region, 1974, 1979, and 1985.

Region	All State Legislators N	Number and Percent of Blacks					
		1974		1979		1985[a]	
		N	%	N	%	N	%
South	2,453	90	3.7	143	5.8	211	8.6
Northeast	1,908	47	2.5	51	2.7	65	3.4
North Central	1,756	77	4.4	80	4.6	83	4.7
West	1,329	22	1.7	20	1.5	25	1.9
Total	7,446	236	3.2	294	3.9	384	5.2

Source: Adapted from Joint Center for Political Studies, Black Elected Officials, 1974, 1979, and 1985.

[a]Increase in total number of legislators by 1985 to 1,332 in the West and 1,910 in the Northeast giving a total of 7,451 for all regions.

with the highest increase, 18 members, occurring in the Northeast region during the same period. Nevertheless, the ratio of black underrepresentation in the Northeast is −63.4 in 1985, a decline of only 5 percent from 1974.

Although the greatest gains have been made in the South, blacks in this region are still underrepresented in state legislatures. An additional 189 seats are needed in order for blacks in the South to attain the 400 state legislators in keeping with their representation in the voting age population. Blacks in 1974 constituted 3.7 percent of the state legislators and 16 percent of the voting age population in the South, a difference of 12.3 percent. By 1985 blacks in the South constituted 8.6 percent of the state legislators and 16.3 percent of the voting age population, a difference of 7.7 percent. This represents a net gain of 4.6 percent in a decade. Perhaps in another twenty to thirty years, provided all things remain the same, blacks in the South will achieve parity or near parity with whites in the relative number of State Legislators.

Table 7-3 also shows that of the four regions, the North Central has the lowest underrepresentation of black state legislators, −39, −36, and −44 percent for the respective years, despite a slight increase in underrepresentation in 1985. Other regions have remained fairly constant over the ten-year period, with a slight decline of 5 percent or less in underrepresentation. This suggests that under present circumstances, there may be a point below which it becomes increasingly difficult to reduce black underrepresentation. Consequently, this may bring about renewed efforts in the areas of voter registration, getting people out to vote, and pursuit of court action to achieve more equitable representation. In addition, more attention may be given to coalition politics as a process by which blacks may seek to achieve their social and economic goals in the legislative chambers of state governments.

Economic Trends

Principal indicators of trends in black-white relations and progress toward equality for blacks are relative employment, unemployment, and income among whites and blacks. (For a discussion of these indicators and the measurement of relative and absolute change in the examination of racial data, particularly income, see Farley 1984, 13–15). Employment is the primary source of group and

Table 7-3. Percent of Voting Age Population, State Legislators, and Underrepresentation of Blacks, by Region, Race, Year, and Dates, 1974, 1979, and 1985.

Years and Regions	Percent of Voting Age Population		Percent of State Legislators		Black Under-representation
	White	Black	White	Black	Percent
1974					
West	95.4	4.6	98.3	1.7	-63.0
North Central	92.8	7.2	95.6	4.4	-38.9
Northeast	92.1	7.9	97.5	2.5	-68.4
South	84.0	16.0	96.3	3.7	-76.9
All Regions	90.3	9.7	96.8	3.2	-67.0
1979					
West	95.6	4.4	98.5	1.5	-65.9
North Central	92.8	7.2	95.4	4.6	-36.1
Northeast	92.1	7.9	97.3	2.7	-65.8
South	84.0	16.0	94.2	5.8	-63.8
All Regions	90.4	9.6	96.0	4.0	-58.3
1985					
West	94.8	5.2	98.1	1.9	-63.5
North Central	91.6	8.4	95.3	4.7	-44.0
Northeast	90.7	9.3	96.6	3.4	-63.4
South	83.7	16.3	91.4	8.6	-47.2
All Regions	89.4	10.6	95.1	4.9	-53.8

Source: Adapted from Joint Center for Political Studies, Black Elected Officials, 1974, 1979, and 1985.

individual identity, as well as a major determinant of family income and well being. Historically, in the South and throughout America, blacks have been the "last to be hired and the first to be fired" or laid off. In addition, they have been restricted to employment in the more menial, demeaning, and low-paying positions (Myrdal 1944, Chapter 9; Fein 1965, 116–17; Moland 1981, 479). Blacks are impacted to a much greater extent than whites by changes in the economy that produce a general increase in unemployment or a general reduction in unemployment (Tobin 1965, 454; Farley 1977).

In response to pressure from blacks, President Roosevelt in June of 1941 issued an executive order prohibiting discrimination in employment in government and in industries with Federal contracts (Woodard 1966, 135). He created the Fair Employment Practices Committee (FEPC) to effectuate the provisions of the order. Congressional action in 1946 killed the FEPC; nevertheless, in February 1948 President Truman urged Congress to pass recommendations coming from his Committee on Civil Rights, including the establishment of a permanent FEPC. His request met with strong resistance in Congress. Under pressure from the racial turmoil of the 1960s, John F. Kennedy in 1961 issued an executive order on equal opportunity in Federal and Federally connected employment. According to Fleming (1965, 383), this order "greatly strengthened standards of compliance and methods of enforcement applying to contractors and Federal Agencies."

The passage of the Civil Rights Act of 1964 gave Congressional support to equal employment opportunities for blacks. Affirmative action, as a major thrust to promote equal employment opportunities for blacks and other minorities, became a major policy of the U.S. government during the 1970s. Under this policy, if blacks and other minorities are underrepresented in private businesses, employers may be required to give preference in hiring and promotions to members of the minority until the minority in question is fairly represented among employees. The very nature of this policy acknowledges the underlying struggle that persists for blacks in their effort to achieve parity with whites in employment and income.

Given the civil rights legislation and the operation of the Affirmative Action Program over the past two decades, what is the relative position of blacks to whites with respect to employment, unemployment, and income? How do the occupations of employed blacks in the South compare with those of employed whites in the South and employed blacks in other regions of the United States?

Occupation of Employed Persons by Race

Blacks in the United States have always been concentrated in the lowest paying, least skilled occupations, largely as service workers and laborers (Howe and Widick 1969; Drake and Cayton 1945, Chapter 9; U.S. Bureau of Census 1979, 60–62). Table 7-4 reveals that in 1960, slightly more than one-third (34.7 percent) of all employed blacks in the United States were service (household, protective, other) workers, compared to fewer than one-tenth (9.3 percent) of the whites. About half of all black service workers were employed as private household workers (16.4 percent), while only 1 percent of the whites were private household workers. A similar pattern is revealed in the South, where more than one-third of the employed blacks (36.6 percent) were service workers, and of those more than half were engaged in private household work (19.6 percent). On the other hand, fewer than one-tenth (7.7 percent) of the whites were service workers; of these, only 1 percent were employed as private household workers.

In 1960, one-fifth (19.5 percent) of the employed blacks in the United States were laborers (farm, nonfarm), compared to fewer than one-tenth (6.1 percent) of the whites. For the South, one out of four employed blacks and fewer than one out of ten whites were laborers. Thus, in 1960, slightly more than half (54.2 percent) of the employed blacks in the United States and fewer than one-fifth (15.4 percent) of the employed whites were service workers or laborers. For the same period in the South, three out of five employed blacks (61 percent) and about one out of ten whites (13 percent) were service workers or laborers.

Over the twenty-year period from 1960 to 1980, the percentage of employed blacks in the Nation in service occupations decreased from 34.7 to 23.1. For the same period blacks engaged in private household services decreased from 16.4 to 2.6 percent. During the same twenty-year period, the proportion of white workers in the country engaged in service occupations increased from 9.3 to 11.6 percent. This increase reflects the growth of professional and technical work in the service occupations.

The same pattern is revealed in the South. Between 1960 and 1980, the percentage of black service workers in the South declined from 36.6 to 24.1. However, the percentage of household workers fell more sharply, from 19.6 to 3.5. For whites the percentage of service workers increased from 7.7 to 10.0. Again, these changes reflect the growth of professional and technical activities in the ranks of service occupations.

Table 7-4. Percent of Employed Persons by Occupation, Region, and
          Race, 1960

Occupations	United States Percent		Northeast Percent	
	White	Black	White	Black
Professional	12.4	5.1	13.1	5.5
Managerial, except farm	9.6	1.6	9.1	2.1
Farmers and farm managers	4.2	3.0	1.1	0.1
Salesworkers	8.2	1.5	8.1	2.3
Clerical and kindred	16.0	6.4	17.6	11.8
Craftsmen and foremen	15.0	6.7	15.2	7.8
Operatives and kindred	19.2	21.4	21.4	28.3
Service occupations	9.3	34.7	9.5	31.4
Farm laborers	2.0	5.8	0.8	0.6
Laborers, except farm	4.1	13.7	4.1	10.1

Source: U.S. Bureau of the Census. 1960. Detailed Characteristics:
          1960, Table 257, pp. 717-19.

Throughout the United States in 1960, blacks were greatly underrepresented in the white-collar occupations (managerial, professional, technical, sales, and administrative-support, including
clerical). However, the percentage of blacks in white-collar occupations in the country rose from 14.6 in 1960 to 39.3 in 1980 (see Table
7-5). This represents a gain of 24.7 percent. The percentage of blacks
in white-collar positions in the South rose from 10.6 in 1960 to 33.3
in 1980. This reflects a 22.7 percent increase. For the same period
the percentage of whites in white-collar positions in the United
States rose from 46.2 to 55, an increase of 8.8 percent, while for

North Central		West		South	
Percent		Percent		Percent	
White	Black	White	Black	White	Black
11.5	5.1	14.2	6.4	11.8	5.0
8.5	1.8	10.6	2.1	10.6	1.3
6.6	0.2	2.7	0.3	5.4	5.0
7.9	2.0	8.2	1.9	8.7	1.0
15.3	10.2	16.3	10.8	15.2	3.3
14.9	8.2	15.0	9.0	15.0	5.6
19.3	27.2	15.0	20.1	19.3	17.8
9.7	31.7	10.6	35.0	7.7	36.6
2.2	0.5	2.8	1.7	2.4	9.3
4.1	13.1	4.8	12.7	3.9	15.1

whites in the South the percentage rose from 46.3 to 54.8, an increase of 8.5 percent.

Although the percentage increase for blacks in white-collar occupations more than doubled that of whites between 1960 and 1980, the ratio of black-to-white workers equals only 60 percent. The concept "ratio" is employed here to make quantitative comparisons between conditions of whites and blacks by assuming the fact for whites as the basic referent and dividing this number or percentage into the same number or percentage for blacks. The result is a figure that reveals the degree or amount of difference between the two groups in a specific aspect. The smallest representations of blacks in white-collar positions occur in the executive, administrative, and managerial occupations; and the sales categories, with ratios of 39

Table 7-5. Percent of Employed Persons by Occupation, Region, and
Race, 1970 and 1980

	1970			
	United States Percent		Northeast Percent	
Occupations	White	Black	White	Black
Managerial and professional specialty	20.0	9.1	20.9	9.9
Technical, sales, and administrative support	30.4	18.2	31.7	26.2
Service	11.0	27.8	11.0	24.2
Farming, forestry and fishing	3.7	4.2	1.5	1.0
Precision production craft and repair	14.6	9.6	14.0	9.7
Operators, fabricators, and laborers	20.2	31.0	20.9	29.0
	1980			
	United States Percent		Northeast Percent	
Occupations	White	Black	White	Black
Managerial and professional specialty	23.9	14.1	25.3	15.7
Technical, sales, and administrative support	31.1	25.2	31.9	31.2
Service	11.6	23.1	11.8	23.2
Farming, forestry and fishing	2.9	2.0	1.4	0.4
Precision production craft and repair	13.4	8.9	12.3	7.9
Operators, fabricators, and laborers	17.1	26.7	17.3	21.6

Source: U.S. Bureau of the Census. 1980. General Social and
Economic Characteristics, Table 89, pp. 45, 46.

Table 7-5. continued.

1970					
North Central		West		South	
Percent		Percent		Percent	
White	Black	White	Black	White	Black
18.3	9.0	22.3	12.1	19.6	8.5
28.6	22.0	31.2	26.4	30.7	12.3
11.7	23.7	12.4	25.6	9.4	31.1
5.1	1.0	4.0	1.3	4.1	7.1
14.7	10.0	13.7	10.4	15.7	9.4
21.6	34.2	16.4	23.7	20.5	31.6

1980					
North Central		West		South	
Percent		Percent		Percent	
White	Black	White	Black	White	Black
21.7	14.7	26.1	17.8	23.4	12.7
29.4	28.1	32.2	34.0	31.4	20.6
12.6	21.3	12.3	20.3	10.1	24.1
4.2	0.4	2.9	1.1	2.9	3.2
13.0	8.2	13.1	9.3	14.7	9.5
19.0	27.2	13.3	17.2	17.5	29.9

and 41 percent, respectively. The highest representations for blacks employed in white-collar occupations occur in the administrative support occupations, including clerical; and technical and support occupations, 80 and 75 percent, respectively.

The blue-collar occupations include precision production, craft, and repair workers; and operators, fabricators, and laborers. Although blacks in the South are overrepresented among blue-collar workers in general, they are underrepresented in the precision production, craft, and repair occupations, with ratios of 60 percent in 1970 and 65 percent in 1980. On the other hand, blacks are over-represented as operators, fabricators, and laborers. As machine operators, assemblers, and inspectors, 14.4 percent of the blacks (compared to 8.6 of the whites) are in these occupations. The highest overrepresentation of blacks as compared to whites (two to one) is found in the subcategory of handlers, equipment cleaners, helpers, and laborers (see Table 7-5).

Occupational Dissimilarity and Issues of Inequality

Although progress is being made toward reducing the racial disparity of occupational status in the South, the rate of progress is slow and varies by occupation. By comparison with whites, blacks remain underrepresented in the high status occupational categories and overrepresented in the lower status occupational categories. This observation holds for white and black workers in all regions. For a summary picture of the changes of occupational statuses of blacks and whites, indexes of racial status dissimilarities in occupational categories (see Duncan and Duncan 1955; Gross 1968; Fossett et al. 1986) were calculated by regions for 1960, 1970, and 1980. The data presented in Tables 7-4 and 7-5 provided the basis for calculating the index of racial status dissimilarities in occupations for each year. These findings are presented in Table 7-6.

An inspection of Table 7-6 indicates that in 1960 almost half (48.6 percent) of the Southern black workers would have to be up-graded to achieve occupational parity with whites. The situation in the other regions is substantially better than in the South. More than a third but fewer than two-fifths of the blacks in the other regions would have to change occupations in order to achieve racial parity. By 1980, the index for the South had dropped from 48.6 to 26.7, while the indexes for other regions dropped less sharply. Between

Table 7-6. Indexes of Dissimilarity in Occupations between Blacks and Whites by Region, 1960, 1970, and 1980[a]

Region	Index of Dissimilarity			Difference between 1960 and 1980
	1960	1970	1980	
Northeast	35.2	22.0	20.2	-15.0
North Central	39.2	24.7	20.4	-18.8
South	48.6	42.2	26.7	-21.9
West	38.1	22.3	19.0	-19.1
All	41.8	28.3	21.3	-20.5

[a]These indexes were calculated from occupational categories given in Tables 7-4 and 7-5 by summing the percentage differences between blacks and whites for a given year and dividing by 2.

1960 and 1970, each region except the South experienced a decline of between 13 and 16 percent in its index of racial dissimilarity. The reduction in the South was only 6.4 percent during that period. However, between 1970 and 1980 the reduction in the index for the South was nearly 16 percent, while a reduction of only about 4 percent or less was experienced in other regions. These findings suggest that under present circumstances there may be a point below which it becomes extremely difficult to achieve status parity. Related concerns are: What are the factors contributing to this difficulty? How do they operate and under what conditions?

The above findings suggest that trends toward occupational equity for blacks may be greatly influenced by changes in economic conditions of the Nation and of each region. Generally, periods of economic prosperity and high employment accelerate trends toward parity while periods of economic depressions and high unemployment have the opposite effect. The economic growth in the South during the 1970s along with the Affirmative Action Program supported the trend toward occupational equity. At the same time the economic decline in major industries of the North Central region slowed down the trend and reversed it in certain occupations.

Changes in occupational disparity are not uniform across the Nation. Thus, Fossett and Swicegood (1982) report that cities differ in racial occupational inequality. Variations in occupational inequity are related to differences in the economic structure and types of jobs available. Some data suggest that the occupational inequalities in the South will diminish as the South becomes more urbanized, industrialized, and high-technology oriented (see Chapters 2 and 3 above).

Fossett and Swicegood (1986) point out, however, that national economic prosperity does not automatically reduce racial occupational inequality. They report (p. 428) that although the decade of the 1940s was a period of strong economic growth, inequities in occupations nevertheless increased in both the South and non-South. However, during the 1950s, a period of relatively poor economic growth, occupational inequality declined in the non-South but continued to increase in the South. Occupational disparity declined in both the South and non-South during the 1960s, a period of rapid economic growth. It continued to decline in the 1970s, when economic growth was relatively slow and uneven. In connection with these economic variations and occupational conditions Fossett and Swicegood write (p. 428) "our data do provide evidence consistent with the assumption that civil rights legislation, court decisions, and other interventions during the 1960s and 1970s contributed significantly to moving the nation toward racial equality." These findings are consistent with the position taken in this chapter that continued progress toward achieving equality for blacks, and the rate of such progress, depend greatly upon governmental policy and intervention as well as upon continuous social and legal pressures from blacks and supporting groups. Yet, even with social engineering programs like affirmative action, change is slow (Feinberg 1985). In early 1989 the Reagan Supreme Court went further and reduced much of the effectiveness of existing affirmative action legislation.

Given the unfavorable position of blacks in the social structure, Lieberson and Fuguit (1967, 188) point out that the absence of racial discrimination in the job market would not mean the elimination of racial differences in occupations, since related social process factors, such as education, job training, and work experience are linked to intergenerational processes of family social mobility, socialization, and change. Assuming that the reduction of discrimination in employment persists, and that current rates of intergenerational mobility persist, Lieberson and Fuguit conclude that "it would take about eighty years before racial occupational inequality would be virtually nil." However, they further state: ". . . if the current relationship between education and occupation for nonwhites were to remain unaltered, the racial index of dissimilarity in occupations would decline from 38 to 29 after eight generations, but never get lower than that" (p. 197). Consequently, there is need for more social action programs addressing various aspects of racial inequities, especially education.

Income by Race and Region

In 1960 the median family income of blacks in the United States was 54 percent of that of whites; in 1970 it was 61 percent, and in 1980 it was 60 percent (see Table 7-7). Among the four regions in 1960, the median family incomes of blacks in the West was slightly more than three-fourths that of whites (77 percent) followed by the North Central with a ratio of 72 percent, the Northeast 69 percent, and the South 46 percent. Between 1960 and 1980 the median family income of blacks as a percentage of white income declined in all

Table 7-7. Median Family Income by Race and Region and Black Income as a Percentage of White, 1960, 1970, 1980, and 1982

Region	1960			1970		
	White	Black	% of White	White	Black	% of White
United States	$ 14,675	$ 7,872	54	$ 19,722	$ 12,012	61
Northeast	15,733	10,885	69	21,227	14,507	68
North Central	14,927	10,758	72	20,390	15,372	75
West	16,047	12,294	77	20,540	14,610	71
South	12,474	5,782	46	17,267	9,702	56

Table 7-7. continued.

Region	1980			1982		
	White	Black	% of White	White	Black	% of White
United States	$ 20,835	$ 12,598	60	$ 24,603	$ 13,599	55
Northeast	21,492	13,288	62	25,815	14,735	57
North Central	21,462	14,694	68	24,903	12,374	50
West	21,713	14,888	68	25,249	16,508	65
South	19,257	11,595	60	23,089	13,044	56

Sources: Bureau of the Census. 1980. General Social and Economic Characteristics: 1980, Table 93, p. 51.

Bureau of the Census. 1982. Money, Income, and Poverty Status of Families and Persons in the United States: 1982, Current Population Reports, Series P-60, No. 140, Table 1.

regions except the South. The greatest decline, nearly 10 percent, was experienced in the West. For the South, however, the median family income of blacks as a percentage of whites increased from 46 percent in 1960 to 60 percent in 1980.

In 1982, however, the median family income of blacks as a percentage of whites declined in all regions, including the South. The greatest decline (18 percent) occurred in the North Central region, where median black family income dropped from 68 to 50 percent of that of whites (U.S. Bureau of Census 1982b). The median family income ratios of blacks to whites dropped to 57 percent in the Northeast, 65 percent in the West, and 56 percent in the South by 1982. Consequently, the North Central region exchanged places with the South for the lowest dollar income ($12,374 and $13,044 respectively) as well as the lowest ratio of black to white median family income. The 1986 report of median family income by race and region (U.S. Bureau of Census 1986) revealed a 6 percent increase in the median family income ratio of black to white in each region except the South, where the ratio remained the same as in 1982. Again, this picture reflects the traditional impact of economic decline upon black employment and income. These data and findings may point to the continuing influence of racism on income and employment for blacks. Perhaps nothing less than affirmative action, economic growth, and legal and public pressure can bring about economic parity for blacks.

Unemployment Percentages by Race, Age, and Region

The unemployment rates for blacks in the United States declined to lows of 6.7 and 6.4 percent in 1968 and 1969, respectively (U.S. Bureau of Census 1979, 61). In 1971, the unemployment rates for blacks and whites in the United States were 7.9 and 4.5, respectively, with a black to white ratio of 1.8 (see Table 7-8). Generally speaking, throughout the Nation during the 1970s, the unemployment rate for blacks in white-collar positions was twice as high as the rate for whites in similar positions. For blacks in blue-collar and service positions the unemployment rate was about one-and-one-half times greater than that for whites (U.S. Department of Labor 1983).

By 1983 the unemployment rates for blacks and whites in the United States had increased to 19.5 and 9.4, respectively, with a ratio of 2.1. Although the unemployment rates declined in 1987 for both

Table 7-8. Unemployment Rates and Civilian Labor Force by Race and Region for Those Aged 20 Years and Older, 1971, 1983, and 1987

	1971			1983		
Region	Black	White	Ratio: Black to White	Black	White	Ratio: Black to White
United States	7.9	4.5	1.8	19.5	9.4	2.1
Northeast	7.7	5.1	1.5	16.8	10.0	1.7
North Central	10.4	3.9	2.7	26.0	9.5	2.7
West	9.4	6.6	1.4	19.3	8.9	2.2
South	6.6	3.2	2.1	18.2	7.4	2.4

	1987		
Region	Black	White	Ratio: Black to White
United States	13.0	5.3	2.4
Northeast	9.1	4.0	2.3
North Central	17.9	5.6	3.2
West	11.4	6.0	1.9
South	12.7	5.5	2.3

Sources: Department of Labor. 1983. Geographic Profile of Employment and Unemployment, 1983, Bulletin 2216.

Department of Labor. 1987. Geographic Profile of Employment and Unemployment, 1987, Bulletin 2305.

races, the black to white unemployment ratio increased to a high of 2.4.

An examination of unemployment rates for blacks by region in 1971 (see Table 7-8) reveals that the South had the lowest unemployment rate for blacks, followed by the Northeast, the West, and the North Central regions. The ratio of black to white unemployment was the lowest in the West at 1.4, followed by the Northeast with 1.5, the South at 2.1 and the North Central region with 2.7. By 1983 the unemployment rate for blacks had increased in all regions by 9 to 16 percentage points and the ratio of black to white unemployment had also increased. Although the unemployment rates dropped for both races in all regions in 1987, the ratio of black to white unemployment increased in the Northeast and North Central regions and declined in the West and South.

Table 7-9 presents the unemployment rates for youth 16 to 19 years of age. Black teenagers have had the highest unemployment rates and the sharpest increases in these rates as compared with any unemployed group in any region. The lowest unemployment rate for youths in 1971 was in the South, 30.2 for blacks, compared with 12.9 for whites. The highest black teenage unemployment rate, 40.6, was in the North Central region, where the white rate was 14.3. By 1983 the unemployment rate for black teenagers in the South had increased by 16.1 percent to 46.3, while the increase for whites was only 5.7 percent, up to 18.6. Although black teenagers in the South experienced a substantial increase in unemployment, the percentage increase was greater for black youth in other regions. The highest percentage increase, 18.7, occurred in the West, resulting in a 46.4 unemployment rate among black teenagers. The unemployment rate among black teenagers in 1983 was lowest in the South (46.3) and highest in the North Central region (58.0), where the black-to-white teenage unemployment ratio of 3.0 was also the highest of the four regions. Although the teenage unemployment rates dropped for both races in all regions in 1987, the ratio of black to white unemployment remained at a level higher than that of 1971 in each region except the South.

The high unemployment rate among black teenagers has significant implications for present and future black-white relations in the South and the United States as a whole. An extremely large number of young blacks are denied the opportunity, at an early age in life, to have the necessary work experiences so crucial for the formation and maintenance of habits essential for personal development and

Table 7-9. Unemployment Rates for Civilian Labor Force by Race and Region for Those Aged 16-19, 1971, 1983, and 1987

Region	1971			1983		
	Black	White	Ratio: Black to White	Black	White	Ratio: Black to White
United States	31.7	15.1	2.1	48.5	19.3	2.5
Northeast	31.1	15.7	2.0	47.6	19.6	2.4
North Central	40.6	14.3	2.8	58.0	19.6	3.0
West	27.7	19.0	1.5	46.4	19.7	2.4
South	30.2	12.9	2.3	46.3	18.6	2.5

Region	1987		
	Black	White	Ratio: Black to White
United States	34.7	14.4	2.4
Northeast	22.2	10.4	2.1
North Central	44.3	13.4	3.3
West	27.2	17.1	1.6
South	35.5	16.3	2.2

Sources: Department of Labor. 1983. Geographic Profile of Employment and Unemployment, 1983, Bulletin 2216.

Department of Labor. 1987. Geographic Profile of Employment and Unemployment, 1987, Bulletin 2305.

the achievement of a stable family and community life. Given the absence of work opportunities, these youths are denied the chance to form habits of punctuality, dependability, and responsibility while acquiring skills and knowledge of the world of work (Moland 1981). Wilson (1987b) points out also that these young people form a substantial sector of the "truly disadvantaged" found in the inner-city ghetto underclasses. Although they have come of age for employment and self-maintenance, they remain as dependents in families who are experiencing extreme economic hardships. Consequently, without jobs, they are found loitering on the street corners, where the potential for involvement in deviant behavior is high, thereby contributing to the perpetuation of the life-style of the urban underclass. Many become involved in activities that lead to frequent arrests and possible imprisonment. The disproportionately high unemployment rate among black youth and young adults of the urban underclass, and the high representation of blacks in ghettos, provide the potential for violent reaction to situations of racial injustice in all regions of the United States (Ball-Rokeach and Short 1985).

Unemployment and underemployment tend to generate poverty. When the war on poverty was initiated under the Kennedy-Johnson Administrations, the poverty rate in the South was twice that in most regions. Table 7-10 shows a substantial decline in the poverty rate in the South between 1959 and 1979. Nevertheless, in the South in 1979, three times more blacks than whites were in poverty, for a ratio of 2.9. (For the same year, the poverty ratio was 3.5 in both the Northeast and North Central regions.) For whites in 1986, the poverty rates had increased by 1 to 3 percent in each region. For blacks there was an increase of 6 percent in the North Central and 2 percent in the South, and a decrease of 1 percent and 4 percent in the West and Northeast, respectively.

Despite the disparities that still exist in occupations, income, unemployment, and poverty by race, blacks in the South have made gains in these areas over the past two decades or more. These gains have brought the South to a position relatively comparable with other regions of the United States on all dimensions of economic activities.

Trends in Education

The Supreme Court Decision of May 17, 1954, exerted a dramatic effect, stimulating many school districts to desegregate and provok-

Table 7-10. Numbers and Percents of Persons Below Poverty Level, by Regions, Race, and Years, 1959, 1969, 1979

	1959				1969			
	White		Black		White		Black	
Region	N	%	N	%	N	%	N	%
United States	27,719	18	10,965	55	18,935	11	7,680	35
Northeast	5,207	13	1,042	34	3,741	9	1,026	24
North Central	7,535	16	1,418	41	4,750	9	1,132	25
West	3,687	15	690	33	3,264	11	406	25
South	11,290	27	7,815	70	7,179	15	5,115	44

	1979			
	White		Black	
Region	N	%	N	%
United States	17,332	9	7,649	30
Northeast	3,485	8	1,315	28
North Central	4,323	8	1,431	28
West	3,163	9	488	23
South	6,360	11	4,415	32

Source: Bureau of the Census. 1980. General Social and Economic Characteristics: 1980, Table 96, pp. 61-62.

ing most Southern districts to resist or delay desegregation. As a consequence, by 1963, 98 percent of black students in the South were still in all-black schools (Orfield 1983, 5). It was only after passage of the 1964 Civil Rights Act and several court decisions that the percentage of blacks in segregated schools in the South was substantially reduced. By 1974 the percentage of students enrolled in all-black schools in the South had dropped from 98 to 8.1 (see Table 7-11).

On the whole, Southern public schools are more completely desegregated than those in other regions. For example, while only 21 percent of the black public school students in the South attended schools with 95–100 percent black enrollment in 1974, this percentage was 48 in the Northeast, 58 in the North Central, and 38 in the West. On the other hand, though, more black students in the South than in the other regions attended schools that were half black or less.

Both the rate and volume of school desegregation among the Southern States have been uneven. Initially, change came in the border states, e.g., Delaware and Kentucky. By 1980 more than 50 percent of black students were attending classes in predominately white schools. Orfield (1983, 3) reported that in 1980 white students were far more likely to be attending substantially desegregated schools in the South than in other regions, especially the Northeast.

On the other hand, institutions of higher learning opened to blacks later, in response to pressures from the black community, court actions, and the Civil Rights Act of 1964. Policies of many Northern colleges and universities were relaxed, and state and private universities in the South were desegregated under duress. Young people in the black community were encouraged to take advantage of these new opportunities for marketable graduate, professional, service, and clerical training. The response to this activity was reflected in enrollment and graduation statistics from all regions of the country.

Supported by the black leadership organizations and the Affirmative Action legislation, appropriately trained young blacks began to move into lower-level administrative, professional-service, technical, and clerical occupations in both industry and business. Progress was slow and came as the result of continual pressure by the government and the black civil rights organizations. In the late 1970s and 1980s the entry of young blacks into these occupational categories was supported by pressure from another direction. By this

Table 7-11. Percentage of Black Enrollment in Public Elementary and Secondary Schools by Region[a] and Increasing Levels of Isolation, 1974

Regions	50 Percent	50-100 Percent	95-100 Percent	100 Percent
Northeast	21.5	78.5	47.7	8.5
North Central	20.3	79.7	57.6	24.3
West	29.0	71.0	38.1	4.5
South	45.0	55.0	21.1	8.1

Source: Adapted from Statistical Abstract of the United States. 1977, Table 236, p. 146.

[a]Excluding the District of Columbia.

time the labor resource of the white "Baby Boom" generation was being exhausted. Faced by this dilemma, major industries and businesses turned to the growing crop of young, appropriately trained blacks (and other minority persons) to meet the white-collar labor vacuum. In time, employers began to compete for these new workers. Various programs to recruit and facilitate the training of young blacks were estabished by many firms. The results of this flurry of activity are indicated by the figures shown in Table 7-6.

It was said above that ups and downs of economic activity tend to stimulate and retard progress toward occupational equity of black workers. Other national economic trends and problems also affect this equalizing process. During the 1960s–80s some rapidly advancing countries in Europe, South America, and Asia have become able to compete successfully with several basic American industries—steel, automobiles, rubber, clothing, shoes, and the like. As a consequence, the United States has lost many jobs to these competitors. Although most of the jobs thus lost are low-skill operative, some of the middle-range administrative, professional, technical, white-collar service, and clerical jobs are also gone. The loss of these jobs affected blacks just when they were getting footholds in American industries and businesses.

Another national economic problem that affects aspiring young black workers is the burgeoning national deficit. This almost unmanageable trend depresses the national rate of economic growth and so also the rate of increase of the white-collar middle-range occupations where blacks find greatest opportunities. In addition, in early 1989 the Reagan Supreme Court acted to weaken the efficacy of the Affirmative Action acts, decisions, and programs.

Prospects and Projections

Limited removal of the legal shackles of segregation in the South has enlarged the opportunity for blacks to pursue equity in the political, economic, and educational arenas. Consequently, the South has advanced and no longer ranks last among the regions on all of the indicators of racial inequality. Nevertheless, blacks still experience serious inequities in all the areas of social and economic endeavor. (See Williams and Jaynes 1989, 3–25.)

The basic situation has stimulated widespread reaction and a variety of predictions regarding the future development of race relations in the nation and in the region. Some of these are summarized and described briefly in the following paragraphs. In some situations predictions may be interpreted as alternatives. In other situations they should be regarded as strategic approaches that may be acted out simultaneously in the same or different localities.

Continuing and growing unemployment of today accentuates the "color line" between blacks and whites (Blumer 1986; Deutsch 1987). In my view, the struggle for civil rights by blacks in the South has led them to a constant awareness and assessment of their disadvantaged social position while bringing into sharper focus the illegalities and injustices imposed upon them. Past gains have required great struggle by blacks and support by the federal government. As mentioned above, attempts are now being made to undermine and remove some of these supports. Consequently, the struggle for full opportunity on the part of blacks in the South may intensify during the coming years. Also, the unevenness of the rate of progress in various parts of the South and in various institutional areas may lead to focusing the civil rights struggle in local areas.

The continuing disparities in employment, income, housing, imprisonment, treatment before the law, and so on will serve as constant reminders that equity for blacks has not been achieved. Many blacks may respond to these inequities through the use of nonviolent strategies, e.g., boycotts, protest demonstrations, and legal proceedings, which may at times erupt in violence. At the same time, however, as Ball-Rokeach and Short (1985) predicted, other blacks, particularly those in the underclass, may be driven to extreme violence. These actions may occur in various localities throughout the South for another forty to fifty years as blacks seek to maintain the gains already made.

On the basis of various trend data and findings presented in this chapter, I can offer the following predictions of change in the future. Examination of the present proportion of black elected officials in the South, as well as the rate of increase relative to the proportion of blacks in the voting age population, suggests that fifty years from now blacks would have achieved only about 70 percent of parity with whites. Over the past twenty years the greatest increase in the number of black state legislators has occurred in the South, where the number has grown from 16 in 1964 to 211 in 1985. Other regions have experienced only slight gains in the number of black state legislators. Although the greatest gains have been made in the South, blacks in the South, and in other regions as well, are still underrepresented in state legislatures. This suggests that under present circumstances there may be a point below which it becomes exceedingly difficult to reduce black underrepresentation. Consequently, during the next fifty years, increased attention may be given to coalition politics as the process by which blacks seek to achieve their social and economic goals in the legislative chambers of state government.

Although progress is being made toward reducing the disparity in occupational status for blacks in the South, they still remain underrepresented in the high status occupations in each occupational area and overrepresented in the lower status occupations in each area. This observation holds for employed blacks in all regions. During the next fifty years occupational inequalities experienced by blacks in the South will continue to decline as the South keeps on modernizing, as blacks get better educated, and as the supply of white "baby boomers" diminishes. On the other hand, the Reagan Supreme Court and the Bush racial policy may continue to attack Affirmative Action and other supports for this equalizing trend.

Over the past two decades the trend in the South has been for the median family income of blacks as a percentage of that of whites to increase. However, in 1982, the median family income of blacks vis à vis that of whites declined in all regions, including the South. This reflects the traditional impact of economic decline upon black employment and income. In 1983 the South had the lowest regional teenage unemployment rate among blacks, still two and a half times greater than that of whites. The high unemployment rate among black teenagers in all regions has significant implications for present and future black-white relations in the South and the United States as a whole. Given the increasing teenage population among blacks and the continuing general racial disparities in employment, income, poverty, and treatment before the law as well as the growing recent conservatism of national policy in this area, the stage appears to be set for intensifying the struggle for black equality during the next two decades, especially in the South. This struggle, including potential for violence, may result in a further diminishing of the inequalities between blacks and whites in the South over the next fifty years. The struggle may also exacerbate racism and increase resistance to efforts by blacks.

The strategy of coalition politics, as exposed by some leaders, constitutes a nonviolent approach to the remedy of these problems in the region. Some moderate Southern whites feel free to speak out and act on behalf of blacks and the region's image in the United States and abroad. Hispanics, Asians, and Native Americans, as minorities, may be drawn into the coalition along with blacks. Slowly, also, poor whites in cities as well as on farms may discover that they have common cause with other poor people. One dramatic illustration of this alternative is embodied in Jesse Jackson's "rainbow coalition" (Jackson 1986).

On the other hand, successful competition by blacks through the coalition tactic may also stimulate racist attitudes and feelings. This reaction is expressed in the complaints of "reverse racism" and favoritism. Similarly, some political observers explained the heavy vote for Albert Gore in certain Southern states on "Super Tuesday" 1988 as a racist reaction. It was said that these voters resented the success of Jackson's "rainbow coalition" and expressed their resentment by a vote for Gore. Such responses to the successes of blacks may increase in the future.

The traditional nonviolent action strategy is espoused by the NAACP, Urban League, and other leadership organizations of the black community. They propose continued and sophisticated use of the traditional tactics of protest, boycott, legal action, and the like. Their immediate aim is to arrest and reverse the negative thrust of the Reagan Administration and to place the movement of liberal change back on track. The long-range goal is to accelerate, in the near future, the broad national thrust toward equity treatment of blacks and other minorities.

Some other observers foresee a violent and destructive development in the near future. Ball-Rokeach and Short (1985) ground this prediction in the expansion, stabilization, and institutionalization of a permanent national urban underclass, composed substantially of poor blacks. They argue that if the present trend continues unchecked, the United States may experience mob violence on a scale never before encountered in this country. Some of the consequences of such violence may be grim. On the other hand, such explosions of violence may trigger long-term programs of societal reorganization and liberalization.

Some other observers offer predictions related to various sectors or aspects of social life in the black community. For example, many leaders and experts point to problems of black families as a factor that may significantly affect the course of race relations in the future. They stress, particularly, poverty, unwed motherhood, poor housing and health, adolescent unemployment, high level juvenile delinquency, drugs and alcohol, and predatory violence in the under-class metropolitan ghettos, South as well as North. Moynihan (1965) attributed this problem to inherent "weakness" of black families. Landry (1986) recognizes the economic polarization of the black community between the poor and disadvantaged families and the economically advancing and more successful black middle class families as another factor contributing to this development. Although their predictions are very gloomy, they do not suggest violent intergroup relations; however, in the absence of changes in social and economic policy that would effect changes in the economic and social situations of this growing underclass (Wilson 1987a), it is my opinion that the potential for violence is ever present. This approach brings us full circle to the conclusion that the active intervention of government at all levels, in concert with skillful efforts of the black organizations, will continue to be essential in retrieving black families from the disabilities and problems with which they are now harassed. Leaders advancing this approach would claim that "strengthening" black families would be the key effort to advancement along political, economic, educational, and social fronts.

I can conclude this discussion of Prospects and Projections by sketching the framework of thought that has guided me. I have suggested that the practice of race relations in the United States is determined in large part by the policies that are generated by the federal government—the Congress, the Administration, and the Courts. Citizens endeavor to influence these policies by means of conservative ideological groups (e.g., the Chamber of Commerce, the Republican party, and the Moral Majority) and by the liberal ideological groups (e.g., CIO labor unions, the Democratic Party, and civil rights organizations). Generating race relations policy, therefore, is a continuous process of struggle that is not always aware of the Constitutional principles that underlie the government and the society. Although the tradition commits the groups to nonviolent struggle for change, recent history and current metropolitan central city conditions warn that massive collective racial violence is not unexpected. (See Williams and Jaynes 1989, 28–30.)

Speaking in the mid-1980s, I expect that until the end of the century or later, the Reagan ideological conservatism will continue to qualify American race relations. I predict therefore that progress in the liberal direction will be slow and policy-compliance will be more voluntary and less mandatory than it was two decades ago.

However, it is more risky to predict what turn change may take in the twenty-first century. In speculating about change in these years ahead where foresight is limited and untrustworthy, I can use the hypothesis of a cyclical pattern of change in society (see Mitchell 1941). By the second quarter of the twenty-first century, according to this model, we may see a reversal of the swing to the conservative orientation. Change may be in the liberal direction, and race relations may become more democratic and conditions for blacks more equitable than in the 1970s and 1980s.

Part III

Social Orientations

The two chapters in this part examine changes in the main orientations that characterize social action in the region. In Chapter 8, Reed characterizes the orientation with the concept of culture. He shows that with urban industrialization, a spreading and pervasive layer of "mass culture" qualifies the lives of most people in the region. Underneath, the traditional culture persists but is more and more relegated to rural and small town places. People have learned to live with both kinds of culture; thus Reed can conclude that even though the South is changing, it is nevertheless recognizably the South.

In examining the issue of conservatism versus liberalism in Chapter 9, Luebke employs the concept of power rather than culture as the vehicle of analysis. He reveals that both "modernizer" elites and "traditionalist" elites are power-oriented; nevertheless, the modernizers are more pragmatic and flexible than the indigenous traditionalists. With both categories of leaders, liberal organizations and leaders get little sympathy. It is predicted that the situation is not likely to change significantly in the foreseeable future.

8

New South or No South? Regional Culture in 2036

John Shelton Reed

The fiftieth year of the Southern Sociological Society, 1986, marked several other significant Southern anniversaries. It had also been fifty years since the publication of *Gone With the Wind*; fifty years since Howard W. Odum's classic *Southern Regions of the United States* (1936); and, not least, an even century since Henry Grady, editor of the Atlanta *Constitution*, gave a speech in Boston (Grady 1890) that popularized the phrase "the New South." There is a sort of numerological magic about the round numbers, these half centuries and centuries (not to mention millennia, as we will have occasion to observe soon enough), and we probably ought to remind ourselves that these divisions are social conventions, reflecting only the evolutionary accident or divine whim that gave us ten fingers. Still, it has been a hundred years since Grady's speech, which does mean that very few who were living then are still with us; certainly nobody remembers the speech firsthand.

But, since 1886, many of us have heard a great deal about its subject. Different versions of the New South have come and gone, as Edwin Yoder (1984, 191) put it, "like French constitutions and theories of the decline of Rome." Talk of a New South probably reached its high point in 1976, when Americans elected the first undeniably Southern president since Andrew Johnson. So much was said about it then that Walker Percy (1977, 170) was driven to complain: "Of all the things I'm fed up with, I think I'm fed up most with hearing about the New South. . . . One of the first things I can remember in my life was hearing about the New South. I was three years old, in Alabama. Not a year has passed since that I haven't heard about a new South. I would dearly love never to hear the New South mentioned again. In fact my definition of a new South would be a South in which it never occurred to anybody to mention the New South."

Percy is right, of course. But the phrase is convenient shorthand for whatever the South is becoming. And I want to ask a question about the next "New South," specifically: how much and in what respects will its culture be assimilated to national patterns?

Continuing Southern Distinctiveness?

There was a time when few even thought to ask that question about Southern culture. Nearly everyone just *assumed* that the South would remain culturally distinctive. Certainly Henry Grady did. In his "New South" speech, Grady made some concession to the fact that the North had won the Civil War; he was willing, even eager, to adopt Northeastern economic ways, to build an urban, industrial economy like the one that had defeated his own. But scholars like Paul Gaston (1976) have pointed out quite rightly that Grady and his many admirers intended to pour the old cultural wine of planter rule and white supremacy into those new economic and demographic bottles. It apparently never crossed their minds to wonder whether traditional Southern ways were consistent with life in a radically altered society.

Later, though, particularly as Grady's economic prescriptions actually began to take effect, others began to wonder. As Broadus Mitchell put it in 1928 (quoted in Singal 1982), will "these great industrial developments . . . banish the personality of the South," or will industrialism "submit to be modified by a persistent Southern temperament?" Scholars from many disciplines—historians and anthropologists, folklorists and students of literature, geographers and political scientists—all have applied their disciplines' characteristic modes of inquiry to this question. Many brilliant and sensitive journalists have asked that question, too, and it is foolishness, mere academic snobbery, to ignore what they have written. Their work can be called "impressionistic" by those who wish to dismiss it, but at its best it is brilliant and sensitive ethnography.

One of the greatest of those journalists, W. J. Cash, put the case for cultural persistence as strongly as it has ever been put, in his masterpiece, *The Mind of the South* (1941). Cash thought even Southern skyscrapers were expressions of continuity, reflecting an old tradition of civic pride and the search for glory. "Softly," he asked, "do you not hear behind that the gallop of Jeb Stuart's cavalrymen?" (1941, 219). Not everyone has agreed, of course—C. Vann Woodward (1969, 34) replied to Cash's rhetorical question: "The answer is 'no'! Not one ghostly echo of a gallop"—and that argument itself is on the way to becoming a persistent feature of our region's culture.

Few these days deny that the South has always been changing, and will continue to change as it moves into the next century. The disagreement today is about the extent and nature of the changes. The question has become: Does "New South" mean *no* South? In a volume devoted to sociological understandings of the South, it seems appropriate to see what sociologists have contributed to this discussion.

The Sociological Contribution

Oddly enough, it is only recently that sociologists have really had anything to say about this, despite the fact that it would seem on the face of it to be a sociological question. (The "regional sociologists" of the 1930s and 1940s had other concerns, pressing ones related to the South's painfully evident social problems.) But the past quarter century has seen the emergence of what is now a fairly large body of sociological literature, based primarily on survey research into attitudes and values. (See, e.g., Glenn 1967; Glenn and Simmons 1967; Holloway and Robinson 1981; Hurlbert 1984; Killian 1985; Reed 1986.)

For the most part, these studies have adopted the rough-and-ready expedient of defining "Southerners" as residents of the Southern states (themselves variously defined), and comparing these respondents to other Americans on various measures of attitudes, values, and behavior. Some studies have examined trends in regional differences over time; others have compared regional differences among younger Americans to those found among older ones; most have introduced controls for such confounding factors as education, occupation, and size-of-place. The methodological shortcomings of these studies are obvious enough, I should think, but they may be offset by the fact that the question of convergence is by its nature quantitative; survey methods can address it with a precision no other approach offers, a precision that may be misleading but one that at least establishes which side of the argument must bear the burden of proof.

In any case, this accumulating literature demonstrates that some important regional differences in the United States are getting smaller: many of them because the South is coming to resemble the rest of the United States; a few because the rest of the United States is starting to look like the South. But, at the same time, it shows that large regional differences still exist, in a great many respects. Some of these differences are not going away, and some, indeed, are increasing. In other words, nearly all of the logical possibilities of what could be happening, *are* happening in one respect or another.

Can anything sensible be said about which differences are doing what? I think we can begin to make sense of this mass of data by distinguishing between two different sorts of attitudes and values that have, until recently, been "Southern" ones—by which I mean only that they have been found more often among Southerners than among other Americans.

Disappearing Traditional Values

In the first place, Southerners in the aggregate, black and white, have been characterized by a constellation of values that are common to folk, village, and peasant cultures everywhere in the world (Reed 1983, 47–53)—not surprisingly, since that is what the whole South was as recently as fifty years ago, and what parts of it still are today. Any student of modernization could list these attributes; it seems perfectly clear that they are linked to economic development, and we do not have to take sides here in the quarrel about whether they are cause or effect. Among these attributes would be such things as fatalism and suspicion of innovation. Other traditional values seem to involve emphasizing firm and fixed boundaries between categories: between family members and others, for instance; between local people and strangers, or between ethnic brethren and aliens; between men and women, leaders and followers, and so forth. Indeed, cultural modernization seems to consist largely of learning to live with fuzzy and ambiguous boundaries.

Harold Grasmick (1973), whose literature review and research on this subject I have leaned on heavily, calls this cluster of values "the" traditional value orientation, and he shows that, among

Southerners, it is eroded by urban life, by education, by travel and residence outside the South, by exposure to the mass media. Since all of these experiences are more common in each new generation of Southerners, it is not surprising to find that the traditional value orientation is less common among young Southerners than old ones, and less common now than a generation ago.

Other contributors to this volume document the continuing economic and demographic convergence between the South and the rest of the United States. One consequence of that process will surely be regional convergence with respect to these traditional values as well. Indeed, the process has been going on slowly but steadily for some time now, and there is no reason to suppose that convergence will not soon be complete. Already regional differences in religious prejudice have virtually vanished, and differences in racial prejudice are so much smaller now than twenty years ago that they can almost be ignored (see, e.g., Reed 1986, 92–95; Reed and Black 1985). (Some of the demographic differences, however, have disappeared only to reemerge as differences in the opposite direction [see Rindfuss 1978], and there is always the possibility that the same may happen with some of the decreasing cultural differences.)

Another factor to consider, of course, is the migration to the South that is examined in the early chapters of this book. If it continues at anything like its present level, it will also nudge regional convergence along, because migrants to the South are conspicuously "untraditional": they are, that is, much less likely to display these characteristics than native Southerners, white or (especially) black (see Reed 1983, 122–46). (By most of these measures, incidentally, blacks are the most "Southern" of all Southerners.)

Enduring Differences

But there have been other regional differences. Some "Southern" characteristics are not linked in any obvious way to rural residence, agricultural pursuits, poor education and not much of it, limited exposure to the "wider world." In a book called *The Enduring South* (Reed 1986), I examined some of them, and ventured to predict that regional differences in some of these characteristics are going to be with us for a while.

Although it is presumptuous for me to mention *The Enduring South* in the same breath as Cash's classic, *The Mind of the South*, there is at least a genetic connection between the two books that I would like to put on the record. When I first read *The Mind of the South* for recreation, in graduate school, I found it methodologically exasperating. I kept asking (as I was being trained to ask) "How does he *know* that?" When it came time to write a dissertation, I set out to study the "mind of the South" the way Paul Lazarsfeld and Wagner Thielens (1958) had studied "the academic mind"—that is, with survey data. The result became *The Enduring South*. And I must say I emerged from the experience with a new respect for the achievement, and the "methodology," of W. J. Cash.

The differences my book documented would not have surprised Cash at all. Most of them can be seen as manifestations of the individualism that Cash saw as central to Southern culture (see also Reed 1982, 162–85). They reflect an anti-institutional ethic that says: In the last analysis, you are on your own—and *should* be. Two generations after Cash, another Southern journalist, Roy Reed (1976, 103–04), described this mentality for the readers of the *New York Times*. "For all the American encroachments," he wrote, the South is "inhabited and given [its] dominant tone by men—and women who acquiesce in this matter—who carry in their hearts or genes or livers or lights an ancient, God-credited belief that a man has a right to do as he pleases. A right to be let alone in whatever plain of triumph he has staked out and won for his own. A right to go to hell or climb to the stars or sit still and do nothing, just as he damn well pleases, without restraint from anybody else and most assuredly without interference from any government anywhere." For example, Reed suggested, consider attitudes toward land-use legislation: "It is no accident that the most determined holdouts against [such] legislation in the United States are country people from the South. They will take care of their own land, and let the next man take care of his. If the next man puts in a rendering plant or a junkyard, that is his business." Reed believes this orientation is doomed—that the fight was lost "about the time [a man] lost the irretrievable right to take a leak off his own front porch"—but "they have not yet taken [Southerners'] right to curse and defy. . . ."

Well, Walter Hines Page said once that "Next to fried foods, the South has suffered most from oratory" (quoted in Smith 1985), and maybe Reed got carried away. Cash may have overstated it, too. But certainly an individualistic, anti-institutional note is evident in many aspects of Southern life. It is obvious, for example, in the Evangelical Protestantism to which most Southerners subscribe, a form of religion that sees salvation as something to be worked out by the individual, in a direct, unmediated relationship with Jesus. As Tom T. Hall sings it, in a classic country song: "Me and Jesus got our own thing goin'. / Don't need anybody to tell us what it's all about."

The same pattern is evident, I think, in a disposition to redress grievances privately, which sometimes means violently—a disposition that gives black and white Southerners homicide rates at which the rest of the civilized world marvels. Anti-institutionalism can also be seen in a sort of localism and familism that reflects, not ignorance of the alternatives (as in the traditional value orientation), but simple preference for the palpable and close at hand, as opposed to the distant and formal. And, finally, individualism may be reflected in a sort of economic libertarianism that was apparently suppressed during the hard times of the past 120 years, but that seems to be coming back strong in our own times, at least among Southern whites (see, e.g., Botsch 1980).

All of these are "Southern" attributes, more common in the South than elsewhere. And in these respects the South is *not* becoming more like the rest of the country: indeed, in some of them, regional differences are increasing. Unlike the traditional value orientation, these attributes are by no means universal among "folk societies," nor are they limited to such societies. And their statistical behavior is different, too: some of these traits are more common among educated Southerners than uneducated ones, or among urban Southerners than rural ones. Economic conservatism, as Robert Freymeyer (1982) has shown, is even more common among migrants to the South than among natives, so one cannot expect migration to reduce *that* difference.

Origins of Southern Anti-Institutionalism

Where these traits came from in the first place is an interesting question, but it is obviously a historical one—and it is tempting to leave it to the historians, especially since they disagree among themselves. Some point to the ethnic origins of Southerners and argue a Celtic influence (see McWhiney and Jamieson 1982, 170–91 and the works cited therein) or an African one (e.g., Cash 1941, 49–50; Pinckney 1934, 45–46), or some catalytic interaction of the two—each an explanation that at least moves the problem back across the Atlantic and out of the hair of *American* historians. Others point to the legacy of the plantation, or the persistence of the frontier, or one of a half-dozen other "central themes" of Southern history. A sociologist would be foolhardy indeed to step into that fracas, but I will venture to suspect that the explanation for continuing Southern distinctiveness does repose somehow in the fact that black and white Southerners are *groups to whom things have happened,* groups whose members have learned lessons from their collective histories.

In one version of this argument, C. Vann Woodward (1968) has suggested that the un-American experiences of defeat, military occupation, poverty, frustration, and moral guilt have given white Southerners an outlook qualitatively different from that of other Americans. Obviously, a similar argument could easily be made for black Southerners (leave aside the moral guilt). This has been a very appealing line of thought, and there may be something to it, although it leaves a number of questions unanswered. This is not the place for a critique of Woodward's argument, much less a test of his hypothesis, but let me just observe that he does not spell out how events and experiences of a century or more ago are supposed to affect values and attitudes today. My own research (Reed 1983, 70–94) suggests that it is seldom a matter of lessons continuing to be learned from reflections on that history: indeed, artists and historians aside, few Southerners of either race seem to know or to care much about their groups' histories. Rather, it appears that lessons drawn from group experience may have been passed on to succeeding generations without knowledge of the facts from which the conclusions were drawn.

It is not clear either exactly what lessons Southern history is supposed to have taught. Returning to our pattern of individualism and anti-institutionalism, however, it seems to me that long experience with an environment seemingly uncaring or even hostile could produce or reinforce traits like those to be explained (see Reed 1986, 101–02). And both black and white Southerners, in their different ways, have had good reason in the past to view their environments as unresponsive, if not actually malevolent.

Implications for the Future of Regional Differences

So what? What difference does it make where this pattern of individualism comes from? Well, it has some implications for what we can expect as we move into the next century. Regional differences brought about by different historical experiences will not go away simply because Southerners come to have economic and demographic circumstances like those of other Americans. This sort of "Southern characteristic" could prove much more durable—apparently is proving much more durable—than traits that reflect simply economic underdevelopment. Some might want to argue that group differences tend to decrease in the absence of forces operating to maintain them—sort of a cultural version of the Second Law of Thermodynamics—but that is not at all a self-evident proposition; at least its validity needs to be demonstrated.

All of this is speculation, of course, but if this view is correct, regional differences of this sort will decrease if history teaches its lessons more indiscriminately. Some course of events might cause Southerners to forget the lessons of their past, or teach other Americans what have heretofore been "Southern" lessons. Either way, regional differences would decrease.

A recent, revised edition of *The Enduring South* brought many of the data in the book forward another twenty years, from about the mid-sixties to the 1980s (Reed 1986, 91–100). For the most part, the book's original analysis held up pretty well. The regional differences that should have become smaller did so. Some cultural differences were largely due to Southerners' lower incomes and educational levels, to their predominantly rural and small-town residence, to their concentration in agricultural and low-level industrial occupations. Those differences were smaller in the 1960s than they had been in the past, and they are smaller still today. A few, indeed, have vanished altogether. There are important respects in which Southerners look more like other Americans, culturally, than they have at any time for decades, if ever.

On the other hand, differences that were persisting in the 1960s— in localism (as *The Enduring South* measured it), in attitudes toward some sorts of violence, in a number of religious and quasi-religious beliefs and behaviors—are mostly still with us, usually as large as they were then, and occasionally larger. This, I believe, supports the book's conclusion that those are differences of a quasi-ethnic sort, with their origins in the different histories of American regional groups, not merely epiphenomena of different levels of current economic and demographic "modernization."

There were, however, a few—only a very few—instances where these differences, too, were smaller than a generation before. And where that happened *it was not because the South became less*

Southern, but because the non-South changed to resemble the South.

This pattern is evident in survey items of several different sorts, but my favorite example involves responses to the question, "What man that you have heard or read about, living today in any part of the world, do you admire the most?" (see Reed 1986, 96–97). When the Gallup Poll asks this question, as it often does, it is obviously fishing for the name of a public figure. Nevertheless, many Southerners perversely insist on naming somebody the interviewer never heard of: relatives, friends, miscellaneous local figures. In 1965, nearly a third of white Southern respondents did that, and they were almost twice as likely as non-Southerners to do so.

If this response indicates a species of localism, by this measure the regional difference in localism had decreased by 1980, from fourteen points to five. But not because Southerners had become less localistic. The percentage of Southerners who refused to name a public figure had actually risen, from 32 percent to 38 percent, but the percentage of non-Southerners who gave this kind of response had risen, too, even faster: from 18 percent to 33 percent. (The same pattern can be observed, by the way, with a similar question about the most-admired *woman.*)

This is not the model of regional convergence that most observers have had in mind. But the 1960s and 1970s gave all Americans some un-American experiences: Viet Nam, Watergate, Iran, assassinations, urban riots, economic stagnation, double-digit inflation, rising crime rates, urban decay, and a host of other distressing, frustrating, alienating developments. Is it stretching a point to speculate that many non-Southerners have begun to believe, as many Southerners already did, that they cannot always get what they want or even keep what they have, that hard work and good intentions are not always enough, that politicians and bureaucracies are not to be trusted, that people out there don't like them? And if non-Southerners come to believe that, would it be surprising if they took up the values of a nearby subculture that came to those conclusions some time ago—for example, the value that says your family, friends, and neighbors are more reliably admirable than people you have only "heard or read about"?

Let me close with a general point. It is fairly easy to predict the future of regional cultural differences that are merely reflections of economic and demographic differences. All it takes are economic and demographic projections (and the willingness to trust them, which is the hard part). But if we allow that group culture can also be shaped by history, by *events*, prediction becomes much more difficult (see Rindfuss, Reed, and St. John 1978). It becomes nothing less than a matter of predicting events. If sociologists could do that any better than anyone else, we could put a lot of stockbrokers and fortune-tellers out of work.

9

Southern Conservatism and Liberalism: Past and Future

Paul Luebke

The massive changes in race relations in the South manifested by the decline of institutional Jim Crow segregation have contributed mightily to an image of a New South. The popular press often presents this New South as a boom region determined to lay aside its conservative past.

In this chapter, I take issue with such a public-relations view of the South. I argue that the ideology of the dominant elite has changed since 1936 primarily in its level of sophistication. While the Southern political-economic elite has diversified in recent decades, it has not been forced to share power significantly with any other societal group. The elite has certainly conceded to the demands for racial equality from the civil rights movement and the federal government, but in a key economic area, labor relations, it has made few changes. The elite promotes a conservative ideology of individual achievement, in which political debate centers over how much government should promote the region's economic development. Liberals' desire to use government to aid and empower the disadvantaged receives short shrift in most Southern legislatures. Trends suggest that this dominant elite, and thus Southern politics, will not be significantly less conservative in 2036.

In his 1949 classic, *Southern Politics,* V. O. Key predicted that further industrialization of the South would lead to an increase in social and political liberalism. In accord with Key, this chapter first examines the major pressures from liberal social movements for changes in race and labor relations. The chapter considers the differing ways in which two wings of the Southern conservative elite reacted to these demands for admission to the elite, and how the influence of these two wings changed.

Second, the chapter examines the part played by conservatism and liberalism in the Democratic and Republican parties of the South. The third section looks to the future. Can blacks, unionists, or other liberals dislodge the conservative elite from the left? Alternatively, does the South provide enough fertile ground for conservative populism, from the right, to challenge the elite successfully?

This chapter defines conservatism and liberalism primarily as political-economic constructs. However, political or economic conservatism in the South is often associated with a status-quo orientation in family roles, child-rearing norms, educational philosophy, and religious practice. Liberalism, both in the political-economic and general spheres, usually supports greater equality in social relations, and conservatism advocates less equality.

While a few blacks and white women may be said to have entered the Southern political elite since the civil rights movement, overwhelmingly members of the Southern political-economic elite are white and male. The elite is therefore used in this chapter to mean affluent and powerful white males. The discussion relies on studies of race relations, labor relations, and political parties in the post-World War II South.

Other chapters in this book also touch on conservatism and liberalism. For example, in the preceding chapter, Reed identifies conservatism with the traditional folk pattern and liberalism as an element of the new mass culture. For Reed, these orientations are collective representations rather than manifestations of social power. In Chapter 7, Moland demonstrates that conservatism in the sense used here constitutes a major element in Southern race relations. In Chapter 5, Martin et al. comment on the conservative economic elite's suppression of women. They also perceive conservatism as a key component of male dominance in interpersonal and domestic relations. Further, in Chapter 4, Streib briefly explores the relationship between the region's dominant conservative elite and the political protests of the growing elderly population.

Modernizers and Traditionalists

The Southern elite has long been split into two camps, which sometimes compete with one another for political-economic dominance—and sometimes reach a compromise to allow for continued control (Black and Black 1987; Elazar 1972). The first group, whom I call *traditionalists*, are rooted in the small-town and rural conservative culture of the region. Economically, traditionalists generally support continuation of the past, whether agricultural or industrial, rather than change, because they fear they cannot control the change. The industrial base of traditionalism today is in the labor-intensive, low-wage sectors, such as textiles, apparel, and furniture-manufacturing. Traditionalists oppose demands for change from black or labor groups, arguing that the traditional "free-enterprise" basis for social, political, and economic organization has served the region well. Change is usually threatening (Luebke, Peters, and Wilson 1985; Luebke 1985; Goldman and Luebke 1985).

Modernizers, the second group, are increasingly dominant in the region. Disproportionately regional in-migrants, they tend to be both urban and urbane (see Chapter 1). They seek to bring the South increasingly into the national economy. The modernizing elite does not reject demands from blacks or labor out-of-hand, but rather seeks an accommodation with such groups in the interest of social stability, social control, and economic gain.

Contending Views: Racial Politics

During the New Deal years, the traditionalist elite pressured Southern Congressmen to oppose many of the liberal federal programs proposed by Northern Democrats. Traditionalists feared that federal programs could force changes in either race or labor relations in the region (Key 1949, 351–9; and Wright 1986, 259–60).

In the 1940s, modernizers, then in control, spent a disproportionate amount of government money, compared to non-Southern states, trying to convince outside capital to come South (Cobb 1982, 91). In the 1945–55 decade, the modernizers did as little to challenge Jim Crow segregation as did the traditionalists. However, following the 1954 *Brown* v. *Topeka Board of Education* decision and the negative publicity that Southern communities, notably Little Rock in 1957, received in the years thereafter (Cobb 1982, 125–26), modernizing Southern businessmen slowly began to recognize that Jim Crow was an impediment to economic growth (Jacoway 1982, 5). Among the elite, modernizers recognized the importance of state subsidies to corporations, including increased support of schools and major investments in highways, water and sewer lines, and the like. As in South Africa today, members of the elite began to debate the desirability of further changes, such as quasi-official arrangements to respond to blacks' demands for (and white resistance to) changes in race relations structures.

The traditionalist elite held sway in certain parts of the South, affirming the importance of Jim Crow structures and vowing never to allow changes in race relations, even if that meant economic stagnation for Southern communities. Following the 1954 *Brown* decision, Virginia pledged massive resistance; Mississippi encouraged the formation of White Citizens Councils. And local governments, especially in the Deep South, did not discourage violence against black school-desegregation advocates (Cobb 1984, 110–13).

By contrast, the modernizing elite recognized that hard-core resistance to desegregation would give the region a bad reputation, which could interfere with economic development (Black 1976). Some modernizers sought stratagems to obstruct desegregation without open opposition, while giving the appearance of accepting racial change. For example, in the mid-1950s, North Carolina governor Luther Hodges, who subsequently would be identified with the formation of the Research Triangle Park development between Raleigh and Durham, supported the Pearsall Plan, a complicated General Assembly legislation that put the burden of school desegregation upon black parents while leaving the impression that North Carolina had chosen a moderate path (Chafe 1981, Chapter 2). A Little Rock school official wrote admiringly to a North Carolina colleague about the Pearsall Plan, in contrast to Little Rock's attempt at open defiance: "You North Carolinians have devised one of the cleverest techniques of perpetuating segregation that we have seen" (Chafe, 1981, 70).

Politicians and businessmen in various Southern cities also adopted public postures that sought to build their national reputations as exceptions to the Jim Crow rule. Atlanta's slogan as "the city too busy to hate" made Northern capital feel more comfortable, but it belied the reality that the city's public accommodations remained almost entirely segregated until the 1964 federal civil rights law demanded a change (Cobb 1984, 112; Hunter 1980, Chapter 5).

At the same time, even the modernizing leadership held securely to the belief that civil rights protesters were improperly challenging Southern folkways. North Carolina business and governmental leaders interviewed in 1977 agreed that the 1960 Greensboro sit-ins were necessary. But they also acknowledged, almost unanimously, that at the time they opposed the civil rights movement's desegregation goals as too radical (Luebke 1981). North Carolina's U.S. senator Terry Sanford reminded voters in his 1986 campaign spots that he stood up for civil rights when it was risky to do so. While that statement is true, in that the traditionalist North Carolina elite branded Sanford a dangerous "liberal race-mixer," the fact is that Sanford as governor in 1963 actually opposed Greensboro and Chapel Hill demonstrations against segregated restaurants (Chafe, 1981, Chapter 5). Sanford epitomized the promise-without-performance characteristic of modernizers' response to the civil rights movement.

Elizabeth Jacoway argues in *Southern Businessmen and Desegregation* (1982, 9) that Columbia, South Carolina, Tampa, and Dallas constitute three examples beyond Atlanta and the North Carolina cities in which modernizers recognized the futility of resistance. In the same year in which Sanford sought to control civil rights demands in North Carolina, leading South Carolina industrialists worked successfully to prevent anti-black violence during the desegregation of Clemson College (Lofton 1982, 80). Tampa's voluntary desegregation of public facilities in the early 1960s emerged consciously as an alternative to the well-publicized violence in another Florida city, St. Augustine, and the stigma associated with Little Rock. A white Tampa businessman wrote in 1960 that an "objective look at Little Rock will show us that such policies mean economic deterioration of a very substantial kind" (Lawson 1982, 266).

Dallas's reputation as a reactionary city resulted from the 1963 Kennedy assassination, but before that, beginning in 1960, white and black leaders had endorsed a controlled desegregation plan that struck an intermediate course between the civil rights movement on the left and the Ku Klux Klan on the right. The modernizing elite recognized the adverse effects of open support for Jim Crow, but it also refused to accede to the anti-segregation program of the civil rights movement. Dallas's biracial committee endorsed the white elite's agenda, that the white majority would have to tolerate limited change, in exchange for black citizens' acceptance of change that was limited (Brophy 1982, 150).

By the mid-1960s, modernizing elites in most parts of the urban

South had defeated the traditionalist elites for control of racial politics. Most white Southern leaders recognized that the old Jim Crow social order could not be maintained. Some of these leaders re-educated themselves to recognizing that segregationist values were immoral (Jacoway 1982, 14). But a key to the discussion of why government policy in the Southern states since the civil rights movement has remained conservative is found in the white modernizers' orientation toward the racial equality movement. The movement by the mid-1960s had forced the modernizing elite to accept that Jim Crow would have to die. But modernizers began to realize that the abolition of Jim Crow did not fundamentally alter the essential power relationship between white majority and black minority. And, wherever possible, the modernizing elite avoided sharing power with the movement at the level of local and state politics.

However, federal intervention via passage of the 1964 Civil Rights Act outlawing segregated public facilities promoted racial change at a faster pace than either the modernizing or traditionalist elite wanted. Pressure was greater upon those traditionalist business leaders and politicians who had expected to be able to resist the civil rights demands. Birmingham, New Orleans, and Jackson, Mississippi, were three such examples of cities in Deep South states that had hewed to the hard line on segregation (Cobb 1984, 113).

Traditionalists faced the dilemma in the late 1960s that obedience to the public accommodations provisions of federal law no longer sufficed to attain a reputation for being moderate. This was ironic because, less than a decade before, other Southern cities, with modernizing elites at the helm, had captured the progressive image with far less radical change (Cobb 1984, 112). The Jackson example illustrates how the ante had been raised, so that the white elite not only had to acquiesce in desegregated public accommodations, but also had to ensure that the public schools did not become all-black. Northern corporate leaders had told Jackson's elite that if the segregated academies sponsored by the White Citizens Council flourished while the city's public schools had negligible white enrollment, those corporations could not risk the bad publicity of a major investment in Jackson (Sallis and Adams 1982).

The Jackson Chamber of Commerce responded to the Northern corporate criticism by joining forces with the Jackson Urban League. In October 1970 these unlikely partners co-filed an *amicus curiae* brief for the plaintiffs in the *Swann* v. *Charlotte-Mecklenburg* school busing case, which was before the U.S. Supreme Court. Jackson's white elite wanted a quick Supreme Court decision, so that continued questions over attendance zones in Jackson would not lead to a further decline in white enrollment. The Supreme Court's April 1971 decision in the Charlotte case enabled Jackson's plans to become firm. As in other Southern cities in which economic modernization was the elite's priority, white leaders joined blacks in publicizing the virtues of school desegregation (Sallis and Adams 1982, 254; Chafe 1981, 222–34). Shortly thereafter, both Allis-Chalmers and General Motors announced plant construction plans for the Jackson area.

In Jackson, pressures from both the federal government, via civil rights legislation and Supreme Court decisions, and multinational corporations, which could not afford the bad press, transformed the behavior of the local elite. In some cases, white leaders appeared to change their racial philosophy from supporting Jim Crow to welcoming its demise (Sallis and Adams 249–53). In short, national political and economic institutions may have forced some white Southern leaders to change from traditionalist to modernizer. Some critics have charged that the elite's change was not genuine (Bartley 1969, 342–43). Nevertheless, the civil rights movement, in alliance with the federal government, forced the Southern white elite to alter its open complicity with Jim Crow institutional racism (Badger 1984, 109).

The 1970s and 1980s demonstrated subsequently that the white elite's changed approach to race relations by no means ensured either black economic power or an end to black poverty in the South. The challenge of the next fifty years is whether blacks in the South, devoid of its Jim Crow caste system, will integrate into the mainstream economy any better than have blacks in the Northeast, Midwest, or West.

Contending Views: The Labor Question

As shown in Chapters 1 and 3, the surge of modern economic development in the South began with the incursion of outside capital and the expansion of industrial operations. This development was accompanied by increased activity of self-conscious workers and labor organizations. Although the economic trend has continued, the experience of labor has been quite different.

Forty years ago in the South, unions won three out of four representation elections. By the early sixties, management and unions were winning in equal numbers, and in the 1980s management in the South defeated unions two-thirds of the time (Marshall 1967, 266; and Kinney 1986). While this trend reflects the national decline in union membership, specific Southern issues have also influenced labor-management conflict. In particular, the question of union power has challenged the white Southern elite throughout the twentieth century. Indeed, at times when Jim Crow structures were intact, workers, especially whites, sought to challenge the elite's dream of a low-wage, nonunion environment that would lure Northern capital (Cobb 1984, 68).

The 1935 Wagner Act and the later National War Labor Board decisions significantly aided the labor movement in the South, for the federal government intervened to ensure neutrality between unions and employers (Marshall 1967, 225). Because the balance of power, without federal intervention, favored local employers, pro-union workers and labor organizers were greatly encouraged. Franklin Roosevelt's image as pro-union appeared to offer a key psychological boost to white workers, the great majority of whom were pro-FDR Democrats (Marshall 1967, Chapter 14).

The passage of the Taft-Hartley Act in 1947 shifted the psychological advantage away from unions (Dempsey 1961, Chapter 1). But both the AFL and the CIO, bitter rivals at the time, believed that the organizing tide in the South would continue to flow with unions. Beginning in 1946, they had launched what the CIO called "Operation Dixie" on the premise (in retrospect, clearly erroneous) that Southern workers would be no more difficult to organize than other Americans (Marshall 1967, Chapter 15).

The traditionalist elite of the South, however, did not believe this would happen. Although modernizers usually accepted unions' presence if organizing drives were successful, traditionalists were fundamentally unwilling to tolerate unions. Traditionalists opposed Operation Dixie by counterattacking at labor's most vulnerable points. One such point was the Southern fundamentalist Protestant hostility to labor unions as secular organizations. The other (and this was worse) was the alleged link of Communists to the CIO. Moreover, traditionalist leaders argued that no firm would establish a plant in an area in which workers had supported a union. As a consequence, traditionalists were determined to do everything they could to prevent Southern workers from responding to labor unions as workers in the North had done (Cobb 1984, 92–95).

A Grenada, Mississippi, editor illustated the harsh anti-union line of traditionalists in a commentary on a CIO organizing drive in his town in 1946: "It is generally assumed that the CIO is shot through with Communism, and I do not like Communism. I do not like to get orders from Washington, much less Moscow" (Marshall 1967, 262). Other community leaders noted the links between union and racial politics, citing the CIO's opposition to poll taxes and segregation, which, it was claimed, "are against American and Southern principles." The CIO lost the organizing drive election overwhelmingly.

More sophisticated Southern corporations such as R. J. Reynolds Tobacco Company, a mainstay of the modernizing elite, illustrated that, even for the modernizers, union power was better eliminated than tolerated. In 1950, Reynolds used the alleged Communist influence within the Food, Tobacco, Agricultural and Allied Workers' Union of America (expelled from the CIO in 1949)—to defeat the union six years after it had gained recognition with strong backing from black tobacco workers (Marshall 1967, 237–38). In part to ensure that a union movement did not revive, the company then improved its personnel practices (Tilley 1985, 411–14). By the 1950s, Reynolds employees received a wage and benefits package comparable to what unions could negotiate at other cigarette-manufacturing plants in the South (Tilley 1985, 455–80). This model proved to be a precursor of corporate strategies a quarter-century later. Workers simply exchanged their potential power at the workplace for wages and benefits that came without any union dues.

The AFL and CIO, both before and after their 1955 merger, recognized that the textile industry was the key to Southern unionization (Marshall 1967, 246). But textile industrialists chose the traditionalist path of resistance. When textile unions at Dan River Mills in Virginia and Harriet-Henderson Mills in North Carolina called strikes in 1951 and 1958, employers refused to budge. At Dan River the union was much weakened but survived (Marshall 1967, 259). In Henderson, a union organizer was convicted of a bombing conspiracy despite dubious evidence (Payton 1970), and the union was eliminated. North Carolina officials, including Governor Hodges, openly sided with management, fearing that a successful strike would weaken North Carolina's reputation as a union-free environment (Billings 1979; Marshall 1967, 274).

Businessmen in South Carolina probably fought unions most fiercely. It is noteworthy that the traditionalist stance on labor in the late 1950s did not prevent industrialists from tolerating token desegregation at the state's public universities. A modernizing orientation in race relations struck the South Carolina business elite as essential, while a hard-line approach to unions seemed equally necessary (Marshall 1967, 280). In the Spartanburg-Greenville area, Northern firms interested in relocation specifically committed themselves to take all efforts to avoid unionization. The two cities sought to strengthen a local anti-union perspective that linked prosperity to the absence of organized labor (Sloan and Hall 1979). Similarly, the Deering-Milliken firm closed its Darlington, South Carolina, plant in 1956 rather than negotiate with the textile workers' union, which had narrowly won a representation election. The effect of employers' firm stands in Virginia, North Carolina, and South Carolina upon textile union organizing was devastating. Not until 1981, when J. P. Stevens signed a union contract—mostly involving plants with high percentages of black workers at Roanoke Rapids, North Carolina—could labor organizers begin to hope for a positive change (Mullins and Luebke 1982). The history of labor relations in the four decades since World War II demonstrates the crucial role of the federal government as a structural support for change. When traditionalist elites chose to try emphatically to reverse the unionization trend, they succeeded because local power and culture supported their antiunionism and, as was not the case with race relations, the federal government saw no basis upon which to intervene.

World economic trends in the 1970s and 1980s had a significant impact upon the South's economy (see Chapter 1). Lower-wage textile employment declined and relatively high-wage employment in more capital-intensive sectors increased (Wright 1986, 270–71). However, the predictions of greater union power correlating with increased Southern industrialization—by V. O. Key in 1949 and Ray Marshall in 1967—proved erroneous. Two factors best explain the continuing weakness of organized labor. First, across the South, traditionalist and modernizing elites were able to reach a compromise on the unionizing of factories. The same modernizers who recognized the dangers of hard-line resistance to the civil rights movement were also unwilling to oppose unions absolutely. They recognized that collective bargaining was well institutionalized in the labor relations of many Northern and international firms that sought to locate plants in the South. It made no sense to the modernizers to discourage a major corporation that was foolhardy enough to want to let a union organize a Southern plant. On the other hand, modernizers remained sympathetic if a non-South corporation wished to fight labor organzing at a Southern plant even though it engaged in collective bargaining at its non-South factories. Code words such as "competitive wage rates" and "low level of work stoppage" told the out-of-state corporation that Southern states were not friendly to unions. Yet Southern AFL-CIO representatives could not criticize such an industrial-recruitment stance, because it did not *openly* oppose unions.

Modernizers convinced traditionalists that elite neutrality was excellent public relations. At the same time as government industrial recruiters officially took no position on unions, business leaders could express the blunt anti-unionism of traditionalists. For example, in North Carolina in the late 1970s, state government was dominated by modernizing Democratic Governor Jim Hunt, but the statewide Chamber of Commerce, with whom Hunt worked closely, editorialized: "We don't need consumerist and populist movements and agitation by organized labor" (*North Carolina*, February 1978, 18).

Democratic governors across the South—such as Hunt in North Carolina (1977–85), Richard Riley in South Carolina (1979–87), or William Winter in Mississippi (1980–84)—managed to win the support of the AFL–CIO while actually excluding unions from the kinds of government-management-labor tri-partite discussions that were commonplace in the North, Midwest, and West. Both these modernizing governors and state union leaders recognized that unions lacked legitimacy in the eyes of the traditionalist and modernizing business leaders, even though the modernizing elite was more tolerant. In sum, unions lacked institutional legitimacy in the South, and business leaders wanted them to remain illegitimate. When tri-partite discussions were held in Southern states, government and business were usually joined by representatives of universities, not labor unions (Goldman and Luebke 1985, 24).

Contending Views: The Political Parties

Historically, the political and business leaders of the South have been Democrats. The Democratic Party in the South until the civil rights movement served as the party of business and white supremacy. Even as higher-status whites turned to voting for Republicans in national elections, beginning especially with Eisenhower in 1952 (Bartley and Graham 1975) and culminating in Reagan's South-wide success in 1984, much of the business elite still found it useful to remain active in the local and state Democratic Party. Southern business leaders, although committed Republicans in national elections, often felt they had no alternative because many county-level and state legislative offices were decided in the Democratic primary elections inasmuch as Republicans had no operating party at the local level (Luebke 1985).

In most Southern states in the 1980s, the Democratic Party sought to woo the modernizing economic elite away from its flirtation with state Republicanism. This modernizing elite lives in the region's larger cities, and many of its members are not native Southerners. It has its economic base disproportionately in the high-technology, capital-intensive industrial, and service sectors. White modernizers recognize that affirmative action policies can reduce the overwhelming concentration of blacks in lower-status positions and increase the number of blacks in white-collar jobs. Statewide Democratic political leaders, who rely on black votes for election, accept the necessity of affirmative action, even if they are not enthusiastic public promoters of the concept. Democratic governors of the 1980s, among them North Carolina's Hunt, South Carolina's Riley, Mississippi's Winter, and Florida's Bob Graham, found much more enthusiasm for the high-technology economic development that business modernizers promoted. With less fanfare, all of these governors appointed unprecedented numbers of blacks to governmental positions, including judgeships. In fact, high-technology and some deference to black political power are hallmarks of the Democratic modernizing elite.

As the label suggests, modernizers strongly support state government's underwriting of infrastructure costs for education, transportation, and public utilities (water and sewer). Modernizers constitute what Key called a "progressive" government-business alliance, which seeks to maintain a pro-business political climate and tries to pass legislation, such as community college training programs, often as a direct subsidy to nearby factories (Key 1949, 214; Luebke and Schneider 1987).

When Southern Democratic governors actively promote the modernizer alliance, they are often labeled liberals by journalists, especially Northerners, who are mesmerized by the busy governmental sector which contradicts stereotypes of the sleepy South.

This is ironic because these Democrats in fact are relying on direct benefits to business that they hope will trickle down to workers, and because the taxes that pay for the government programs tend to be regressive. The favorite tax of Southern politicians over the last fifty years has been the sales tax, allegedly a fair tax because "everyone pays the same." Traditionalists, with a none-too-subtle racist slant, support sales tax increases, especially the sales tax on groceries, because it is known as "the only tax *they* (poor blacks) pay." The modernizing Democrats and their business allies show no interest in raising personal or corporate income taxes, even though the corporate share of taxes at the state level has declined steadily since 1960. Business at the state legislatures lobbies for tax breaks and to demand better public schools and other government infrastructure expenditures. Yet the modernizer alliance does not ask business to pay for these services through increased taxes, because this allegedly would hurt the competitive position of each Southern state's economic recruitment efforts (Luebke 1985).

Modernizers' sympathy for affirmative action is a second reason why they are often pegged liberal. In fact, affirmative action is a symbolic position which modernizer Democrats, who need the support of black leaders, have no choice but to support. This acceptance of affirmative action is not the same as placing black unemployment and related problems of housing and health-care at the top of a white Democrat's political agenda. Nevertheless, even this tolerance of black demands does constitute political change, which some white voters resent. While the modernizer Democrats can usually count on black electoral support, white voters who resent the accommodation to black demands have sought another political home. This traditionalist perspective on race relations has increasingly found a home in the Republican parties of the South.

Especially in statewide races for governor or the U.S. Senate, Republicans offer a more traditionalist, more anti-government, and more socially conservative alternative to the ideology of the dominant Democrats. Traditionalist ideology challenges the activist government ideas of modernizing progressives. The traditionalists question the legitimacy of government's explicit commitment to financial support of an expanding infrastructure, a support that can bring new kinds of employment to a state (Luebke, Peters, and Wilson 1986).

The traditionalist elite in the South of the 1980s is disproportionately associated with low-wage, labor-intensive industries such as textiles and apparel, which feels keenly the wage competition from across town or across the ocean (Goldman and Luebke 1985; Luebke, McMahon, and Risberg 1979). This elite therefore believes that Democratic modernizers have unfairly favored out-of-state industry. North Carolina's Republican Governor Jim Martin, who benefited from traditionalist elite support in his 1984 election, appointed an "assistant secretary of commerce for traditional industry" shortly after his inauguration. Some observers have questioned how this new job title helps low-wage industry, but the significant point is Martin's acknowledgment of a political debt to this economic elite (Luebke, Peters, and Wilson 1986).

In the state legislatures of the South, traditionalists oppose the evolution of state government into a more social-services-oriented welfare state. As advocates of voluntarism and defenders of the belief that poverty is one's own fault, traditionalists take issue with the modernizers' commitment to a greater state role in social services just as much as they dislike state government's subsidy of economic development.

But the demands upon state government often require traditionalist politicians to compromise with modernizers on both the content and size of budgets. Traditionalist ideology is better expressed by Southern Republicans in the U.S. Senate such as North Carolina's Jesse Helms, South Carolina's Strom Thurmond, or, from 1981 to 1987, Alabama's Jeremiah Denton. The U.S. Senate provides more space for the principled politician who wishes to adopt unpopular stands in order to make a point.

At the elite level across the South, Democratic politicians have convinced most modernizing business leaders that the future in state politics remains with Democrats, not Republicans. Their dilemma is that the mass electorate is less convinced (Toner 1986). The boon that GOP presidential candidacies provide statewide Southern candidates has aided the election of significant numbers of Republicans to the U.S. Senate. Fortunately for the Democratic elite, only one Southern state (North Carolina) elects its governor in the presidential election year (*Almanac* 1986). Even when Republicans succeed in winning the governor's seat, as they did in 1986 in South Carolina and Alabama, they face the reality that the majority of state senators and representatives as well as the attorneys general and lieutenant governors in these states are Democrats.

Historically in the South, the challenge to entrenched power has come from liberal social movements demanding changes in race and labor relations. The liberal demands over the decades have weakened the traditionalist wing of the elite. The modernizing elite has consolidated power throughout the South because modernizers are more receptive to change. Because modernizers appear flexible, they are far more capable than traditionalists of deflecting liberal challenges.

In the 1980s, modernizers faced an attack from a traditionalist social movement, the New Christian Right (N.C.R.), which criticized especially the modernization of society in noneconomic realms. The NCR blamed the modernizing elite for what it perceived as an illegitimate secularization trend in family relations, sexual mores, and the public schools. Jerry Falwell and his religious-political organization, the Moral Majority (based in Lynchburg, Virginia), became best-known nationwide as a spokesperson for a politicized fundamentalism, but other white Southern preachers were active as well (Hadden 1981).

The N.C.R. tried to build a mass-elite political alliance of lower-to-middle income whites and the traditionalist elite. The mass appeal emphasized social issues such as abortion while the elite was motivated by an anti-government ideology centered on economic issues. The N.C.R's goal was to elect legislators who would promote both social and economic traditionalism. The most successful example of the New Right political alliance emerged in North Carolina, where Republican Jesse Helms was elected three times to the U.S. Senate between 1972 and 1984. Helms received crucial support, especially in his 1984 race against modernizer Democratic Governor Jim Hunt, from the Raleigh-based National Congressional Club. The Club's thirty-second television spots attacked Hunt for "Mondale liberalism," a label that apparently stuck enough that many undecided white voters in that election chose the Republican ticket.

But Helms's success appears ephemeral, based on his own charismatic appeal to adherents of both noneconomic and economic traditionalism. Fundamentalist Christians liked Helms's *advocacy* of a big-government prohibition of abortion while traditionalist businessmen were most impressed with Helms's *opposition* to big-government economic programs. When, in 1986 and 1987, the Congressional Club sought to replicate that fundamentalist-business alliance by seeking control of the North Carolina Republican party, the Club's candidates, even though they held firmly to Jesse Helms's political principles, were soundly trounced by modernizer Republicans.

In Mississippi in 1983, Republicans sought to use traditionalist life-style appeals, claiming that Democratic gubernatorial candidate Bill Allain had engaged in homosexual acts while on a visit to Atlanta. Allain was nonetheless elected. In South Carolina, N.C.R. candidates ran in Republican primaries in 1986 for both Congress and the state legislature from the Greenville area, home of fundamentalist Bob Jones University, but none was successful.

In Alabama the N.C.R. won a victory at the U.S. District Court level in early 1987 against alleged "secular humanist" content in public school books. But overall, the N.C.R. appears unlikely to be able to stop the increasing modernization of Southern society for several reasons. First, the N.C.R. is advocating restrictions on life-style. As Reed has noted at the mass level, contemporary Southern culture increasingly advocates choice, even if not all choices are equally acceptable. Second, at the elite level, modernizers have shown little support for a restrictive social ideology, preferring instead a laissez-faire orientation toward the noneconomic realms. Third, the strongest social base of the N.C.R. is among older, less-educated Southerners. As we move toward 2036, those favoring a Bible-based definition of appropriate social relations should be even fewer than in the 1980s.

Toward 2036: The Ascendancy of the Modernizer Elite

The prospects for liberalism in the next half century appear as unlikely as the chances of the New Christian Right. Liberalism's ascendancy in the South requires a definition of common interest among less affluent black and white Southerners. This black-white coalition would be a late-twentieth century update of classical economic populism, in which the electoral majority decides that its self-interest demands less power for the incumbent conservative elite and more programs that directly benefit the majority. A successful liberal movement would generate programs in support of adequate housing and health care, extended job opportunities, and equitable taxation. In these policy areas across the South, politicians regularly pay lip service to the need for reform, but policies rarely change (Southern Growth Policies Board 1985). If candidates advocated such liberal programs and won—whether or not the somewhat risky label of *liberal* was used—legislative coalitions could be forged to achieve such goals. As the Southern Growth Policies Board research demonstrates, there is no shortage of equity-oriented proposals. Political will is the problem.

In *Southern Politics*, published shortly after South Carolina Dixiecrat (and now Republican) Strom Thurmond ran for president in 1948 with little success, V. O. Key argued that the politics of racial resentment would die out shortly. Key believed that economic self-interest would bring together white and black working-class Southerners. In fact, in his three races for the presidency in 1964, 1968, and 1972, especially as a third-party candidate in 1972, George Wallace demonstrated that racial appeals were still potent among white Southerners.

As racial appeals decline with new generations of white Southerners, the *theoretical* possibility of a biracial liberal alliance increases. But in practice, neither blacks nor unions have the clout to promote such a political program. Most important, Democratic parties in the Southern states have little sympathy for a biracial economic justice ideology. The parameters of political debate in the contemporary South almost always exclude serious consideration of a redistributive program.

One exception currently is Texas, where liberal-populist Jim Hightower, as state Agricultural Commissioner, advocates an interracial alliance to fight against corporate food and farm interests. In most Southern settings, however, the modernizing elite has captured the rhetoric of equity from the liberal social movements. Because liberalism has no strong base in any Southern legislature, the modernizing elite can co-opt the best of liberal political ideas but not be forced to share significant power with liberals. Just as modernizers responded in the 1960s and 1970s to black demands for equal opportunity, modernizers over the next half century can be expected to co-opt the best liberal ideas for more equity in areas such as housing, health care, economic development, or public education—while refusing to share power with liberals.

In the 1970s and 1980s Southern blacks struggled to gain political representation at state legislatures, often winning significant numbers of seats (although still far below their proportion in the population) only after winning voting rights law suits or threatening to pursue such litigation. If black leaders moved beyond issues of racial equity to a program of economic liberalism—in which racial equality is directly tied into economic equality—perhaps liberalism would have a brighter future in the South.

But Southern black political leaders appear uncertain whether to endorse economic liberalism or the modernizing elite's program, which relies almost entirely on the private sector to generate prosperity through economic expansion. Former Atlanta mayors Maynard Jackson and Andrew Young are closely identified with the modernizer ideology, while Jesse Jackson has campaigned for President, especially in 1988, as an advocate of an interracial economic-justice program. Jesse Jackson frequently attacked multinational corporations and stressed the economic common ground between white and black less-affluent citizens (one Jackson appeal was for "the little fish regardless of color to unite against the corporate barracuda"). Nevertheless, fewer than 10 percent of Southern whites supported Jackson on Super Tuesday in March 1988, the presidential primary day in virtually all Southern states. His advocacy of increased black political power apparently was a more salient message than his liberal-populist economics. Jackson's limited appeal to working-class whites strikes at the dilemma for advocates of the biracial liberal alliance.

Barring an unexpected upturn in labor unions' chances among white Southerners, there appears no majority-white organization in Southern society that could, along with black political groups, advocate economic liberalism. Consequently, the institutional bases of economic liberalism appear too weak to have a major impact upon the less-affluent white South. Does the modernizing elite's ideology of individual achievement prevail because most white Southerners reject arguments of economic equity, or because Democratic party leaders in the South define equity as an unacceptable political alternative (Black and Black 1987; Luebke and Zipp 1983)? The question strikes at the heart of the relationship between elite and mass in a democratic society.

The modernizing elite is likely to prevail in the next decades in the South, because it has successfully established the argument that prosperity will trickle down to all Southerners through a public policy predicated on government subsidizing individual entrepreneurial and corporate investment. This dominant ideology has more staying power than either economic liberalism, which would restrict private prerogatives in order to aid the less affluent, or traditionalist economic and noneconomic conservatism, each of which opposes one variant of the choices inherent in modernization.

Part IV

Social Change, Social Prediction, Social Action

This part conceptualizes the major changes and summarizes the central predictions that are presented in the eight empirical chapters above, and discusses some of the actions social scientists can take to control and direct the future course of change. In Chapter 10 it is said that the transformation of the South is analogous in its depth to the Industrial Revolution in eighteenth- and nineteenth-century Western Europe and America. The essential character of this change is conceptualized as the transformation of the social organization, the stratification pattern and the power structure of the region. The region was then a New South.

The second part of Chapter 10 summarizes the major developmental and problematical predictions set forth in the eight research chapters. It is predicted that the South may become the largest of the four regions; over four-fifths metropolitan/urban; with a quarter of its population elderly; nearly one-third ethnic/racial minority; much like the rest of the nation in gender pattern and equity for women; dominated by mass culture, with traditional culture relegated to small towns and rural areas, leaving the region still recognizably Southern; and typically conservative, with little sympathy for liberal efforts. It is also predicted that old and new problems may intensify—for example, resource exhaustion, increasing strains on local government, fiscal problems from both internal and foreign sources, environmental and health problems, and so on.

Chapter 11 recognizes that social change is widely initiated by collective social action. In this connection, social scientists have both an opportunity and a responsibility to use their knowledge and skill to direct the course of change. In this chapter Ferriss examines the ways social scientists can help and asserts that "it does make a difference" that they participate.

10

Summary:
Societal Transformations
and Social Predictions

Joseph S. Himes

This chapter is intended to perform two tasks for this book. First, it identifies and describes the societal changes of the South documented in the empirical sections of the foregoing chapters. The major societal changes considered here include alterations of social organization, stratification system, and power structure. Change of these societal elements functions to transform the region from an autocratic, rigidly stratified, communal, agrarian society into a mass, urban, industrial, associational society.

The other task is to summarize and report the developmental and problematical predictions offered by the chapter authors. Developmental predictions comprise statements of those creative or adaptive directions and ways in which the region may change and evolve in the foreseeable future. On the other hand, problematical predictions refer to those dysfunctional and undesirable ways in which the region may alter during the foreseeable future.

Societal Transformations

As the Old South was transformed, it became a new kind of society. The change was as fundamental as that which issued from the Industrial Revolution in Western Europe and North America. Each author in the book was conscious that he (she) was reporting one aspect of this fundamental transformation. Each predicted also that

257

the transformation may be accelerated in the half century yet to come.

Social Organization

The members of all societies have the same basic needs or "dependencies"—for example, security, subsistence, companionship, and so on (Wilson and Wilson 1945, 45). These needs drive or entice people to act, usually in interaction with others. Thus motivated, people act in typical or habitual ways called *social roles.* Roles equip individuals for regular relations with others—for example, in interactions with spouses, cooperations of foreman and worker, or struggle of subordinates with superordinates. Most relations are patterned and regulated by social rules. For example, the small-town wife may carry her basket or shopping bag when she visits the general store; however, the big-city housewife at the supermarket formally pays the cashier who operates the computer cash register and expects her purchases to be stored in a brown or plastic bag that the company furnishes.

The concepts employed here—needs, roles, relations and rules— are the essential elements of social organization (Wilson 1971, v–x). Social organization is the product of the relatively systematic arrangement of these elements. Organization reveals many different contrasting forms—informal and formal, traditional and conventional, as folkways and mores, as norms and values, and so on. When conditions—for example, migration, economic growth, aging, demographic composition, and so on—change, social organization is adaptively modified.

This conceptual model provides an appropriate analytic instrument for demonstrating how Southern social organization changed in the course of the transformation of the region. In 1950 more than half the Southern population lived in small rural and village communities. They engaged in farming or farm-servicing occupations. Most relations revolved around farming, forestry, fishing, and mining (rural-oriented jobs and family-home). Intensity of relations was implemented by village institutions (school, church, store, post office), limited travel, visitors, and media. Most relations were face-to-face, both personal and general.

In these years most social roles were inclusive and relatively informal, consistent with the nature of social relations. In the familistic arena what one individual knew every individual tended to know. In Southern villages and small towns a few specialized roles emerged— school teacher, minister, storekeeper, mechanic. These roles and re- lations fitted the small groups that characterized rural life. Like- wise, social rules tended to be general, relatively unspecialized, and informal. The major arenas of specialized rules were government (as it touched the local community) and institutionalized activities in schools, churches, stores, and the like.

In the thirty-five years between 1950 and 1985 the proportion of rural dwellers in the South declined to 33 percent (see Chapter 2). Though officially classified as rural, some of these people lived by an urban way of life. However diverse and detached, by 1985 two thirds of Southern people lived congested in urban and metropolitan areas. Social relations clustered around work, private and public interests, and family-home. Although most specialized relations occurred within metro communities, they tended to be laterally and longitudinally impersonal. Personal and impersonal contacts were maintained across and throughout the metro area. Mobility and media extended them far beyond the regional boundaries. Accumulated art and ar- chaeological excavations projected relations backwards thousands of years. Relations, though informal and intimate in family and friend- ship settings, became impersonal, formal, specialized, and often technical. The typical setting of such relations is the formal organi- zation, the large association, the institutional agency.

Such systems of relations require cadres of categoric roles. Each individual plays a number of these roles in contacting the number of people required to achieve satisfaction of his corps of dependencies. In the new South, social rules became typically specific and tech- nical, formal and impersonal, and orderly and codified. They crystal- lize and coalesce into inclusive subsystems to guide and discipline individuals as they participate in the network of relations. In daily life they are confronted as state and local laws, organizational pol- icies and procedures, regulations and guidelines, work orders, and the like. They pattern and discipline activity in most spheres of Southern urban life. These rules differ fundamentally from the gen- eral, informal, and personal commands that guided life in the earlier world of primary relations in families, neighborhoods, play- and pal- groups, work groups, and the like. The character of these earlier so- cial rules is revealed by such terms as *folkways* and *mores, custom* and *usage, tradition* and *convention.*

Continuation of these processes as predicted will ensure full transformation of the South into another type of society. The traditional folk pattern that characterized the region until the middle of the twentieth century will have been replaced by a new societal form. The South will have joined the rest of the nation, especially the Northeast and Midwest, as another manifestation of urban industrial society. Traditionalism, as suggested by some authors (see Chapter 8), will survive as relatively isolated vestiges. The South will resemble the inclusive society more than it differs from it.

Stratification

The individual and collective members of social systems are differentiated, aggregated, and socially ranked by the use of evaluating characteristics or criteria. In the South the important criteria for these purposes have traditionally included race, sex, family lineage, education, wealth, income, residence, and religious affiliation. These factors and processes produced an autocratic, agrarian, race-based, rigid social class system that was not fundamentally altered by the Civil War. However, the forces of change that transformed the region after World War II expanded, relaxed, and opened the stratification system to the new economy, population, and culture of the New South.

Traditionally, the upper class included wealthy planters, business executives and bankers, high federal and state officials, freestanding professionals (doctors, lawyers), education and church leaders (Episcopal), outstanding journalists, and female scions of great families. These individuals and families had prestige, wealth, and power. They dominated the region and set the standard and pace of life for all.

A small middle class included administrators on plantations and factories, principals and teachers in public and private schools, directors of service agencies, professionals in the media, state and lower government, and so on. These people never experienced the luster of "high society" nor wielded policy-controlling power. They had working contacts with the uppers but did not share sociability relations.

Traditionally, the families and individuals who fell below the middle class were not always sharply differentiated into working-lower or other classes. People in this position were poor, lacked prestige, and had little power. Some of them owned small farms or operated small businesses or craft shops. They possessed small accumulations of wealth and managed their work and lives. A great many of the people at this level, both white and black, worked on plantations and owned very little property of any kind. They were dependent upon and controlled by the planters. In the small cities of the region there were some poor people whose problems derived from moral and social deviances—for example, crime and alcoholism.

After World War II the stratification structure of the South changed radically. Industrialization, in-migration, and urbanization were major causes of this transformation. In the years after the Second World War the South grew to one of the largest regions of the country (see Chapter 2). The new population settled in cities and worked in the new industries. Kasarda et al. (see Chapter 3) showed that between 1950 and 1985 employment in the primary industries (agriculture, forestry, fisheries, and mining) declined by 17.5 percent. Nevertheless, the number of workers in the construction and service activities grew by 15.9 percent. In this period, more than nine tenths (93 percent) of the growth in employment occurred in these industries.

As a consequence of these changes, a large new sector was added to the regional upper class. Industrial executives of a new inmigrant type (modernizers) extended the class. To a significant extent leadership slipped out of control of the traditionalists into the hands of the new members. At the same time, the older categories of upper-class persons lost power and prestige in the region.

The population and occupational changes issuing from this basic economic transformation generated several new sectors within the regional middle class. These new middle-class workers came from the new high-tech, service, and wholesale-retail industries. They were part of the white-collar middle class that C. Wright Mills (1959) has identified in the 1950s. They were bureaucratic managers, salaried professionals, consultants and counselors in health and human services, government, communications, high-tech services, lodging accommodations, and so on. This new white-collar sector had internal layers—for example, administrative professionals, technical professionals, scientific professionals, and lower level technicians such as computer service technicians. At the same time—largely as a consequence of the civil rights movement—women, blacks, Hispanics, and other minorities in increasing numbers moved into these new middle-class sectors (see Chapters 5–7). As a result of these changes, the Southern middle class has become the largest component of the regional class system.

In the new Southern class system, it is possible to differentiate working class from lower class. Typically, the working class includes persons with limited education and training who are employed at low rates of pay. Because of the current "minimum wage," some of these persons and families fall within the official poverty category. Race prejudice, segregation, and discrimination exacerbate this experience for blacks (see Chapter 7). Working-class people tend to live within the structures of the law and moral rules. The working class can also be said to include persons and families who live on public welfare, but within the legal and moral norms of the society.

The lower class is differentiated from the working class by economic and moral criteria. At the bottom of the structure is a genuine lower class, popularly called the "permanent underclass." This is the "unrespectable" lower class. It contains the unfortunates of all races who have fallen from popular social grace. This group includes the perennially unemployed; the health-impoverished; those in the drug, alcohol, and crime culture; and other deviants from the rules of the law and morality. It is said that they have been trapped in this socioeconomic situation from which they cannot escape. A permanent underclass can be observed in such large Southern cities as Miami, Tampa, Atlanta, Charlotte, Richmond, Washington, Baltimore, Nashville, Birmingham, New Orleans, and the large cities of Texas.

Power

Transformation of regional organization and stratification was accompanied by change in the power structure. Dominance of the traditional agrarian and professional elites was challenged and eroded from several directions. As a consequence, the regional power structure became more diffuse and impersonal than it had been previously.

The industrial in-migrants who followed World War II challenged the traditional familistic power structure of the region. This new sector of power leaders included the executives and managers of the new manufacturing, service, and high-tech activities that developed in the 1950s and later. In Chapter 9, Luebke calls these leaders "modernizers" and contrasts their style with that of the earlier leaders whom he calls "traditionalists." These new leaders generated the power that had not been mobilized at an earlier time.

The burgeoning white-collar professional, technical, and service middle classes acquired the bureaucratic authority needed for the performance of their jobs. This was threatening to the traditionalist elites but raised little problem for the modernizers. With continued change, increasing power in the economic arena tended to emanate through politics from state and local governments. This trend further eroded the fealty of tenants and servants that the planter traditionalists enjoyed.

The modernizers had a further advantage in the South. Social power of all kinds came to be more and more associated with the influence of national power structures. The modernizers had prior and better connections than the traditionalists with this power source.

Private economic and social power as wielded by the traditionalists and modernizers was further challenged by political power exercised by the U.S. government. The first major application of this source of power is demonstrated in the New Deal during the Great Depression. The government utilized national political authority to deal with the massive economic and social problems of the times. Almost naturally, after World War II, the government turned again to this power source to cope with the problems of rapid social change and burgeoning economic growth. In this way the U.S. government became an alternate dominant actor in the Southern power game.

Meanwhile, transformation of the South generated a series of special interest sectors—business/industry, labor, political parties, social classes, women, the aged, minority groups, education, religion, and so on—with variable goals and ancillary power centers. These subsystems cluster around the two major systems in variable pluralistic patterns. They employ countervailing power in complex processes of struggle to protect and advance their individual interest. In sum it can be said that as the South was transformed, the sources, the amount, the forms, the distribution, and the structure of social power were fundamentally altered.

Predictions of Social Changes

The aim of this part of the chapter is to summarize the predictions of change in the region that are set forth in the preceding chapters. First, the major developmental predictions will be succinctly inventoried and summarized. The second part will summarize the problematical, i.e., undesirable changes that may occur in the foreseeable future of the South. As will be suggested in the next chapter these predictions may help Southerners to guide and control their march into their future.

Leading Developmental Changes

The leading developmental changes are summarized in the following list:

After World War II the Southern population grew rapidly, mainly by in-migration, in size and regional percentage; becoming older and more female; and including larger proportions of blacks, Hispanics, and Asians.

Simultaneously, the population changed in settlement from two-thirds rural in 1950 to more than four-fifths urban a century later.

With in-migrant capital and leadership from the North, the economy will move from mainly extractive to manufacturing, high tech, and service and sales in the near future.

The national elderly population will continue to concentrate in the South, mainly Florida, where it has become a strong influence in political and social affairs.

It is predicted that the continuing struggle (a) between women and men may minimize the influence of race and male traditionalism on gender, improve female economic equity, and, with federal assistance, better their legal status; (b) between Hispanics and Anglos will move relations toward structural assimilation of (Cubans fully, Mexicans rapidly, Puerto Ricans slowly); (c) between blacks and whites, with public policy support and self-help, will move relations toward equity (briskly in the black urban middle-classes and slowly in the black working- and under-classes).

The culture of the region will continue to change by accelerated expansion of the mass layer and contraction of the traditional base in small places, thus moving the South toward similarity with the rest of the country.

However, the regional conservative orientation will continue to dominate both the new and especially the old economic elites, while the thrust of liberal groups remains weak and defensive.

In the years ahead the number of new jobs will increase, especially in the high-tech and service industries. The resulting urbanization will link moderate-sized places by good communication into cities and will extend into metropolitan growth, which may include three-fourths of total population before the middle of the next century. These dramatic changes will affect virtually all social, cultural, and personal aspects of life in the region.

The present settlement pattern of the region began evolving just after World War II. In the future it is predicted to continue and accelerate. Rapid expansion of the economy, especially in the high-tech and service industries, will accentuate the attraction of urban places for in-migrant leaders and workers. It is predicted that a third of the way into the twenty-first century most of the regional population will reside in metropolitan areas. This trend will aggravate problems that are relatively new to the region. Metropolitan growth will stimulate the burgeoning of suburban areas and will further isolate middle-class and upper-middle-class sectors from the urban poor. Central cities will continue to spawn and stabilize multiracial underclasses in the old deteriorated sections of cities. These trends will generate and accentuate some of the regional problems discussed below.

The growing regional population will diversify in composition. One major class of in-migrants will be, increasingly, elderly people who retire in the Gulf-rim states—Florida, Arizona, and New Mexico. The middle states of Virginia, North Carolina, and Kentucky will also attract some of the in-coming elderly people. This growing elderly sector will be increasingly composed of women, typically widowed and retired. The feminization of the elderly population will generate and exacerbate some problems for the region.

Aging of the Southern population will produce diverse economic and social consequences. Through government and private pension plans (e.g., Social Security, Railroad retirement, other government programs, and industrial retirement), the gross income of several states, especially Florida, will be significantly increased and stabilized. At the same time, the burden of taxation to support public services for the elderly will be borne mainly by the younger working class. This trend generates still other problems.

Demographic changes also foster increasing racial and ethnic heterogeneity in the region. These trends will affect the patterns of relations between sectors of the population. It is likely also that this trend of change may affect the political organization and behavior of the region in the years just ahead. In addition, gender relations between men and women will be affected by other changes in the region and will further blur or erase the imprint of the antebellum plantation family.

Rapid in-migration and industrialization of the region will continue to exert an influence on the change of Southern culture. The traditional conservative, individualistic, and paternalistic pattern will be challenged by pragmatic, instrumental ways brought in from the outside. This new "mass culture" will continue to take strong root in the growing urban sector of the region, driving the traditional pattern into isolation in small towns and rural areas, both of which are shrinking in size. Although this trend will increase in the near future, the region will retain enough of traditionalism to be recognizable as the South. The "new South" will be more like the general American society than formerly, yet it will still be recognizably the South for some years to come.

Related to the issue of culture is the matter of sociopolitical orientation. The in-migrant, modernizing economic leaders tend to be economically conservative. However, while joining the traditional elites in control of the regional economy, they tend to resist and ignore some of the socioreligious conservatism of the traditional dominants. Both classes of leaders are resistant to political and economic liberalism. The resistance toward "liberalism" is strongly affected by traditional regional norms on labor union action, demands for women's rights, and racial protest activity. This Southern dilemma continues and will yield only grudgingly to the winds and forces of change.

Leading Problematical Changes for the South

As suggested above, changes in the nation and region are also dysfunctional and produce socioeconomic problems. These problems are all evident enough, in reality or in expectation, to consider seriously. Most of them are not unique to the South, but they are likely to become more severe as the region moves into its future. Some of the more obvious issues are presented below:

Increasing urban concentration of population will exacerbate pollution of air, water, and other resources.
Growing collective needs will intensify pressure on communities

to provide resources (e.g., water, energy, fuel, available land).

Growing demand for public services will continue to outrun public funds to provide them.

Feminization and aging of the Southern population will aggravate their problems in the region.

Individualistic and anti-institutional values of the needy and frail elderly will clash with collective solutions of collective problems by communities.

Increasing demands for public services will intensify the strain with major tax-paying community sectors.

These tendencies will intensify political tension between age categories and social classes.

Concentration of underprepared individuals in slow-growth areas will generate problems of need and frustration.

The growth of new health problems—AIDS, degenerative diseases, seasonal epidemics—will exacerbate the economic, political, and service dilemmas of the region.

The national balance of trade, the national debt, foreign economic competition, and high defense expenditures will aggravate or extend economic problems.

Underprepared workers will be increasingly handicapped by the spread of high-tech and service industries.

Problems of intergroup relations—ethnic, racial, age, gender, class, and so on—will strain existing human relations resources.

Managing the disposal of toxic waste materials will become more and more urgent.

In the years ahead the South is likely to have problems grounded in expanding use of natural resources. Accelerated urbanization will cause increasing pollution of the basic resources of air, water, and soil. Related to these issues is the matter of disposing of various kinds of toxic waste. Such problems will make a growing demand upon the leadership and resourcefulness of the region.

Other sources of problems are the demands of citizens upon government agencies for service. These demands have grown and will outrun the fiscal capacity of government (particularly local government) to meet them. This issue is variably affected by sectors of the population—the frail elderly, women, minorities, the unemployed, low-income persons, and so on. The problem develops a political dimension (e.g., the elderly vs. young workers) when one group or the other assumes a possessive approach to the matter. Streib (Chapter 4) perceives this problem as prophetic of the changing future of the region.

The minority sectors of the regional population will become an area of increasing tension. Each of these groups, women, Hispanics, and blacks, is striving uniquely for full entry into the life of the region. Each is faced to one degree or another with resistance. These aspects of the regional problems are likely in the future to become increasingly an aspect of the political arena. Intergroup struggles such as these will accentuate change of the region as it moves into its future.

A crop of relatively new national problems also affects the South. The region is affected by the fiscal problems of the federal government—the unfavorable balance of payments, the unbalanced national budget, and the competition in various industrial areas from foreign companies. All these problems will affect the South generally as part of the nation, and uniquely in terms of the regional industries (e.g., textiles). New and worsening diseases of various kinds, AIDS, cancer and heart disease, will affect the South as they affect the other regions. These diseases will be intensified by aging of the population. Some agricultural pests and diseases affect Southern crops uniquely (e.g., tobacco, citrus fruit). Traditionally the South had a disproportionate share of the underprepared workers in the country. They will be uniquely affected by the spread of high-tech and service industries, both of which present fairly high educational demands.

Very naturally predictions like those just presented and discussed raise the question of what, if anything, can be done to avoid the problematic future developments and ensure desirable or preferred outcomes of change? All social scientists face this same question many times in the course of their professional careers. In the following chapter an experienced and thoughtful sociologist examines this issue. He replies that there are various steps that can be taken to direct the course of social change and assist the outcome of preferred ends. He assures us that it does indeed "make a difference" to try.

11

Making a Difference: The Role of the Social Sciences

Abbott L. Ferriss

As John F. Kennedy was fond of saying, a single person may make a difference in the affairs of society. At a particular time and place, circumstances may require someone with leadership or innovative talents—and that someone may happen along to alter the situation and make a difference in the future course of history. A profession may also make a difference, for it may inculcate a certain philosophy in its members, provide training, develop skills, and pass along certain tools and a tradition of "making a difference." Through values, concern with the general welfare of society, and understanding of social organization and change, the social sciences, especially sociology, have made a difference in the South. Sociologists have contributed in planning and stimulating change, in pointing to opportunities, and in helping set up organizations that have been influential in the South.

Making a Difference through Two Regional Organizations

Fifty years ago, the South was mired in its deepest depression, its economy stalemated, its people characterized by Franklin D. Roosevelt (January 20, 1937) as "one-third of the Nation, ill-housed, ill-clad, and ill-nourished." Some years earlier sociologist Howard W. Odum had published an analysis of the deficiencies and resources of the South that served to characterize the region: "as to resources—superabundance; as to science, skills, technology, organization—deficiency; as to general economy—waste; as to culture—richness, with immaturity and multiple handicaps; as to trends—hesitancy and relative retrogression in many aspects of culture" (Odum 1936, 151). He saw social planning as the key to regional regeneration and education as the means of improving the human resources of the South.

Sociologists and Race Relations: The Southern Regional Council

Race relations traditionally have pervaded most social and economic concerns of the South. They have often hindered efforts to bring about needed social and cultural change. In studying these problems, sociologists have played prominent roles by fostering programs to improve race relations. They have not been alone, of course. A variety of organizations in the South—churches and foundations, youth organizations, and community groups—and other professional people have worked to avoid conflict and effect peaceful social and cultural change. Chief among these has been the Commission on Interracial Cooperation (CIC) and its successor, the Southern Regional Council (SRC).

After World War I, as soldiers returned to civilian life, an Interracial Commission was formed to seek to avoid racial conflict and bring blacks and whites together to reduce tension. Formed in 1919, the name was changed in 1921 to the Commission on Interracial Cooperation. Support of the work initially came from the Julius Rosenwald Fund and the Phelps-Stokes Fund (directed by Thomas Jesse Jones, a sociologist). Also prominent in its formation and program development were sociologists Will W. Alexander and Ira De A. Reid. In the 1920s CIC began to "devote most of its energies to research, publicity and education of southern blacks and whites in the achievements of blacks and the need for cooperation between the races" (Ducey 1984a). During this period CIC also advocated establishing better schools and health facilities, and improving general living conditions of blacks. A systematic program of legal aid to blacks was initiated, and studies were begun of segregation in the South. A biracial conference at the local level was the organizational device then advanced, with the objects of education, establishing a pattern of discussion and interaction, and seeking solutions to racial problems on a long-term basis. Annual meetings, begun in 1921, were attended by thousands.

In this early phase, research figured prominently. T. J. Woofter, Jr., a young sociologist, and Arthur Raper, fresh from sociology training at the University of North Carolina, came to the program. Woofter's *The Basis of Racial Adjustment* (1925) and Raper's *Preface to Peasantry* (1936) are representative of their work. Raper, with Walter Chivers, a young sociology professor at Morehouse College, conducted a study of lynching in the South. Raper's *The Tragedy of Lynching* (1933) became one of the landmarks of its time. Arthur Raper and Ira De A. Reid published *Sharecroppers All*, an indictment of the Southern agricultural system. In addition to research, the CIC program sought to correct injustices wherever possible, influence the public through press releases, and stimulate university study of race relations (Dykeman and Stokely 1962).

In 1930 the Carnegie Corporation provided funds to develop teaching materials for race-relations courses in the South. Summer sessions for teachers were held at George Peabody College, Mississippi College, Blue Ridge, North Carolina, and Louisiana State University. The purpose was to infuse the curriculum with race relations materials.

In 1937 the CIC program began "reorganizing interracial committees at the state and local levels." Research was temporarily subordinated in favor of sponsoring local conferences and institutes on race relations. A publication, *The Southern Frontier*, was the voice of the program.

"Under the influence of Howard Odum of the University of North Carolina, a movement within the CIC grew to establish an organization that would focus on the particular needs of the South as a region—needs which included but went beyond the pervasive problem of race. Odum . . . was president of the CIC from 1937 until its dissolution in 1944 . . ." (Ducey 1984b). He and black sociologist Charles S. Johnson, president of Fisk University, co-chaired a Continuation Committee which led to the organization of the Southern Regional Council.

Mrs. Jessie Daniel Ames of the CIC urged Gordon B. Hancock, sociologist of Virginia Union University, to bring blacks together to draw up a statement of grievances, promising to arrange a response from white leaders. At this meeting on October 20, 1942, in Durham, North Carolina, black leaders, including Charles S. Johnson, prepared the "Durham Statement." In turn, white leaders met in Atlanta, April 8, 1943, and issued a response. This led to a meeting of both groups on June 16, 1943, in Richmond, Virginia, supported by Johnson, Odum, Alexander, and others (Hancock 1964, 12). These and other conferences eventuated in the development of a charter for the Southern Regional Council, which was accepted June 6, 1944. The Council assumed the property of the CIC and enlarged its work. Under this charter the SRC undertook efforts "for improvement of economic, civic and racial conditions in the South . . . to promote a greater unity in the South in all efforts toward regional and racial development; to attain through research and action programs the ideals and practices of equal opportunity for all peoples in the region; to reduce race tension, the bases of racial tension, racial misunderstanding, and racial distrust; to develop and integrate leadership in the South on new levels of regional development and fellowship" (SRC 1944).

Odum, president of CIC from 1937, became president of SRC in 1944, and Charles S. Johnson became chair of the Executive Committee. Sociologist Guy B. Johnson was executive director of SRC from 1944 to 1947, followed by George S. Mitchell, an economist. Ira De A. Reid was associate director beginning in 1944. Other sociologists involved in the work of the Council, either on staff, engaged in research for the Council, or in some other capacity, included Fred C. Frey, William E. Cole, Moselle Hill, Hylan Lewis, Robin Williams, John Maclachlan, E. Franklin Frazier, John A. Griffin, and Charles M. Grigg.

The educational aims of the Council were furthered through *The Southern Frontier*, which in 1946 became *The New South*; in the late 1960s it changed to the *South Today*, later to *Southern Voices*, and currently, *Southern Changes*.

The most significant lasting accomplishment of CIC and SRC was the bringing together of blacks and whites at the state and local levels to consider their mutual problems. Later this activity was conducted by the State Councils on Human Relations. Following World War II these interracial groups sought to detect and defuse tensions occasioned by the return of servicemen to civilian life. As a consequence, few incidents of racial conflict occurred in the South, in contrast to considerable conflict in Midwestern and Eastern cities. During the postwar period, the Veterans Services Project (1944–51) also sought to encourage blacks to enroll in colleges and take advantage of the veterans education bill. A statistical review of public educational disparities was sponsored by SRC (Swanson and Griffin 1955).

The accumulation of information at the Council offices on the conditions of blacks has been extensive; consequently writers and journalists have turned to the staff when working on race-relations stories or projects. The Council also has used this information to develop and sponsor some 300 program activities for improvement of race relations in the region. The nature of some of them may be inferred from their titles:

Urban Planning Project, 1954–72

Women's Work and Fellowship of the Concerned Voter Education Project, 1954–71

Voter Education Project, 1954–61

Crime and Correction Project, 1954–69

Health and Public Education, 1958–61

Organizations Assisting Schools in September, 1955–1962

Community Organization Project, 1963–67

Operation Opportunity, 1959–64

Under this list, the Voter Education Project has exerted the greatest influence on the South. It has augmented the political electorate by bringing about the registration of 1.5 million voters. Headed by Wiley Brandon during its final years with SRC, it spun off to become an independent agency under leadership of Vernon Jordan, John Lewis, and others. Its work continues with support from various philanthropies.

The long-term success of the Southern Regional Council and the many other organizations that affected the civil rights movement led supporting organizations to believe that the SRC mission had been accomplished. For a time during the 1970s, support for its work was slim, indeed; it appeared to have reached its nadir during 1977–78. With Steve Suitt's assumption of the executive directorship, however, the broader mission of SRC for civil rights and equality began to reassert itself, and the program began to move forward once again.

In 1986 the work continued—The Voting Rights Project, an Institute for Political Participation, and The Southern Legislative Research Project. In the workplace also there were projects: The Southern Labor Institute and the Cooperative Democracy and Development Project. A Southern Justice Program was concerned with administration of justice equitably to blacks and whites. Education was the focus of a School Drop-out Prevention Project, as was a Project on Segregation and Christian Academies.

Plans for continuing work on governmental issues in 1988 included developing an electronic data base on political information and development of communications technologies for increasing nonpartisan political participation. Consistent with this popular function of the past, the Council also continued as a source of ideas and information for the press and other communications media.

From the 1920s, through persistent, informed programs of social science research and study, education, and action, the Southern Regional Council has made a difference in race relations and the quality of life in the South.

Sociologists and Higher Education: The Southern Regional Education Board

The Southern Regional Education Board (SREB) provides the basis for fifteen southern states to cooperate "to advance knowledge and to improve the social and economic level of the region." It developed through the combined efforts of politicians (especially state governors), educational organizations (e.g., the American Council on Education), and social scientists. SREB was formally established July 11, 1949.

Interest in interstate cooperation in higher education was generated in the South during the 1930s by the example of the Tennessee Valley Authority (T.V.A.), through studies of deficiencies in southern education—particularly those of Odum and Rupert Vance at the University of North Carolina—and by the anticipated increase in demand for higher education occasioned by the discharge of World War II military veterans. These concerns led to establishment of a committee on Southern Regional Studies and Education in the American Council of Education in 1943, with John E. Ivy, Jr.—a sociologist at the University of North Carolina—as executive secretary. To stimulate and facilitate interstate cooperation, compacts had to be made between states and ratified by legislatures.

An early instance of cooperation among Southern states was a compact between West Virginia and Virginia to transfer fifteen to twenty students a year from the University of West Virginia to the Medical College of Virginia, West Virginia paying the costs "over and above those normally incurred by students of Virginia" (Sugg and Jones 1960, 9). Through this compact, West Virginia, although it had no medical school, could provide its students a medical education.

Although trained medical specialists were needed, many states did not have facilities for higher education in certain specialized fields. Interstate contracts provided a way to meet this need. Beginning in the early 1950s, contracts were arranged through SREB for transfer of students in veterinary medical education; medical education for Negroes (predating the 1954 Supreme Court decision); training in dentistry, nursing, pharmacy, forestry, and social work; training in several specialized areas of the sciences; and programs in other fields. States agreed "to provide adequate services and facilities to the graduate, professional and technical education for the benefit of the citizens of the respective States" (Sugg and Jones 1960, 21). Beginning in 1952 the Board experimented with a variety of programs, involving altogether some thirty academic fields.

By 1950, $495,625 ($2,257,465 in 1986 dollars) were exchanged between Southern states for the education of some 360 individuals; in 1955, $1,314,175 ($5,381,235 in 1986 dollars) were expended for education of 1,004 Southerners; in 1958, the figure was $1,168,625 ($4,431,599 in 1986 dollars) for 910 students. Other fields involving academic planning or student exchange included graduate nursing, petroleum sciences, statistics, city planning, foreign affairs, agricultural sciences, architectural education, special education, clinical psychology, nuclear energy, and mental health.

Beyond the transfer of students from one state to another, SREB developed programs for the joint use of library resources, the expansion of educational television, and a mental health program. The mental health program had as its objectives to attract mental health professionals to the region, to stimulate mental health research, to improve communication among mental health professionals, and to consult on mental health problems. As SREB grew, its emphasis moved into broader, more vital areas of educational planning and cooperation.

Later the New England states created an organization parallel to SREB, the New England Board of Higher Education, and Western states organized the Western Interstate Commission on Higher Education. Thus, other states "have followed the Southern lead in many respects . . ." (Sugg and Jones 1960, 152), extending the impact of the program nation-wide.

Another sociologist who had worked with SREB was Robert C. Anderson (sociologist/educator); other directors serving between 1957 and 1962 include John K. Folger, Harry Williams, E. F. Schietinger, and Winfred L. Godwin, currently president of the Board. Other sociologists have conducted studies that have facilitated development of the SREB program—among these are Charles M. Grigg, Florida State University; Nahm Z. Medalia, Georgia Institute of Technology; and Daniel O. Price, University of North Carolina (Miller 1967).

During the 1960s, through conferences and studies, SREB expanded its planning functions. It advocated statewide planning and coordination in higher education and stressed expansion and improvement of postsecondary educational opportunities for black students. This emphasis was further abetted during the 1970s by a grant of $9,000,000 from the William R. Kenan, Jr., Charitable Trust to help black colleges and nearby school systems better prepare black students for college. The interstate and interinstitutional sharing of academic programs, as the SREB Academic Common Market, now offered more than 1,000 programs through 128 senior colleges and universities. Over the forty-year life of this program SREB has enabled the graduate education of some 10,000 students who have received higher degrees.

In the 1970s an Office of State Services was established to provide information to state education officials on approaches and developments to improve quality of education under conditions of stable enrollments.

During the present period, SREB has led the nation in proposals for educational reform through pursuing higher standards in teaching and learning and through attention to the interface between secondary school and college programs. SREB has advocated early identification during secondary school of the most able students in order to help them prepare for college-level study. It has recommended steps to strengthen the academic background of teachers by revamping teacher education programs. Vocational education has also come within the SREB's scope. The SREB-State Vocational Educational Consortium focuses upon raising the competencies of students in high school vocational education by developing model programs to test applied approaches for teaching communications, mathematics, and science. Efforts to improve educational quality are being evaluated through a three-year pilot program to test student achievement and enable comparisons by region and by state through the National Assessment of Educational Progress (SREB 1988).

In short, SREB has stimulated interstate cooperation in sharing scarce educational resources and has led the Southern states into broader educational planning, evaluation, and achievement of quality education. SREB has "made a difference." Skills, competencies, and technical capabilities have been developed that otherwise would have lain dormant, and the South is richer for it. Sociologists, educators, and other social scientists have contributed prominently to the conception, development, and administration of this program.

Other Ways in Which Southern Social Scientists Have Made a Difference

In addition to the two examples of organized activity described above, social scientists, sociologists, economists, and so forth have made a difference in a wide variety of public activities. Public recognition has crowned many for their activities or research work. Many contributions to community and society through extracurricular service activities as well as research publications can be cited. They include work on human and civil rights; activities that improve the quality of life; humanitarian contributions in mental health; services to the aged; help to the criminally insane and to drug abusers; work to prevent crime; ideas on organization, leadership, and motivation to improve industrial productivity; services to black families; efforts to improve the system of higher education; and services to church organizations. Their contributions have been legitimized by being formally recognized by community groups or agencies through citations or awards (*The Southern Sociologist*, 1981–84).

Motivation, skill, and training are keys to creative professional leadership. Many come to the social sciences already motivated to contribute to the general welfare; others acquire motivation from studying sociological and economic research on social problems. Such studies inculcate this impulse and also provide theories of social change that point to the steps intervention should take. The social sciences orient students to objective analyses of problems and enables them to dig deeply to find root causes, if such can be found, of societal issues. Thus, the norms, theories, information, and motivations of social science professions lead to identifying and working for societal adjustments along the way to a more smoothly functioning society. The combined efforts of scientific analyses, politics, economics, sociology—and, often, religion—are needed to effect social change. When goals are identified, planning the steps necessary for their achievement becomes the first step in the direction of change.

Planning the South's Future:
The Southern Growth Policies Board

Planning today in the South largely proceeds along specialized avenues—recreational resource planning by federal agencies, river basin planning by erosion control and navigation agencies, and the like. Educational planning anticipates demographic change in order to guide school construction, teacher training, and budgets for education. Local multi-purpose planning by a consortium of governmental units is rare: the Atlanta Regional Commission is an example, a seven-county effort to guide economic development of the metropolitan area. The Tennessee Valley Authority involves multi-purpose regional planning that has wrought tremendous transformations of life and industry during its fifty-year history. Today, the Commission on the Future of the South of the Southern Growth Policies Board (SGPB) is guiding the considerable resources at its disposal toward multi-purpose planning. The program is sensitive to political and economic influences of the twelve Southern states and Puerto Rico participating in the program. The scope of its work may be seen in The Ten Regional Objectives recently endorsed by the Commission:

"Provide a nationally competitive education for all Southern states by 1992;

"Mobilize resources to eliminate adult functional illiteracy by 1992;

"Prepare a flexible, globally competitive work force by 1992;

"Strengthen society as a whole by strengthening at-risk families by 1992;

"Increase the South's capacity to generate and use technology by 1992;

"Implement new economic development strategies aimed at home-grown business and industry by 1992;

"Enhance the South's natural and cultural resources by 1992;

"Develop pragmatic leaders with a global vision by 1992;

"Improve the structure and performance of state and local govern-ments by 1992" (Betts 1986).

As Howard Odum pointed out, implementation of such far-reach-ing objectives requires state and local (particularly local) participa-tion. It will be recalled that the success of the Southern Regional Council rested heavily upon state and local committees, working groups, and "human relations councils." If the objectives of the SGPB are likewise activated through planning at the state and local levels, incorporating local considerations into plans, and adjusting to the means and resources locally available, the ten objectives may indeed have a chance of being realized by 1992.

The broad scope of SGPB's work is further illustrated by its pub-lication series: *Foresight* on human resource development; *Alert* on emerging economic issues; *Southern International Perspectives,* which explores opportunities for international trade; *Growth and Environmental Management;* and *Local Insight,* through which is-sues in local government and development are discussed. The Board's Committee on Southern Trends annually issues "Looking Forward: Visions of the Future of the South," which brings together many of these interrelated threads.

In addition to this publication program, the Board pursues its ob-jectives by assembling conferences of leaders, and by stimulating planning and development at state and local levels. Examples in-clude the following activities:

Developing leadership in the rural South has been furthered through calling attention to four ongoing programs in the South that stimulate local leadership. The SGPB publication *Foresight* de-scribes the "Look Up Gaston" program of Gaston County, North Carolina, which sponsors programs to encourage countywide eco-nomic development; a New Market, Tennessee, program, "Southern Appalachian Leadership Training," which addresses the needs of low-income rural leaders with limited formal education; the "LeadAR" program of Little Rock, Arkansas, which gives economic and community development training to rural leaders across the state; the T.V.A. "Power Distributor Economic Technical Assistance Program," which trains staff of electric co-ops to assist local leaders; and a community development program to raise the quality of life in a fifteen-county area of northeast Mississippi under sociologist Vaughn L. Grisham at the University of Mississippi.

In 1982 the SGPB launched an interstate banking movement. By 1987 it had assembled representatives of the banking community, federal and state officials, and others to assess the impact of the development. Bank consolidations occurring since 1982 were examined. The available credit supply for small and medium-sized banks was studied. Competition was reviewed and recommendations were developed for state governors and legislatures to improve availability of capital assets for development.

The guidance of growth also has been a topic of continuing study. In "Guiding Growth in the South: A Decade Later," SGPB analyzes and reports upon the innovative programs of the states designed to manage growth. Growth management affects the location, rate, type, amount, and quality or timing of development, based upon statewide plans for large regional developments as well as sensitivity to environmental preservation.

SGPB recently formed a Southern Technology Council to advise on issues of augmenting the technological capacity of the South. Funded by special assessments of states and corporate members, the Council is creating a consortium of two-year postsecondary schools in each state to become technology transfer points for innovative manufacturing processes, equipment, and training. It aims to revitalize small town and rural factories.

While the Southern Growth Policies Board is organized as a public, interstate agency, supported by the twelve states and Puerto Rico, it also encompasses an Associate Membership Program, dues of which go into a Fund for the Future of the South. Some forty commercial establishments make up a group of "Sustainers," while fifty-five Corporate Members and more than 140 nonprofit members, including universities and colleges, contribute to the support of SGPB. Such widespread participation provides a broad economic and social base for carving out a future for the South.

In such work, economists, political scientists, sociologists, and other social scientists contribute their skills and understanding through conducting studies and engaging in planning. A strategy for their development and utilization will now be examined.

Training to Make a Difference: Strategies for the Future

The social sciences continue to play a role of influence in the direction and movement of the future of the South. Political science, economics, sociology, and other social sciences, through planning and by anticipating the consequences of societal changes, are helping commercial and political leaders forge the future.

The principle of continuity in historical sequences, the interlocking of events from the past to the present and into the future, compels us to recognize that the future of social sciences in the South can be shaped by strategies now beginning to be implemented. These strategies will equip social scientists to be important and skillful agents in directing the future of the region's growth and development. They involve formal education at the undergraduate and graduate levels, and the channeling of graduates into nonacademic (as well as academic) employment.

Smaller numbers of entering college freshmen in the next decade will mean fewer undergraduate enrollments in the social sciences nationwide; the low point may be expected in the mid-1990s, followed by a steady increase. The college-age population of the South will continue to decline to 1990 and increase slightly from that date to the year 2000 (Huber 1984; Bowen 1981).

However, declining enrollments will not affect all institutions uniformly. As a result of their control over student intake, private institutions may be able to maintain enrollment levels. In addition, two-year institutions, community colleges, and institutions with student bodies who live at home may be able to maintain enrollment levels by providing educational opportunities for persons older than typical students and by other programs (Plisko 1983, 100). Vietnamese and other Asian-Americans, Spanish-speaking migrants, and their children actually may acquire stronger motivations for higher education than native Southerners (Bureau of the Census 1982, Table 166; Frisbee in Chapter 6, above). Service courses for engineers, nurses, business administrators, and other professions may be attractive to these in-migrant groups.

A strategy for undergraduate education requires the development of courses and teachers to serve the interests of a student body that is changing in its demographic composition. Moreover, course content requires adaptation to the altered character of human interactions and societal problems under the impact of technological and ideological change. These issues are legion—for example, the organization of the rural social system to improve food production; the understanding of human motivation and behavior to control population increases in undeveloped areas of the world; the control of individual and industrial behaviors to reduce pollution and improve the air, water, and soil of the environment; conservation and utilization of limited resources of energy and raw materials; reducing morbidity and mortality from causes generated by the sociocultural behavioral patterns that affect such conditions as cardiovascular disease, tobacco smoking, drug abuse, poor dietary habits, suicide, automobile and industrial accidents, the myriad disorders resulting from stresses generated by the social system; and, finally, the societal maladjustments resulting from changes in science and technology.

In this connection graduate education in the social sciences, especially sociology, has several responsibilities. Initially, those who go into academia must be prepared and committed to offer the kind of undergraduate training described in the preceding paragraph. More than this, however, university professors must train students for the practical jobs in the communities of a growing and developing region. At least three strategies for accomplishing this end can be described briefly.

First, graduate education has the task of preparing future professionals who can serve in a wide range of nonacademic areas. This training is designed to apply social science knowledge and skill in such areas as evaluation research, transfer of technological knowledge into social action, developing human relations understanding, and social organizing skills.

Second, graduate education must offer training in research: developing research designs and research strategies intimately related to the problems of people, imposing relevant theories upon the masses of survey data now available, and devising and carrying out experiments in both the laboratory and in the field.

Third, in application, graduate education must find the means to bring sociological and social science understanding to bear upon such current problems as drug abuse, poverty and hunger, environmental pollution, interpersonal conflict and marital breakdown, subcultural intolerance of grievances, the plight of minorities, and a host of other social problems.

It is encouraging to report that increasing numbers of sociology Ph.D.s in the South are entering nonacademic occupations, many of which relate specifically to planning and directing the region's move into its future. Currently, 22 percent of new sociology Ph.D. recipients in the South have entered these nonacademic occupations. Of the South's Ph.D. class of 1980–81, 20 percent entered nonacademic employment as their first postdoctoral positions. The comparable class of 1983–84 sent 30 percent of its members into these occupations (Ferriss 1986).

All who enter academic employment do not remain there. After teaching for two years or more, the young professional may enter survey or market research (Smith 1983); become a computer or statistical specialist (Mizell 1983); work for federal, state, or local government in research or administration (Terry 1981, 1982, 1983); serve other agencies or associations; find employment in corporations; practice privately as a family counselor or sampling consultant (Swanson 1983); or, finally, leave sociology to join the secure business of one's own family or the family of one's spouse. This trend of employment augurs well for the increasing role and usefulness of sociologists in the business of regional growth and development.

Conclusion

Howard Odum's vision of "regional reintegration in the nation" (1936, 594), whether through planning or otherwise, gradually is being realized. Communication media now knit the nation together, interregional capital investments emphasize interdependencies while stimulating local development, internal migrations infuse the South with diverse population and cultural types, large Southern cities exert dominance over a widening hinterland—and, in many instances, decisions come down from national centers of power to affect socioeconomic life, even in small towns: Main Street comes to look the same everywhere. While these trends represent integration of the South with the rest of the nation, simultaneously they overpower and deplete the subregional cultures, the source of the South's pride and vitality. Yet there remains a South different from other regions, a South with a distinctive cultural flavor. The more vital parts Odum would seek to preserve while adapting the more debilitating elements to the demands of modern society. As Reed (1986) points out, the traditional folk culture of the South will persist along with the predominant industrialized mass culture of the urban South. To ensure continued development of the South and to preserve and adapt the life-giving traditions of the folk culture will require active planning and organization of the kinds in which sociologists and other social scientists have been involved.

In striding into the future, the South will require the combined efforts of the diverse professional talents at its disposal—economists and sociologists, business professionals and ministers, politicians and social workers. Planning and development require multidisciplinary talents working in harness. Resolving problems of the future, as attested by the essays in this volume, will demand the best each profession has to offer.

The nature and extent of the problems of planning and control that face the region as it moves into its future can be illustrated in many ways. For example, one problem already on the horizon lies in the increasing diversity of racial and ethnic types in the South's population (See Kasarda, Chapter 3; Frisbie, Chapter 6; and Moland, Chapter 7). Ethnic differences are tolerated when separated by time and place, but the increasing density of the population in the South, the close proximity of people in urban conglomerates, may give rise to intolerance and conflict. Deliberate education to generate understanding of strangers and tolerance of differences will be needed. The National Conference on Peacemaking and Conflict Resolution, developed by sociologist Margaret S. Herrman (and now located at George Mason University), moves in the right direction. Programs that facilitate personal adjustment of in-migrants to the South by inculcating understanding of local ways and techniques of adaptation achieve the same end. This is being done for international immigrants at Jubilee Partners near Comer, Georgia, a project of the Habitat for Humanity of Koinonia Partners.

Second, as Streib points out in Chapter 4, the elderly population in Florida and the border areas of the warm Gulf waters will continue to increase. The increase comes not from an aging of the South's population but largely from internal migration of retirees from the Midwest, the Middle States, and the East. The need for community services to the older population will continue to increase in order to manage adjustments to social and health problems, housing and recreational needs, social isolation, and occasional dependency. Efforts will be needed to facilitate their adjustment, as has been done in a number of communities with the help of sociologists and other social scientists. At the same time, the South must not overlook the welfare of other dependents—the culturally and educationally deprived, the strangers from foreign shores with problems of acculturation, and the handicapped.

Third, while the South has been largely spared many environmental problems characteristic of more industrialized regions, this avoidance of contamination by technological processes will not continue. Already some rivers and lakes are unfit for wildlife; the air around some cities is heavy with pollution; and concern is aroused by unsafe water, high noise decibels, and food contaminated with chemicals. Heightened public-awareness programs and legal steps to reduce the sources of pollutants are needed to preserve existing environmental amenities and limit threats to health and to the quality of life. The Oak Ridge National Laboratory in Tennessee is developing devices to monitor these threats scientifically. Social scientists must apply their talents to the organizational problems associated with bringing the community together to take action to purify the environment and reduce pollution. The challenge will require interdisciplinary efforts. Sociologist Tom Hood and associates at the University of Tennessee already are working on some of these problems.

The three problems mentioned above—ethnic conflict, aging population, and environmental contamination—illustrate problems the South must face in the immediate future. These and others must be the focus of the South's planning efforts as the South moves into its promising future.

References

Abbott, Shirley. 1983. *Womenfolks: Growing Up Down South*. New York: Ticknor and Fields.

Achenbaum, W. Andrew. 1978. *Old Age in a New Land*. Baltimore: Johns Hopkins University Press.

Alexander, Thomas B. 1983. "The Dimensions of Continuity across the Civil War." In *The Old South in the Crucible of War*, ed. Harry P. Owens and James J. Cooke, 81–97. Jackson: University Press of Mississippi.

Allport, Gordon W. 1954. *The Nature of Prejudice*. Reading, Mass.: Addison-Wesley.

Almanac of American Politics, 1986. 1985. New York: E. P. Dutton.

Alther, Lisa. 1975. *Kinflicks*. New York: New American Library.

Arendt, Hannah. 1963. *On Revolution*. New York: Viking.

Atchley, Robert C. 1985. *Social Forces and Aging*, 4th ed. Belmont: Wadsworth.

Atkinson, Maxine P., and Jacqueline Boles. 1985. "The Shaky Pedestal: Southern Ladies." *Southern Studies* 24:398–406.

Auletta, K. 1982. *The Underclass*. New York: Random House.

Badger, Tony. 1984. "Segregation and the Southern Business Elite." *Journal of American Studies* 18:105–109.

Ball, Richard E., and Lynn Robbins. 1984. "Marital Status and Life Satisfaction of Black Men." *Journal of Social and Personal Relationships* 1:459–70.

———. 1986. "Black Husbands' Satisfaction with their Family Lives." Paper presented at the Annual Meeting of the Southern Sociological Society, New Orleans, April.

Ball-Rokeach, Sandra J., and James F. Short, Jr. 1985. "Collective Violence: The Redress of Grievance and Public Policy." In *American Violence and Public Policy*, ed. Lynn A. Curtis, 155–80. New Haven: Yale University Press.

Banes, Ruth A. 1981. "Southern Women in Country Songs." *Journal of Regional Culture* (Fall/Winter):57–70.

———. 1985. "Mythology in Music: The Ballad of Loretta Lynn." *The Canadian Review of American Studies* 16(3)(Fall):283–300.

Bartley, Numan V. 1969. *The Rise of Massive Resistance: Race and Politics in the South During the 1950s*. Baton Rouge: Louisiana State University Press.

Bartley, Numan V., and Hugh D. Graham. 1975. *Southern Politics and the Second Reconstruction*. Baltimore: Johns Hopkins University Press.

Bean, Frank D., Harley L. Browning, and W. Parker Frisbie. 1984. "The Sociodemographic Characteristics of Mexican Immigrant Status Groups: Implications for Studying Undocumented Mexicans." *International Migration Review* 18:672–91.

Bean, Frank D., B. Lindsay Lowell, and Lowell Taylor. 1986. "Undocumented Mexican Immigrants and the Earnings of Other Workers in the United States." Revision of a paper presented at the Annual Meeting of the Population Association of America, San Francisco.

Bean, Frank D., Elizabeth H. Stephen, and Wolfgang Opitz. 1985. "The Mexican Origin Population in the United States: A Demographic Overview." In *The Mexican American Experience: An Interdisciplinary Anthology*, ed. Rodolfo O. de la Garza, Frank D. Bean, Charles M. Bonjean, Ricardo Romo, and Rodolfo Alvarez, 57–75. Austin: University of Texas Press.

Bean, Frank D., and Marta Tienda. 1987. *The Hispanic Population of the United States*. New York: Russell-Sage.

Bellows, Barbara L. 1985. "My children, gentlemen, are my own: Poor Women, the Urban Elite, and the Bonds of Obligation in Antebellum Charleston." In *The Web of Southern Social Relations: Women, Family, and Education*, ed. Walter J. Fraser, Jr., R. Frank Saunders, Jr., and Jon L. Waklyn, 52–71. Athens: University of Georgia Press.

Berkeley, Kathleen C. 1985. "Colored ladies also contributed: Black Women's Activities from Benevolence to Social Welfare, 1866–1896." In *The Web of Southern Social Relations: Women, Family, and Education*, ed. W. J. Fraser, R. F. Saunders, and J. L. Waklyn, 181–203. Athens: University of Georgia Press.

Berry, Mary Frances. 1971. *Black Resistance White Law*. New York: Appleton-Century-Crofts.

Betts, Doris. 1986. *Halfway Home and a Long Way to Go*. Research Triangle Park, North Carolina: The Southern Growth Policies Board.

Bianchi, Suzanne M. 1981. *Household Composition and Racial Inequality*. New Brunswick: Rutgers University Press.

Bianchi, Suzanne M., and Reynolds Farley. 1979. "Racial Differences in Family Living Arrangements and Economic Well-being: An Analysis of Recent Trends." *Journal of Marriage and the Family* 41:537–51.

Biggar, Jeanne C. 1979. "The Sunning of America: Migration to the Sunbelt." *Population Bulletin* 34(1). Washington, D.C.: Population Reference Bureau.

——. 1984. *The Graying of the Sunbelt: Population Trends and Public Policy, No. 6*. Washington, D.C.: Population Reference Bureau.

Billings, Dwight B. 1979. Planters and the Making of a "New South." *Class,*

Politics and Development in North Carolina, 1865–1900. Chapel Hill: University of North Carolina Press.

Black, Earl. 1976. *Southern Governors and Civil Rights.* Cambridge: Harvard University Press.

Black, Earl, and Merle Black. 1987. *Politics and Society in the South.* Cambridge: Harvard University Press.

Black, Merle. 1978. "Racial Composition of Congressional Districts and Support for Federal Voting Rights in the American South." *Social Science Quarterly* 59:435–50.

Blackburn, Simon. 1972. *Reason and Prediction.* Cambridge: University Press.

Blalock, Hubert M. 1956. "Economic Discrimination and Negro Increase." *American Sociological Review* 21:584–88.

_____. 1957. "Percent Nonwhite and Discrimination in the South." *American Sociological Review* 22:667–82.

_____. 1967. *Toward a Theory of Minority Group Relations.* New York: Wiley.

Blumer, Herbert. 1986. "The Future of the Color Line." In *The American South Comes of Age,* ed. Jack Bass and Thomas E. Terrill, 388–93. New York: Knopf.

Boles, Jacqueline, and Maxine P. Atkinson. 1986. "Ladies: South by Northwest." *Sociological Spectrum* 6(1):63–81.

Boles, Jacqueline, and Charlotte Tatro. 1979. "The Male Sex Role: Continuity and Change." Paper presented at the Annual Meeting of the American Psychiatric Association, Chicago, May.

Boles, Janet K. 1979. *The Politics of the Equal Rights Amendment: Conflict and the Decision Process.* New York and London: Longman.

Botsch, Robert. 1980. *We Shall Not Overcome: Populism and Southern Blue-Collar Workers.* Chapel Hill: University of North Carolina Press.

Bouvier, Leon F., and Robert W. Gardner. 1986. "Immigration to the U.S.: The Unfinished Story." *Population Bulletin* 41 (November):1–50.

Bowen, William. 1981. *Graduate Education in the Arts and Sciences: Prospectus for the Future, Report of the President.* Princeton, N.J.: Princeton University Press.

Bowers, William J. (with Glenn L. Pierce and John F. McDevitt). 1984. *Legal Homicide: Death as Punishment in America, 1864–1982.* Boston: Northeastern University Press.

Brabant, Sarah. 1986. "Socialization for Change: The Cultural Heritage of the Southern Woman." *Sociological Spectrum* 6(1):51–59.

Bradshaw, Benjamin S., and Frank D. Bean. 1973. "Trends in the Fertility of Mexican Americans, 1950–1970." *Social Science Quarterly* 53:688–96.

Breen, T. H. 1980. "Horses and Gentlemen: The Cultural Significance of Gambling among the Gentry of Virginia." In *The American Man,* ed. E. H. Pleck and J. H. Pleck, 77–106. Englewood Cliffs, N.J.: Prentice-Hall.

Brophy, William. 1982. "Active Acceptance—Active Containment: the

Dallas Story." In *Southern Businessmen and Desegregation,* ed. Elizabeth Jacoway and David L. Colburn, 137–50. Baton Rouge: Louisiana State University Press.

Browning, Harley L., and Ruth M. Cullen. 1983. "The Complex Formation of the U.S. Mexican-Origin Population." Texas Population Research Center Working Paper No. 5.020. Austin: University of Texas.

Bureau of the Census. 1972. *Census of Population: 1970. "General Social and Economic Characteristics." United States Summary.* PC(1)-1C. Washington, D.C.: Government Printing Office.

——. 1973a. *Census of Population: 1970. "Negro Population." Subject Reports.* PC(2)-1B. Washington, D.C.: Government Printing Office.

——. 1973b. *Census of Population: 1970. "Persons of Spanish Origin." Subject Reports.* PC(2)-1C. Washington, D.C.: Government Printing Office.

——. 1973c. "Persons of Spanish Origin in the United States, March 1972 and 1971." *Current Population Reports.* Series P-20, No. 250. Washington, D.C.: Government Printing Office.

——. 1973d. *Census of Population: 1970. "Puerto Ricans in the United States." Subject Reports.* PC(2)-1E. Washington, D.C.: Government Printing Office.

——. 1973e. *Low Income Population.* Subject Report Number PC(2)-9A. Washington, D.C.: Government Printing Office.

——. 1975. *Historical Statistics of the United States.* Vol. 1 and 2. Washington, D.C.: Government Printing Office.

——. 1977. *Statistical Abstract of the United States.* Washington, D.C.: Government Printing Office.

——. 1979. *The Social and Economic Status of the Black Population.* Special Studies Series P-23, No. 80. Washington, D.C.: Government Printing Office.

——. 1980. *General Social and Economic Characteristics: 1980.* Washington, D.C.: Government Printing Office.

——. 1981. *Statistical Abstract of the United States, 1981.* Washington, D.C.: Government Printing Office.

——. 1982a. *1980 Census of Population, General Social and Economic Characteristics, United States Summary.* Part I, PC80-1-C1. Washington, D.C.: Government Printing Office.

——. 1982b. *Money, Income and Poverty Status of Families and Persons in the United States: 1982. Current Population Reports.* Series P-60, No. 140. Washington, D.C.: Government Printing Office.

——. 1982c. *1980 Census of Population. Persons of Spanish Origin: 1980. Supplementary Report.* PC80-S1-7. Washington, D.C.: Government Printing Office.

——. 1983a. *Census of Population 1980: General Population Characteristics.* PC Series, Table 20. "Age by Race and Sex, 1911–80." Washington, D.C.: Government Printing Office.

_____. 1983b. *1980 Census of Population: Characteristics of the Population.* Vol. 1. (Chapter C: General Social and Economic Characteristics.) PC80-1-C1. Washington, D.C.: Government Printing Office.

_____. 1983c. *Supplementary Report. Ancestry of the Population by State: 1980.* PC80-S1-10. Washington, D.C.: Government Printing Office.

_____. 1984. *Characteristics of the Population below the Poverty Level: 1982. Current Population Reports: SA Series.* P-60, Number 144. Washington, D.C.: Government Printing Office.

_____. 1984a. *1980 Census of the Population.* Vol. 1. (Chapter D: Detailed Population Characteristics, United States Summary.) PC80-1-D1-A. Washington, D.C.: Government Printing Office.

_____. 1984b. *1980 Census of the Population.* Vol. 1. (Chapter D: Detailed Population Characteristics, Regions.) PC80-1-D1-B. Washington, D.C.: Government Printing Office.

_____. 1985. *Household and Family. Characteristics: March 1984.* (Current Population Reports. Population Characteristics.) P-20, No. 398. Washington, D.C.: Government Printing Office.

_____. 1985. 1983. 1978. 1976. 1974. *County Business Patterns, File 2.* "Machine-readable data file." Washington, D.C.: Government Printing Office.

_____. 1986. *Current Population Reports.* "Money Income and Poverty Status of Families and Persons in the United States." (P-60, No. 157). Washington, D.C.: Government Printing Office.

_____. 1988. *Poverty in the United States: 1986. Current Population Reports.* Series P-60, No. 160. Washington, D.C.: Government Pinting Office.

Burton, Orville Vernon. 1985. *In My Father's House Are Many Mansions: Family and Community in Edgefield, South Carolina.* Chapel Hill: University of North Carolina Press.

Bynum, Victoria. 1984. "On the Lowest Rung: Court Control over Poor White and Free Black Women." *Southern Exposure* 12:40–44.

Cardoso, Lawrence A. 1980. *Mexican Emigration to the United States, 1897–1931.* Tuscon: University of Arizona Press.

Carolina Times. Durham, North Carolina. 2/3/87. "St. Augustine's College Celebrates 120 Years of Progress."

Carter, Hodding. 1950. *Southern Legacy.* Baton Rouge: Louisiana State University Press.

Carter, Hodding III. 1985. "South Africa at Home: Reagan and the Revival of Racism." *Playboy* 33:106ff.

Cash, W. J. 1941. *The Mind of the South.* New York: Knopf.

Catt, Carrie Chapman, and Nettie Rogers Shuler. 1923. *Woman Suffrage and Politics: The Inner Story of the Suffrage Movement.* Seattle: University of Washington Press.

Center for Research on Women. n.d. *Bibliography on Southern Women.* Memphis, Tenn.: Memphis State University.

Chafe, William, 1980. *Civilities and Civil Rights: Greensboro, North Carolina and the Black Struggle for Freedom.* New York: Oxford.

Chandler, C. R., H. Paul Chalfant, and Craig P. Chalfant. 1984. "Cheaters Sometimes Win: Sexual Infidelity in Country Music." In *Forbidden Fruits: Taboos and Tabooism in Culture,* ed. Ray B. Browne, 133–44. Bowling Green, Ken.: Bowling Green University Press.

Chen, Yung-Ping. 1983. *Social Security in a Changing Society* (2nd ed.). Bryn Mawr, Penn.: McCahan Foundation.

Cherlin, Andrew, and Pamela B. Walters, 1981. "Trends in United States Men's and Women's Sex Role Attitudes, 1972–1978." *American Sociological Review* 46 (August):453–60.

Clinton, Catherine. 1982. *The Plantation Mistress.* New York: Pantheon.

———. 1985. "Caught in the Web of the Big House: Women and Slavery." In *The Web of Southern Social Relations: Women, Family, and Education,* ed. W. J. Fraser, R. F. Saunders, and J. L. Waklyn, 19–34. Athens: University of Georgia Press.

Cobb, James C. 1982. *The Selling of the South: The Southern Crusade for Industrial Development, 1936–1980.* Baton Rouge: Louisiana State University Press.

———. 1984. *Industrialization and Southern Society, 1877–1984.* Lexington: University of Kentucky Press.

Cooney, Rosemary S., and Alice E. C. Warren. 1979. "Declining Female Participation among Puerto Rican New Yorkers: A Comparison with Native White Non-Spanish New Yorkers." *Ethnicity* 6:281–97.

Cotterill, R. S. 1939. *The Old South.* Glendale, Calif.: Arthur H. Clark Co.

Courage, Myrna Morrison. 1987. "Structural Correlates of Views of Women's Work-Family Roles." Unpublished Ph.D. dissertation. Florida State University, Tallahassee.

Current, Richard N., T. Harry Williams, Frank Freidel, and Alan Brinkley. 1983. *American History: A Survey.* New York: Knopf.

Daniell, Rosemary. 1980. *Fatal Flowers: On Sin, Sex, and Suicide in the Deep South.* New York: Holt, Rinehart, and Winston.

Darden, Donna Kelleher. 1986. "Southern Women Writing about Southern Women: Jill McCorkle, Lisa Alther, Ellen Gilchrist, and Lee Smith." *Sociological Spectrum* 6(1):109–16.

Dauer, Manning J. 1972. "Florida: The Different State." In *The Changing Politics of the South,* ed. William C. Havard, 92–164. Baton Rouge: Louisiana State University Press.

Davis, Cary, Carl Haub, and JoAnne Willette. 1983. "U.S. Hispanics: Changing the Face of America." *Population Bulletin* 38:1–43.

Dean, Virginia, Patti Roberts, and Carroll Boone. 1984. "Comparable Worth under Various Federal and State Laws." In *Comparable Worth and Wage Discrimination,* ed. Helen Remick, 238–66. Philadelphia: Temple University Press.

de la Garza, Rodolfo O., and David Vaughn. 1984. "The Political Socialization of Chicano Elites: A Generational Approach." *Social Science Quarterly* 65:290–307.

Dempsey, J. P. 1961. *The Operation of the Right-to-Work Laws.* Milwaukee, Wisc.: Marquette University Press.

Department of Justice. 1961. *Uniform Crime Reports: Crime in the United States, 1960.* Washington, D.C.: Government Printing Office.

———. 1971. *Uniform Crime Reports: Crime in the United States, 1970.* Washington, D.C.: Government Printing Office.

———. 1981. *Uniform Crime Reports: Crime in the United States, 1980.* Washington, D.C.: Government Printing Office.

———. 1985. *Uniform Crime Reports: Crime in the United States, 1984.* Washington, D.C.: Government Printing Office.

Deutsch, Claudia. 1987. "The Ax Falls on Equal Opportunity." *The New York Times,* Jan. 4, Section 3, p. 1.

Dill, Bonnie Thornton. 1983. "Race, Class and Gender: Prospects for an All-Inclusive Sisterhood." *Feminist Studies* 9:131–50.

Dillman, Caroline M. 1986. "The Sparsity of Research and Publications of Southern Women: Definitional Complexities, Methodological Problems, and other Impediments." *Sociological Spectrum* 6:7–29.

Dillman, Caroline Matheny, ed. 1986. "Southern Women." *Sociological Spectrum* (Special Issue) 6:7–24.

Dougherty, Molly C. 1978. *Becoming a Woman in Rural Black Culture.* New York: Holt, Rinehart and Winston.

Dowd, James J., and Vern L. Bengtson. 1978. "Aging Minority Populations: An Examination of the Double Jeopardy Hypothesis." *Journal of Gerontology* 33(3):427–36.

Dowdall, George W. 1974. "White Gains from Black Subordination in 1960 and 1970." *Social Problems* 22:162–83.

Drake, St. Clair, and Horace R. Cayton. 1945. *Black Metropolis, A Study of Negro Life in a Northern City.* New York: Harper & Row.

Du Bois, W. E. B. 1903/1961. *The Souls of Black Folk: Essay and Sketches.* Greenwich, Conn.: Fawcett.

Ducey, Mitchell F. 1984a. *The Commission on Interracial Cooperation Papers, 1919–1944,* and *The Association of Southern Women for the Prevention of Lynching Papers, 1930–1942.* Ann Arbor, Mich.: University Microfilms International.

———. 1984b. *The Southern Regional Council Papers, 1944–1968.* Ann Arbor, Mich.: University Microfilms International.

Duncan, Beverly, and Stanley Lieberson. 1971. *Metropolis and Region in Transition.* Beverly Hills: Sage Publications.

Duncan, Otis Dudley, and Beverly Duncan. 1955. "Residential Distribution and Occupational Stratification." *American Journal of Sociology* 60:493–503.

Dunn, Edgar S. 1960. "A Statistical and Analytical Technique for Regional Analysis." *Papers and Proceedings for the Regional Science Association* 6.

————. 1980. *The Development of the U.S. Urban System.* Baltimore: Johns Hopkins University Press.

Dykeman, Wilma, and James Stokely. 1962. *Seeds of Southern Change: The Life of Will Alexander.* Chicago: University of Chicago Press.

Egerton, John. 1974. *The Americanization of Dixie.* New York: Harper's Magazine Press.

Elazar, Daniel. 1972. *American Federalism.* New York: Crowell.

Emerson, Rupert, and Martin Kilson. 1965. "The American Dilemma in a Changing World: The Rise of Africa and the Negro American." In *The American Negro,* ed. Talcott Parsons and Kenneth B. Clark, 620–55. Boston: Beacon Press.

English, John. W. 1985. "The Making of a Southern Gentleman." *Atlanta Magazine,* pp. 104–106, 180–81.

Escott, Paul D. 1983. "The Failure of Confederate Nationalism: The Old South's Class System in the Crucible of War." In *The Old South in the Crucible of War,* ed. Harry P. Owens and James J. Cooke, 15–28. Jackson: University Press of Mississippi.

Estes, Carroll L. 1979. *The Aging Enterprise.* San Francisco: Jossey-Bass.

Estes, Carroll L., J. H. Swan, and L. E. Gerard. 1982. "Dominant and Competing Paradigms: Toward a Political Economy of Aging." *Aging and Society* 2(2):151–64.

Fahey, Charles, and Mary Ann Lewis. 1984. "Catholics." In *Handbook on the Aged in the United States,* ed. Erdman B. Palmore, 145–54. Westport, Conn.: Greenwood.

Falk, William W., and Thomas A. Lyson. 1988. *High Tech, Low Tech, No Tech.* Ithaca: State University of New York Press.

Farley, Reynolds. 1977. "Trends in Racial Inequalities: Have the Gains of the 1960s Disappeared in the 1970s?" *American Sociological Review* 42:189–208.

————. 1984. *Blacks and Whites: Narrowing the Gap?* Cambridge: Harvard University Press.

Fein, Rashi. 1965. "An Economic and Social Profile of the Negro American." In *The Negro American,* ed. Talcott Parsons and Kenneth B. Clark, 102–33. Boston: Beacon Press.

Feinberg, William E. 1985. "Are Affirmative Action and Economic Growth Alternative Paths to Racial Equality?" *American Sociological Review* 50:561–71.

Ferriss, Abbott L. 1986. "1984 Survey of Post-Doctoral Jobs." *The Southern Sociologist,* 16(Winter–Spring):12.

Fichter, Joseph H., and George L. Maddox. 1965. "Religion in the South, Old and New." In *The South in Continuity and Change,* ed. J. C. McKinney and E. T. Thompson, 357–83. Durham, N.C.: Duke University Press.

Fischer, David H. 1978. *Growing Old in America* (expanded edition). New York: Oxford University Press.

Fishman, Joshua, Vladimir Nahirny, John Hofman, and Robert Hayden. 1966. *Language Loyalty in the United States.* The Hague: Mouton.

Fleming, Harold C. 1965. "The Federal Executive and Civil Rights: 1961–1965." In *The Negro American*, ed. Talcott Parsons and Kenneth B. Clark, 371–400. Boston: Beacon Press.

Flexner, Eleanor. 1959. *Century of Struggle: The Women's Rights Movement in the United States*. Cambridge: Harvard University Press.

Fligstein, Neil. 1981. *Going North: Migration of Blacks and Whites from the South, 1900–1950*. New York: Academic Press.

Florida Committee on Aging. 1986. *Pathways to the Future*, II. Tallahassee: The Executive Office of the Governor, The Capitol.

Flynn, Cynthia B., Charles F. Longino, Jr., Robert F. Wiseman, and Jeanne C. Biggar. 1985. "The Redistribution of America's Older Population: Major Migration Patterns for Three Census Decades, 1960–1980." *The Gerontologist* 25:292–96.

Flynt, J. Wayne. 1985. "Folks Like Us: The Southern Poor White Family, 1965–1985." In *The Web of Southern Social Relations: Women, Family, and Education*, ed. W. J. Fraser, R. F. Saunders, and J. L. Waklyn. Athens: The University of Georgia Press.

Fossett, Mark A., and Gray Swicegood. 1982. "Rediscovering City Differences in Racial Occupational Inequality." *American Sociological Review* 47:681–89.

Fossett, Mark A., et al. 1986. "Racial Occupational Inequality, 1940–1980: National and Regional Trends." *American Sociological Review* 51:421–29.

Fowlkes, Diane L. 1984. "Women in Georgia Electoral Politics: 1970–1978." *The Social Science Journal* 21(January):43–55.

Fox-Genovese, Elizabeth, and Eugene Genovese. 1986. "The Mind of the Southern Slaveholder." *Social Science* 71(Spring):54–57.

Franklin, John Hope. 1980. *From Slavery to Freedom*. New York: Vintage.

Frazier, E. Franklin. 1957. *The Negro in the United States*. New York: Macmillan.

Frederickson, Mary. 1982. "Four Decades of Change: Black Workers in Southern Textiles, 1941–1981." *Radical America* 16:27–44.

Freymeyer, Robert H. 1982. "Republicans Flow South." *American Demographics* 4(June):35–37.

Friedman, Jean E. 1985. *The Enclosed Garden: Women and Community in the Evangelical South, 1830–1900*. Chapel Hill: University of North Carolina Press.

Frisbie, W. Parker, et al. 1985. *Household and Family Demography of Hispanics, Blacks and Anglos*. Final NICHD Report. Austin: University of Texas Population Research Center.

———. 1986. "Variations in Patterns of Marital Instability among Hispanics." *Journal of Marriage and the Family* 48:99–106.

Frisbie, W. Parker, and Frank D. Bean. 1978. "Some Issues in the Demographic Study of Racial and Ethnic Populations." In *The Demography of Racial and Ethnic Groups*, ed. Frank D. Bean and W. Parker Frisbie, 143–63. New York: Academic Press.

Frisbie, W. Parker, and Lisa J. Neidert. 1977. "Inequality and the Relative Size of Minority Populations: A Comparative Analysis: *American Journal of Sociology* 82:1007–30.

The Gallup Report. 1982. *Women.* Report No. 203 (August).

———. 1985. *Religion in America, 50 Years: 1935–1985.* Report No. 236 (May).

Gans, Herbert J. 1962. *The Urban Villagers: Group and Class in the Life of Italian-Americans.* New York: The Free Press.

Garwood, Alfred N. 1986. *Almanac of the 50 States, Basic Data Profiles with Comparative Tables.* Newburyport, Mass.: Information Publications.

Gaston, Paul. 1976. *The New South Creed: A Study in Southern Mythmaking.* Baton Rouge: Louisiana State University Press.

Genovese, Eugene. 1974. *Roll, Jordan, Roll: The World the Slaves Made.* New York: Pantheon Books.

Gibson, Rose C. 1986. "Blacks in an Aging Society." *Daedalus* 115(1): 349–71.

Gilbert, Neil. 1983. *Capitalism and the Welfare State: Dilemmas of Social Benevolence.* New Haven: Yale University Press.

Gittler, Joseph B. 1956. *Understanding Minority Groups.* New York: Wiley.

Glenn, Norval D. 1963. "Occupational Benefits to Whites from the Subordination of Negroes." *American Sociological Review* 28:443–48.

———. 1964. "The Relative Size of the Negro Population and Negro Occupational Status." *Social Forces* 43:42–49.

———. 1966. "White Gains from Negro Subordination." *Social Problems* 14:159–78.

———. 1967. "Massification versus Differentiation: Some Trend Data from National Surveys." *Social Forces* 46(December):172–80.

Glenn, Norval D., and J. L. Simmons. 1967. "Are Regional Cultural Differences Diminishing?" *Public Opinion Quarterly* 31(Summer):176–93.

Glick, Paul. 1984. "Marriage, Divorce and Living Arrangements." *Journal of Family Issues* 5:7–26.

Godbey, Karolyn. 1987. "Comparable Worth in the Fifty States." Unpublished Ph.D. dissertation. Florida State University, Tallahassee.

Goldfield, David M. 1982. *Cotton Fields and Skyscrapers: Southern City and Region, 1607–1980.* Baton Rouge: Louisiana State University Press.

Goldman, Robert, and Paul Luebke. 1985. "Corporate Capital Moves South: Competing Class Interests and Labor Relations in North Carolina's 'New' Political Economy." *Journal of Political and Military Sociology* 13:17–32.

Gordon, Milton M. 1964. *Assimilation in American Life.* New York: Oxford University Press.

Grady, Henry W. 1890. *The New South.* New York: Robert Bonner's Sons.

Granthan, Dewey W. 1983. *Southern Progressivism: The Reconciliation of Progress and Tradition.* Knoxville: University of Tennessee Press.

Grasmick, Harold G. 1973. "Social Change and the Wallace Movement in the South." Unpublished Ph.D. dissertation. University of North Carolina, Chapel Hill.

Grebler, Leo, Joan W. Moore, and Ralph C. Guzman. 1970. *The Mexican American People.* New York: The Free Press.

Grenier, Charles E. 1985. "The Political Mobilization of the Black Electorate in Louisiana, 1932–1980: Black Voter Registration Trends and Correlates." *Social Development Issues* 9(Fall):40–55.

Grenier, Gilles. 1984. "Shifts to English as Usual Language by Americans of Spanish Mother Tongue." *Social Science Quarterly* 65:537–550.

Gross, Edward. 1968. "Plus Ca Change . . . ? The Sexual Structure of Occupations Over Time." *Social Problems* 16:198–208.

Hadden, Jeffrey. 1981. *Prime Time Preachers: The Rising Power of Televangelism.* Reading, Mass.: Addison-Wesley.

Hall, Jacquelyn Dowd. 1984. "The Mind that Burns in Each Body: Women, Rape, and Racial Violence." *Southern Exposure* 12:61–71.

Hamilton, C. Horace. 1964. "The Negro Leaves the South." *Demography* 1:273–95.

Hammond, Matthew. 1897. *The Cotton Industry: An Essay in American Economic History, Part I: The Cotton Culture and the Cotton Trade.* New York: Macmillan Co.

Hancock, Gordon B. 1964. "Writing a 'New Charter of Southern Race Relations.'" *New South* 19(January):18–21.

Havard, William C., ed. 1972. *The Changing Politics of the South.* Baton Rouge: Louisiana State University Press.

Havard, William C., and Manning J. Dauer. 1980. "The Southern Political Science Association: A Fifty Year Legacy." *The Journal of Politics* 42:664–86.

Hawkins, Darnell. 1986. "Black Overimprisonment: South and North." *Social Science* 71(Spring):58–64.

Hawley, Amos. 1981. *Urban Society: An Ecological Approach.* New York: John Wiley and Sons.

Henley, Beth. 1982. *Crimes of the Heart: A Play.* New York: Viking Press, Penguin Books.

Hernandez, Jose, Leo Estrada, and David Alvirez. 1973. "Census Data and the Problem of Conceptually Defining the Mexican American Population." *Social Science Quarterly* 53:671–87.

Hill, Samuel S., Jr., ed. 1984. *Encyclopedia of Religion in the South.* Macon, Ga.: Mercer University Press.

_____. 1985. "Religion and Region in America." *Annals, AAPS* 480: 132–41.

Himes, Joseph S. 1966. "The Functions of Racial Conflict." *Social Forces* 45:1–10.

_____. 1973. *Racial Conflict in American Society.* Columbus, Ohio: Merrill.

Holloway, Harry, and Ted Robinson. 1981. "The Abiding South: White Attitudes and Regionalism Reexamined." In *Perspectives on the American*

South, ed. Merle Black and John Shelton Reed, 227–52. Vol. 1. New York: Gordon and Breach.

Horan, Patrick M., and Charles M. Tolbert II. 1984. *The Organization of Work in Rural and Urban Labor Markets*. Boulder, Colo., and London: Westview Press.

Howe, Irving, and B. J. Widick. 1969. "The U. A. W. Fights Race Prejudice." In *The Making of Black America*, ed. August Meier and Elliot Rudwick, 234–44. New York: Atheneum.

Huber, Betina. 1984. *Employment Patterns in Sociology: Recent Trends and Future Prospects*. Washington, D.C.: American Sociological Association.

Huff-Corzine, Lin, Jay Corzine, and David C. Moore. 1986. "Southern Exposure: Deciphering the South's Influence on Homicide Rates." *Social Forces* 64:906–24.

Hunter, Floyd. 1980. *Community Power Succession: Atlanta's Policy-Makers Revisited*. Chapel Hill: University of North Carolina Press.

Hurlbert, Jeanne S. 1984. "The South as a Subculture: An Empirical Test of the Hypothesis of Cultural Distinctiveness." M.A. thesis, University of North Carolina, Chapel Hill.

Hurston, Zora Neale. 1937/1961. *Their Eyes Were Watching God*. Urbana and Chicago: University of Illinois Press.

Jackson, G., G. Masnick, R. Bolton, S. Bartlett, and J. Pitkin. 1981. *Regional Diversity: Growth in the United States, 1960–1990*. Boston: Auburn House Publishing Co.

Jackson, Jesse. 1986. "The Rainbow Is Emerging." *Focus*. Washington, D.C.: Joint Center for Political Studies.

Jacoway, Elizabeth. 1982. "An Introduction: Civil Rights and the Changing South." In *Southern Businessmen and Desegregation*, ed. Elizabeth Jacoway and David L. Colburn, 1–14. Baton Rouge: Louisiana State University Press.

Jaffe, A. J., Ruth C. Cullen, and Thomas D. Boswell. 1980. *The Changing Demography of Spanish Americans*. New York: Academic Press.

Janiewski, Dolores. 1983. "Sisters under Their Skins: Southern Working Women, 1880–1950." In *Sex, Race, and the Role of Women in the South*, ed. Joanne V. Hawks and Sheila L. Skemp, 13–35. Jackson: University Press of Mississippi.

———. 1985. *Sisterhood Denied: Race, Gender and Class in a South Community*. Philadelphia: Temple University Press.

Jaynes, Gregory. 1983. "In Alabama: Voting Dry and Practicing Wet." *Time Magazine*, March 7, 10–11.

Johnson, Leanor B. 1978. "Sexual Behavior of Southern Blacks." In *The Black Family: Essays and Studies*, ed. Robert Staples, 80–93. 2nd ed. Belmont: Wadsworth.

Johnson, N. E., and C. S. Stokes. 1984. "Southern Traditionalism and Sex-Role Ideology: A Research Note." *Sex Roles* 10:10–17.

Joint Center for Political Studies. 1974. *National Roster of Black Elected*

Officials. Volume 4. Washington, D.C.

———. 1979. *National Roster of Black Elected Officials.* Washington, D.C.

———. 1985. *Black Elected Officials: A National Roster.* New York: UNIPUB.

Jones, Anne Goodwyn. 1983. "Southern Literary Women as Chroniclers of Southern Life." In *Sex, Race, and the Role of Women in the South,* ed. Joanne V. Hawks and Sheila L. Skemp, 75–93. Jackson: University Press of Mississippi.

Jones, Jacqueline. 1985. *Labor of Love, Labor of Sorrow: Black Women, Work and the Family from Slavery to the Present.* New York: Basic Books.

Jorgensen, Carl C. 1978. "The End of 'Institutional Racism'?" *The Black Sociologist* 7:26–30.

Kahana, Eva, and Boaz Kahana. 1984. "Jews." In *Handbook on the Aged in the United States,* ed. Erdman B. Palmore, 155–79. Westport, Conn.: Greenwood.

Kanter, Rosabeth M. 1977. *Men and Women of the Corporation.* New York: Basic Books.

Kasarda, John D. 1980. "The Implications of Contemporary Redistribution Trends for National Urban Policy." *Social Science Quarterly* 61(3): 373–400.

———. 1985. "Urban Change and Minority Opportunities." In *The New Urban Reality,* ed. Paul Peterson, 36–67. Washington, D.C.: Brookings Institution.

———. 1987. "Jobs, Migration, and Emerging Urban Mismatches." In *Urban Change and Poverty,* ed. Michael McGeary and Laurence E. Lynn, 148–98. Washington, D.C.: National Academy Press.

Kasarda, John D., and Michael D. Irwin. 1987. "National Business Cycles and Community Competition for Jobs." Unpublished manuscript. University of North Carolina, Chapel Hill.

Key, V. O., Jr. 1949. *Southern Politics.* New York: Random House.

Killian, Lewis M. 1970. *White Southerners.* New York: Random House.

———. 1985. *White Southerners,* 2nd ed. New York: Random House.

King, Allan G., B. Lindsay Lowell, and Frank D. Bean. 1986. "The Effects of Hispanic Immigrants on the Earnings of Native Hispanic Americans." *Social Science Quarterly* 67:673–89.

King, Florence. 1975. *Southern Ladies and Gentlemen.* New York: Bantam.

Kingson, Eric R. 1983. *Social Security and You.* New York: World Almanac Publications.

Kinney, David. 1986. "Labor Pains." *Business: North Carolina* 6(April): 16–22.

Krout, John A. 1986. *The Aged in Rural America.* Westport, Conn.: Greenwood.

Lawson, Steven F. 1982. "From Sit-in to Race Riot: Businessmen, Blacks and the Pursuit of Moderation in Tampa, 1960–67." In *Southern Businessmen and Desegregation,* ed. Elizabeth Jacoway and David L. Colburn, 257–81. Baton Rouge: Louisiana State University Press.

Lazarsfeld, Paul F., and Wagner Thielens, Jr. 1958. *The Academic Mind: Social Scientists in a Time of Crisis.* Glencoe, Ill.: The Free Press.

Lee, David, and Ronald Schultz. 1982. "Regional Patterns of Female Status in the United States." *Professional Geographer* 34(1):32–41.

Leslie, Kent Anderson. 1986. "A Myth of the Southern Lady: Antebellum Proslavery Rhetoric and the Proper Place of Women." *Sociological Spectrum* 6(1):31–49.

Leuchtenburg, William E. 1963. *Franklin D. Roosevelt and the New Deal 1932–1940.* New York: Harper & Row.

Levin, Jeffrey, and Kyriakos S. Markides. 1986. "Religious Attendance and Subjective Health." *Journal for the Scientific Study of Religion* 25(1): 31–40.

Lieberson, Stanley, and Glenn Fuguit. 1967. "Negro-White Occupational Differences in the Absence of Discrimination." *American Journal of Sociology* 73:188–200.

Litwack, Leon F. 1983. "Many Thousands Gone: Black Southerners and the Confederacy." In *The Old South in the Crucible of War*, ed. Harry P. Owens and James J. Cooke, 46–63. Jackson: University Press of Mississippi.

Lofton, Paul S., Jr. 1982. "Calm and Exemplary: Desegregation in Columbia, South Carolina." In *Southern Businessmen and Desegregation*, ed. Elizabeth Jacoway and David L. Colburn, 70–81. Baton Rouge: Louisiana State University Press.

Longino, C. F., Jr., and J. C. Biggar. 1981. "The Impact of Retirement Migration on the South." *The Gerontologist* 21:283–90.

Longino, Charles F., Jr., et al. 1984. *The Retirement Migration Project. Final Report to the National Institute on Aging.* Washington, D.C.: National Institute on Aging.

Lopez, David. 1978. "Chicano Language Loyalty in an Urban Setting." *Sociology and Social Research* 62:267–78.

Lorber, Judith. 1986. "Dismantling Noah's Ark." *Sex Roles* 14:567–80.

Luebke, Paul. 1981. "Corporate Conservatism and Government Moderation in North Carolina." In *Perspectives on the American South*, ed. Merle Black and John S. Reid, 107–28. New York: Gordon and Breach.

———. 1985. "North Carolina—Still in the Progressive Mold?" North Carolina's 400th Anniversary Special Edition, *The News and Observer.* Raleigh, North Carolina, July.

Luebke, Paul, Bob McMahon, and Jeff Risberg. 1979. "Selective Industrial Recruitment in North Carolina." *Working Papers for a New Society* 6(March–April):14–17.

Luebke, Paul, Steven Peters, and John Wilson. 1986. "The Political Economy of Microelectronics in North Carolina." In *High Hopes for High Tech: The Microelectronics Industry in North Carolina*, ed. Dale Whittington, 310–28. Chapel Hill: University of North Carolina Press.

Luebke, Paul, and Joseph Schneider. 1987. "Economic and Racial Ideology in the North Carolina Elite." In *Perspectives on the American South, 5*, ed.

James C. Cobb and Charles R. Wilson, 129–43. New York: Gordon and Breach Science Publishers.

Luebke, Paul, and John F. Zipp. 1983. "Social Class and Attitudes Toward Big Business in the United States." *Journal of Political and Military Sociology* 11:251–64.

McCleary, Richard, and Richard A. Hay, Jr. 1980. *Applied Time Series Analysis for the Social Sciences*. Beverly Hills: Sage.

McEaddy, Beverly J. 1976. "Women Who Head Families: A Socioeconomic Analysis." *Monthly Labor Review* 99:3–9.

McKern, Sharon S. 1979. *Redneck Mothers, Good Ol' Girls, and Other Southern Belles: A Celebration of the Women of Dixie*. New York: Viking Press.

McKinney, John C., and Linka Brookover Bourque. 1975. "The National Incorporation of a Region." In *Group Identity in the South: Dialogue Between the Technological and the Humanistic*, ed. Harold F. Kaufman, J. Kenneth Morland, and Herbert H. Fockler. Mississippi State University: Mississippi State Department of Sociology (original publication in 1971).

McLemore, S. Dale. 1980. *Racial and Ethnic Relations in America*. Boston: Allyn and Bacon.

McLemore, S. Dale, and Ricardo Romo. 1985. "The Origins and Development of the Mexican American People." In *The Mexican American Experience: An Interdisciplinary Anthology*, ed. Rodolfo O. de la Garza, Frank D. Bean, Charles M. Bonjean, Ricardo Romo, and Rodolfo Alvarez, 3–32. Austin: University of Texas Press.

McWhiney, Grady, and Perry D. Jamieson. 1982. *Attack and Die: Civil War Military Tactics and the Southern Heritage*. University, Ala.: University of Alabama Press.

Maddox, George L. 1982. "Challenges for Health Policy and Planning." In *International Perspectives on Aging: Population and Policy Challenges*, ed. Robert H. Binstock, Wing-Sun Chow, and James H. Schulz, 127–58. New York: United Nations Fund for Population Activities.

Main, Eleanor C., Gerard S. Gryski, and Beth S. Schapiro. 1984. "Different Perspectives: Southern State Legislators' Attitudes about Women in Politics." *The Social Science Journal* 21(January):21–28.

Marshall, F. Ray. 1967. *Labor in the South*. Cambridge: Harvard University Press.

Martin, E. P., and J. Martin. 1978. *The Black Extended Family*. Chicago: University of Chicago Press.

Martin, Patricia Yancey, Marie W. Osmond, Susan Hesselbart, and Meredith Wood. 1980. "The Significance of Gender as a Social and Demographic Correlate of Sex-Roles Attitudes." *Sociological Focus* 13(October): 383–96.

Massey, Douglas. 1979. "Effects of Socioeconomic Factors on the Residential Segregation of Black and Spanish Americans in U.S. Urbanized Areas." *American Sociological Review* 44:1015–22.

Massey, Douglas S., and Brooks Bitterman. 1985. "Explaining the Paradox of

Puerto Rican Segregation." *Social Forces* 64(December):306–31.

Matthews, Donald R., and James W. Prothro. 1963. "Social and Economic Factors and Negro Voter Registration in the South." *American Political Science Review* 57:24–44.

Merton, Robert K. 1976. *Sociological Ambivalence and Other Essays.* New York: The Free Press.

Middleton-Kern, Susan. 1986. "Magnolias and Microchips: Regional Subcultural Constructions of Femininity." *Sociological Spectrum* 6(1):83–107.

Miller, James L., Jr. 1967. "The Southern Regional Education Board: Continuity and Change." *School and Society* 95(March):184–85.

Mills, C. Wright. 1959. *White Collar.* New York: Oxford.

Mirowsky, John, and Catherine E. Ross. 1984. "Language Networks and Social Status among Mexican Americans." *Social Science Quarterly* 65:551–64.

Mitchell, Margaret. 1936/1968. *Gone With The Wind.* New York: Macmillan.

Mitchell, Wesley C. 1941. *Business Cycles and Their Causes.* Berkeley: University of California Press.

Mizell, Terry. 1983. "Life Beyond the Grove and How to Get There." *The Southern Sociologist* 15(Winter):16–18.

Moland, John, Jr. 1981. "The Black Population." In *Nonmetropolitan America in Transition,* ed. Amos H. Hawley and Sara Mills Mazie, 464–501. Chapel Hill: University of North Carolina Press.

Monthly Magazine of North Carolina Citizens Association, February 1978. Raleigh, North Carolina.

Moody, Ann. 1968. *Coming of Age in Mississippi.* New York: Dial Press.

Morgan, David. 1972. *Suffragists and Democrats: The Politics of Woman Suffrage in America.* Lansing: Michigan State University Press.

Moynihan, Daniel Patrick. 1965. *The Negro Family, A Case for National Action.* Washington, D.C.: Government Printing Office.

Mullin, Michael. 1976. *American Negro Slavery: A Documentary History.* Columbia: University of South Carolina Press.

Mullins, Terry, and Paul Luebke. 1982. "Symbolic Victory and Political Reality in the Southern Textile Industry: The Meaning of the J. P. Stevens Union Contract." *Journal of Labor Research* 3:81–88.

Myers, George C. 1981. "The Demographically Emergent South." In *The Population of the South: Structure and Change in Social Demographic Context,* ed. Dudley L. Poston, Jr., and Robert H. Weller, 268–82. Austin: University of Texas Press.

Myrdal, Gunnar. 1944. *An American Dilemma: The Negro Problem and Modern Democracy.* New York: Harper and Row, revised 1964, McGraw-Hill.

The National American Women Suffrage Association. 1940. *Victory: How Women Won It. A Centennial Symposium 1840–1940.* New York: H. W. Wilson.

National Commission for Employment Policy. 1982. *Hispanics and Jobs:*

Barriers to Progress. Washington, D.C.: National Commission for Employment Policy.

Neugarten, Bernice L., and Dail A. Neugarten. 1986. "Age in the Aging Society." *Daedalus* 115(1):31–49.

Newman, Dale. 1978. "Work and Community in a Southern Textile Town." *Labor History* 19:204–25.

Newman, Robert J. 1984. *Growth in the American South: Changing Regional Employment and Wage Patterns in the 1960s and 1970s*. New York: New York University Press.

Nickens, Lois Carolyn. 1984. "Functional Assessment and Coping Behaviors Among the Rural Black Elderly." Ph.D. dissertation. University of Florida, Gainesville.

Odum, Howard W. 1936. *Southern Regions of the United States*. Chapel Hill: University of North Carolina Press.

Odum, Howard W., and Harry E. Moore. 1938. *American Regionalism: A Cultural Historical Approach to National Integration*. New York: Henry Holt and Co.

Olmedo, Esteban L. 1979. "Acculturation: A Psychometric Perspective." *American Psychologist* 34:1061–70.

Olson, Laura Katz. 1982. *The Political Economy of Aging*. New York: Columbia University Press.

Orfield, Gary. 1983. *Public School Desegregation in the United States, 1968–1980*. Washington, D.C.: Joint Study for Political Studies.

Ortiz, Vilma. n.d. "Changes in the Characteristics of Puerto Rican Migrants from 1955 to 1980." Madison: University of Wisconsin Center for Demography.

Padilla, Felix M. 1984. "On the Nature of Latino Ethnicity." *Social Science Quarterly* 65:651–64.

Passel, Jeffrey S., and Karen A. Woodrow. 1984. "Geographic Distribution of Undocumented Immigrants: Estimates of Undocumented Aliens Counted in the 1980 Census by State." *International Migration Review* 18:642–71.

Payne, Barbara P. 1984. "Protestants." In *Handbook on the Aged in the United States*, ed. Erdman B. Palmore, 181–98. Westport, Conn.: Greenwood.

Payton, Boyd E. 1970. *Scapegoat: Prejudice-Politics-Prison*. Philadelphia: Whitmore Publishing Co.

Percy, Walker. 1977. "Questions They Never Asked Me." *Esquire* 88(December):170–72, 184–94.

Perez, Lisandro. 1986. "Cubans in the United States." *The Annals of the American Academy of Political and Social Science* 487:126–37.

Perloff, H. S., E. S. Dunn, E. Lampard, and R. F. Muth. 1960. *Regions, Resources, and Economic Growth*. Baltimore: Johns Hopkins University Press.

Pinckney, Josephine. 1934. "Bulwarks against Change." In *Culture in the*

South, ed. W. T. Couch, 40–51. Chapel Hill: University of North Carolina Press.

Plisko, Valena White, ed. 1983. *The Condition of Education*. Washington, D.C.: Office of Education.

Portes, Alejandro. 1978. "Migration and Underdevelopment." *Politics and Society* 8:1–48.

Portes, Alejandro, and Robert Bach. 1985. *Latin Journey: A Longitudinal Study of Cuban and Mexican Immigrants in the United Sates*. Berkeley: University of California Press.

Poston, Dudley L., Jr., and David Alvirez. 1973. "On the Cost of Being a Mexican American Worker." *Social Science Quarterly* 53:697–709.

Potter, David. 1964. "The Idea of the South: Pursuit of a Central Theme." *Journal of Southern History* 30(November):451–62.

Prestage, Jewel L. 1970. "Black Politics and the Kerner Report: Concerns and Directions." In *Black Conflict with White America*, ed. Jack R. Van Der Slik, 325–38. Columbus: Charles E. Merrill.

Preston, Samuel H. 1974. "Differential Fertility, Unwanted Fertility, and Racial Trends in Occupational Achievement." *American Sociological Review* 39:492–506.

Queen, Stuart A., Robert W. Habenstein, and Jill S. Quadagno. 1985. *The Family in Various Cultures*. New York: Harper and Row.

Raper, Arthur F. 1933. *The Tragedy of Lynching*. Chapel Hill: University of North Carolina Press.

———. 1936. *Preface to Peasantry*. Chapel Hill: University of North Carolina Press.

Raper, Arthur F., and Ira De A. Reid. 1941. *Sharecropeprs All*. Chapel Hill: University of North Carolina Press.

Reed, John Shelton. 1974. *The Enduring South: Subcultural Persistence in Mass Society*. Chapel Hill: University of North Carolina Press.

———. 1982. *One South: An Ethnic Approach to Regional Culture*. Baton Rouge: Louisiana State University Press.

———. 1983. *Southerners: The Social Psychology of Sectionalism*. Chapel Hill: University of North Carolina Press.

———. 1986. *The Enduring South: Subcultural Persistance in Mass Society* (rev. ed.). Chapel Hill: University of North Carolina Press.

Reed, John Shelton, and Merle Black. 1985. "How Southerners Gave Up Jim Crow." *New Perspectives* 17(Fall):15–19.

Reed, Roy. 1976. "Revisiting the Southern Mind." *New York Times Magazine* 5(December):42–43, 99–109.

Rindfuss, Ronald R. 1978. "Changing Patterns of Fertility in the South: A Social-Demographic Examination." *Social Forces* 57(December):621–35.

Rindfuss, Ronald R., John Shelton Reed, and Craig St. John. 1978. "A Fertility Reaction to a Historic Event: Southern White Birthrates and the 1954 Desegregation Ruling." *Science* 201 (14 July):178–80.

Roberts, Steven V. 1986. "Phil Gramm's Crusade against the Deficit." *New York Times Magazine* (30 March):20–23, 40, 57, 60.

Robertson, A Haeworth. 1981. *The Coming Revolution in Social Security.* McLean, Va.: Security Press.

Roland, Charles P. 1960. *The Confederacy.* Chicago: University of Chicago Press.

Rosa, Jean-Jacques, ed. 1982. *The World Crisis in Social Security.* San Francisco: Institute for Contemporary Study.

Rose, Richard, and Guy Peters. 1978. *Can Government Go Bankrupt?* New York: Basic Books.

Rose, Willie Lee. 1976. *A Documentary History of Slavery in North America.* New York: Oxford University Press.

Rosenwaike, Ira (with Barbara Logue). 1986. *The Extreme Aged in America: A Portrait of an Expanding Population.* Westport, Conn.: Greenwood.

Ross, Heather L., and Isabel V. Sawhill. 1975. *Time of Transition: The Growth of Families Headed by Women.* Washington D.C.: The Urban Institute.

Rossi, Alice. 1980. "Life-span Theories and Women's Lives." *Signs* 6:4–32.

Russell, Gladys Trentham. n.d. *Call Me Hillbilly.* Alcoa, Tenn.: Russell Publishing Company.

Sallis, Charles, and John Quincy Adams. 1982. "Desegregation in Jackson, Mississippi." In *Southern Businessmen and Desegregation*, ed. Elizabeth Jacoway and David L. Colburn, 236–56. Baton Rouge: Louisiana State University Press.

Scanzoni, J. H. 1971. *The Black Family in Modern Society.* Boston: Allyn and Bacon.

Schermerhorn, R. A. 1970. *Comparative Ethnic Relations: A Framework for Theory and Research.* New York: Random House.

Schoen, Robert. 1978. "Toward a Theory of the Demographic Implications of Ethnic Subordination." *Social Science Quarterly* 59:468–81.

Scott, Anne Firor. 1970. *The Southern Lady: From Pedestal to Politics, 1830–1930.* Chicago: University of Chicago Press.

——. 1983. "Historians Construct the Southern Woman." In *Sex, Race, and the Role of Women in the South*, ed. Joanne V. Hawks and Sheila L. Skemp, 95–110. Jackson: University Press of Mississippi.

——. 1984. *Making the Invisible Woman Visible.* Urbana and Chicago: University of Illinois Press.

Singal, Daniel Joseph. 1982. *The War Within: From Victorian to Modernist Thought in the South, 1919–1945.* Chapel Hill: University of North Carolina Press.

Sloan, Cliff, and Bob Hall. 1979. "It's Good to Be Home in Greenville . . . It's Better If You Hate Unions." *Southern Exposure* 7:82-93.

Smith, A. Emerson. 1983. "Non-Academic, For-Profit Sociologists State Their Case." Letter to William C. Eckerman, dtd. 24 January 1983. *The Southern Sociologist* 14(Fall):16–17.

Smith, Lillian. 1949/1961. *Killers of the Dream*. Garden City, N.Y.: W. W. Norton.

Smith, Stephen A. 1985. *Myth, Media, and the Southern Mind*. Fayetteville: University of Arkansas Press.

Sokoloff, Nattalie J. 1980. *Between Love and Money: The Dialectics of Women's Home and Market Work*. New York: Praeger.

Southeast Women's Employment Coalition. 1986. *Women of the Rural South: Economic Status and Prospects*. Lexington, Ky.: Southeast Women's Employment Coalition.

Southern Growth Policies Board. 1985. *Looking Forward: Visions of the Future of the South*. Research Triangle Park, North Carolina.

Southern Regional Council. 1944. Charter (manuscript), on file at Southern Regional Council offices, 60 Walton Street, N.W., Atlanta, Georgia 30303.

Southern Regional Education Board. 1988. "SREB Milestones." Atlanta: Southern Regional Education Board.

Spruill, Julia Cherry. 1938/1972. *Women's Life and Work in the Southern Colonies* (University of North Carolina). New York: W. W. Norton.

Stack, Carol. 1974. *All Our Kin: Strategies for Survival in a Black Community*. New York: Harper and Row.

Staples, Robert. 1982. *Black Masculinity: The Black Male's Role in American Society*. San Francisco: The Black Scholar Press.

Steckel, Richard H. 1980. "Slave Marriages and the Family." *Journal of Family History* 5:406–21.

Stein, Howard F., and Robert F. Hill. 1977. *The Ethnic Imperative*. University Park: Pennsylvania State University Press.

Sterling, Dorothy. 1984. *We Are Your Sisters: Black Women in the Nineteenth Century*. New York: W. W. Norton.

Streib, Gordon F., ed. 1981. *Programs for Older Americans*. Gainesville, Fla.: University Presses of Florida.

———. 1984. "Socioeconomic Strata." In *Handbook on the Aged in the United States*, ed. Erdman B. Palmore, 77–92. Westport, Conn.: Greenwood.

Streib, Gordon F., and W. Edward Folts. 1983. "The Sale of a Mobile Home Retirement Community: Tensions and Resolution." Unpublished paper, Department of Sociology, University of Florida, Gainesville.

Sugg, Redding S., Jr., and George Hilton Jones. 1960. *The Southern Regional Education Board: Ten Years of Regional Cooperation in Higher Education*. Baton Rouge: Louisiana State University Press.

Sullivan, Teresa A. 1984. "The Occupational Prestige of Women Immigrants: A Comparison of Cubans and Mexicans." *International Migration Review* 18:1045–62.

Swain, Martha H. 1983. "The Public Role of Southern Women." In *Sex, Race, and the Role of Women in the South*, ed. Joanne V. Hawks and Sheila L. Skemp, 37–57. Jackson: University Press of Mississippi.

Swanson, Ernst W., and John A. Griffin. 1955. *Public Education in the South*

Today and Tomorrow, A Statistical Survey. Chapel Hill: University of North Carolina Press.

Swanson, William C. 1983. "Confidence and Legitimacy: Two Essentials for Clinical Sociological Practice." *The Southern Sociologist* 14(Summer): 24–25.

Sweet, James A. 1978. "Indicators of Family and Household Structure of Racial and Ethnic Minorities in the United States." In *The Demography of Racial and Ethnic Groups,* ed. Frank D. Bean and W. Parker Frisbie, 221–59. New York: Academic Press.

Taeuber, Irene, and Conrad Taeuber. 1971. *People of the United States in the 20th Century.* Washington, D.C.: U.S. Department of Commerce.

Taylor, Joe Gray. 1982. *Eating, Drinking, and Visiting in the South.* Baton Rouge: Louisiana State University Press.

Terry, Geraldine B. 1981. "Beginning Jobs for Sociology Majors with the State of Tennessee." *The Southern Sociologist* 13(Winter):25–26.

———. 1982. "Directing Graduates Toward Careers in Government." *The Southern Sociologist* 13(Summer):26–27.

———. 1983. "Developing a Program of Study for Sociology Majors Who Anticipate Governmental Careers." *The Southern Sociologist* 14(Spring): 19–20 and (Part 2) 14(Summer):22–23.

Thatcher, Gary. 1978. "Non-Southerners Changing: 'New South.'" *Christian Science Monitor,* April 18, p. 7.

Theodore, Athena. 1986. *The Campus Troublemakers: Academic Women in Protest.* Houston, Tex.: Cap and Gown Press.

Thomas, Emory M. 1979. *The Confederate Nation, 1861–1865.* New York: Harper and Row.

Tienda, Marta, and Lisa J. Neidert. 1984. "Language, Education and the Socioeconomic Achievement of Hispanic Origin Men." *Social Science Quarterly* 65:519–36.

Tilley, Nannie M. 1985. *The R. J. Reynolds Tobacco Company.* Chapel Hill: University of North Carolina Press.

Tobin, James. 1965. "On Improving the Economic Status of the Negro." In *The Negro American,* ed. Talcott Parsons and Kenneth B. Clark, 451–71. Boston: Beacon Press.

Toner, Robin. 1986. "Splintering of Once-Solid South Poses New Problems for Democratic Party." *The New York Times,* October 16, p. 16.

TSS: *The Southern Sociologist,* Vol. 13, 14, and 15 (Fall 1981 through Summer 1984). The Southern Sociological Soceity.

U.S. Department of Labor. 1971. *Geographic Profile of Employment and Unemployment.* Washington, D.C.: Government Printing Office.

———. 1981. *Geographic Profile of Employment and Unemployment.* Washington, D.C.: Government Printing Office.

———. 1983. *Geographic Profile of Employment and Unemployment.* Bulletin 2216. Washington, D.C.: Government Printing Office.

Vance, Rupert B. 1937. *Human Geography.* Chapel Hill: University of North Carolina Press.

van den Berghe, Pierre L. 1967. *Race and Racism.* New York: Wiley.

Vander May, Brenda J., and Ellen S. Bryant. 1983. "Southern Sex Roles: Country Meeting of the Music as the Vehicle for Investigation." Paper presented at the Annual Meeting of the Southern Sociological Society, Atlanta, April.

Van Der Slik, Jack R. 1970. *Black Conflict with White America.* Columbus: Charles E. Merrill.

vander Zanden, James W. 1972. *American Minority Relations.* New York: Ronald.

Van Heek, F. 1974. "The Welfare State and Sociology." *Sociologia Nederlandica* 10(1):3–17.

Verdugo, Naomi T., and Richard R. Verdugo. 1984. "Earnings Differentials Between Mexican American, Black, and White Male Workers." *Social Science Quarterly* 65:417–25.

Walker, Alice. 1982. *The Color Purple.* New York: Washington Square.

Walsh, Lorena S. 1985. "The Experiences and Status of Women in the Chesapeake, 1750–1775." In *The Web of Southern Social Relations: Women, Family, and Education,* ed. Walter J. Fraser, Jr., R. Frank Saunders, Jr., and Jon L. Waklyn, 1–18. Athens: University of Georgia Press.

Weinstein, Bernard, and Robert Firestein. 1978. *Regional Growth and Decline in the United States: The Rise of the Sunbelt and the Decline of the Northeast.* New York: Praeger.

Welch, Susan, and John R. Hibbing. 1984. "Hispanic Representation in Congress." *Social Science Quarterly* 65:328–35.

Welty, Eudora. 1970. *Losing Battles.* New York: Vintage Books.

White, Deborah Gray. 1983. "Female Slaves: Sex Role and Status in the Antebellum Plantation South." *Journal of Family History* 8:248–61.

————. 1985. *Ain't I a Woman? Female Slaves in the Plantation South.* New York: W. W. Norton.

Wilcox, Jerry, and W. Clark Roof. 1978. "Percent Black and Black-White Status Inequality: Southern Versus Nonsouthern Patterns." *Social Science Quarterly* 59:421–34.

Williams, Robin M., Jr., and Gerald D. Jaynes. 1989. *A Common Destiny: Blacks and American Society.* Washington, D.C.: National Academy Press.

Williams, Tennessee. 1947. *A Streetcar Named Desire.* New York: New Directions.

Wilson, Emily H. 1973. *Hope and Dignity: Older Black Women on the South.* Philadelphia: Temple University Press.

Wilson, Everett K. 1971. *Sociology: Rule, Roles and Relations.* Homewood, Ill.: Dorsey.

Wilson, Godfrey, and Monica H. Wilson. 1945. *The Analysis of Social*

Change Based on Observations in Central Africa. Cambridge: The University Press.

Wilson, Kenneth L., and Alejandro Portes. 1980. "Immigrant Enclaves: An Analysis of the Labor Market Experiences of Cubans in Miami." *American Journal of Sociology* 86:295–319.

Wilson, Kenneth W., and Patricia Y. Martin. 1988a. "Regional Differences in Resolving Family Conflicts: The Legacy of Patriarchy in the South?" *Sociological Spectrum.* Forthcoming.

_____. 1988b. "Gender Conceptions by Region: Are Southerners Unique?" Unpublished manuscript. Department of Sociology, East Carolina University, Greenville, North Carolina.

Wilson, William Julius. 1978. *The Declining Significance of Race.* Chicago: University of Chicago Press.

_____. 1986. "Social Change and Racial Progress." *Contemporary Sociology* 15:30–34.

_____. 1987a. "The Hidden Agenda." *The University of Chicago Magazine* 80:2–11.

_____. 1987b. *The Truly Disadvantaged: The Inner City, the Underclass, and Public Policy.* Chicago: University of Chicago Press.

Woodman, Harold D. 1968. *King Cotton and His Retainers.* Lexington: University of Kentucky Press.

Woodward, C. Vann. 1966. *The Strange Career of Jim Crow.* New York: Oxford University Press.

_____. 1968. *The Burden of Southern History* (rev. ed.). Baton Rouge: Louisiana State University Press.

_____. 1969. "W. J. Cash Reconsidered." *New York Review of Books* 13(4 December):28–34.

_____. 1974. *The Origins of the New South.* Baton Rouge: Louisiana State University Press.

_____. 1981. *Mary Chestnut's Civil War.* Binghamton, N.Y.: Vail-Ballou Press.

_____. 1986. *Thinking Back: The Perils of Writing History.* Chapel Hill: University of North Carolina Press.

Woodward, C. Vann, and Elizabeth Muhlenfeld, eds. 1984. *The Private Mary Chesnut: The Unpublished Civil War Diaries.* New York and Oxford: Oxford University Press.

Woofter, Thomas J., Jr. 1925. *The Basis of Racial Adjustment.* Boston: Ginn.

Wright, Gavin. 1986. *Old South, New South: Revolutions in the Southern Economy Since the Civil War.* New York: Basic Books.

Wyatt-Brown, Bertram. 1982. *Southern Honor: Ethics and Behavior in the Old South.* New York: Oxford.

Yetman, N. R., and C. H. Steele. 1975. *Majority and Minority: The Dynamics of Racial and Ethnic Relations,* 2nd ed. Boston: Allyn and Bacon.

Yoder, Edwin M., Jr. 1984. *The Night of the Old South Ball, and Other Essays and Fables.* Oxford, Miss.: Yoknapatawpha Press.

Zollar, Ann Creighton, and J. Sherwood Williams, 1986. "The Contribution of Marriage to the Life Satisfaction of Black Adults." Paper presented at the Annual Meeting of the Southern Sociological Society, New Orleans, April.

Zopf, Paul E., Jr. 1986. *American's Older Population.* Houston, Tex.: Cap and Gown Press.

Contributors

Biggar, Jeanne C. Retired Associate Professor of Sociology, University of Virginia, Charlottesville, Virginia.

Dillman, Caroline Matheny. Associate Professor of Sociology and Director of Off-Campus Programs and Continuing Education, Reinhardt College, Waleska, Georgia.

Ferriss, Abbott L. Professor Emeritus of Sociology, Emory University, and editor and publisher of *Sinet: The Social Indicators Network News*, Atlanta, Georgia.

Frisbie, W. Parker. Professor of Sociology, and Research Associate, Population Research Center, University of Texas, Austin, Texas.

Himes, Joseph S. Excellence Foundation Professor Emeritus of Sociology, University of North Carolina, Greensboro, North Carolina.

Hughes, Holly L. Doctoral Student, University of North Carolina, Chapel Hill, North Carolina.

Irwin, Michael D. Assistant Professor of Sociology, Louisiana State University, Baton Rouge, Louisiana.

Kasarda, John D. Kenan Professor of Business Administration and Sociology, and Director of The Kenan Institute of Private Enterprise, Center for Competitiveness and Employment Growth, University of North Carolina, Chapel Hill, North Carolina.

Luebke, Paul. Associate Professor of Sociology, University of North Carolina, Greensboro, North Carolina.

Martin, Patricia Yancey. Daisy Parker Flory Alumni Professor of Sociology, Florida State University, Tallahassee, Florida.

Moland, John J., Jr. Visiting Professor of Sociology and Interim Director of the Institute for Research in Social Science, Alabama State University, Montgomery, Alabama.

Reed, John Shelton. Professor of Sociology and Adjunct Professor of American Studies, and Director of Institute for Research in Social Sciences, University of North Carolina, Chapel Hill, North Carolina.

Streib, Gordon F. Graduate Research Professor Emeritus of Sociology and Joint Professor, Department of Community Health and Family Medicine, University of Florida, Gainesville, Florida.

Wilson, Kenneth R. Associate Professor of Sociology, East Carolina University, Greenville, North Carolina.

Index

Abolitionist Movement and black
women, 120
Affirmative Action, 188–89, 196, 218,
247–48; legislation, 205, 214; pro-
gram, 196, 204, 214, 216
African origins of individualism, 231
Age of early Southerners, 104
Agricultural workers, Social Security
Act, 86
Alabama, 33, 73, 81, 82, 128, 249, 251
Alcohol: alcoholism, 113–14; use of by
Southerners, 111; drinking by South-
ern white men, 113–14; stereotypes
of Southern white working-class
men, 114–15
Alexander, Will W., 270, 272
Allain, Bill, 251
Allis-Chalmers, 242
American Council on Education, 274
American Federation of Labor (AFL),
243–44, 246
Ames, Mrs. Jessie Daniel, 271
Ancestry of Southerners, 111–12
Anderson, Robert C., 276
Anglos, 149, 160
Antebellum era, 104–05, 107, 110–11
Anti-institutionalism: persistence,
230–31; origins, 231–32; effect of
history, 232; future, 232–35
Area Agencies on Aging, 96

Arizona, 151
Arkansas, 73, 128
Asian, 44, 66
Assimilation: cultural, 150, 161,
180–81; structural, 150, 161, 180–81
Atlanta, 239–40, 251, 253; meeting,
272; Regional Commission, 278

"Baby Boom" generation, 217, 218
Basis of Racial Adjustment, 271
Biracial conference, 270
Birmingham, 241
Birth rate: Southern states, 81
Blacks: education, 161; elderly and income level, 94; elderly women as
family unifiers, 88, 91; extended family, 92; household structure, 177–79;
importance of religion, 88; importance of Social Security, 96;
individual income, 167–71; labor
force participation, 161–66; life expectancy rates, 88; role constancy, 88;
spatial concentration, 174–75; Social
Security Act (1935), 86; family income, 205–08, 219–20
Black Southerners: traditional value
orientation, 229; effect of history, 232
Black-white relations: trends, 188–89;
comparative analysis, 189
Blue Ridge, North Carolina, 271

312

Bob Jones University, 251
Boston, 33, 58
Brandon, Wiley, 273
Brazil, 53
Brown v. *Topeka Board of Education,*
   ix, 187, 238–39
Business cycles, 46–50

California, 72, 81, 151, 152
Caribbean, 61
Carnegie Corporation, 271
Cash, W. J., viii, 226–27, 229–30
Celtic origins of individualism, 231
Census region: elected officials,
   190–95; occupations, 197–204; in-
   come, 205–08; unemployment,
   208–12; poverty, 212, 213; school de-
   segregation, 212–15
Chamber of Commerce, 14
Chapel Hill, North Carolina, 240
Charleston, South Carolina, 33
Charlotte, North Carolina, 242
Cheating by Southern white men, 110
Chicago, 34, 58
Children, 105, 120–21, 129, 132–35
China, 53
Chivers, Walter, 271
Church: as a center of social life, 87,
   110–11, 120; membership in, South
   vs. non-South, 106; Southern funda-
   mentalism, 110–11; black women,
   110–11, 119–20. *See also* Religion
Civil Rights: legislation, 242; move-
   ment, 236, 240–42, 245, 273
Civil Rights Act: of 1957, 187; of 1964,
   ix, 187–88, 196, 214, 239, 241
Civil War, ix–xiv; three consequences,
   xii–xiii; legitimated Southern lead-
   ers, xii–xiii, 105, 107, 112, 117; diary
   of Mary Chesnut, 114; black men,
   119
Clemson College, 240
Coalition politics, 194, 218
Cole, William E., 272
Colorado, 151
Columbia, South Carolina, 240
Commission on Interracial Coopera-
   tion, 270
Committee on Civil Rights, 196
Committee on Southern Trends, 279

Communism, 243–44
Community Organization Project, 273
Concubines, 108, 113
Confederacy, 72, 73
Conflict, 188. *See also* Protest actions;
   Struggle
Congress, 187, 188, 196, 220
Congress of Industrial Organizations
   (CIO), 243–44, 246
Conservatism, 114, 237
Conservative elite, 237
Constitution of the United States, 188
Consumer Price Index, 94
Continuity in historical sequences, 281
Cooperative Democracy and Develop-
   ment Project, 273
Courage, Myrna, 117
Credit: systems, sharecropping, com-
   pany store, and tenancy, 1
Crime and Correction Project, 273
Cubans: population size and growth,
   155–56; historical contact with ma-
   jority, 155, 158; education, 160–61,
   162; labor force participation,
   161–69; income, 167–71; political
   conditions, 169–72; spatial concentration, 174–76; household
   structure, 176–80; language use,
   180–81; return of human capital,
   183–84; future structural assimilation, 184–85
Cultural assimilation, 149
Cultural hegemony, 116–17
Culture: influences on Southern gendering and gender relations, 109–11,
   116–17, 147–48

Dallas, 240
Dan River Mills, 244
Darlington, South Carolina, 245
Death rates, Southern states, 81
Deep South, 239, 241. *See also* South
Deering-Milliken, 245
Democratic Party, 246–52
Demographic consequences: negative
   race relations, feminization, aging, 28
Demographic hypothesis of ethnic pre-
   judice and segregation, 172–74
Denton, Jeremiah, 249
Denver, Colorado, 49

Depression era, 110
Desegregation, 187, 239–40, 245; resis-
tance, 187–88, 211–12; school
desegregation by region, 214
District of Columbia, 76, 80, 190
Divorce: among Southerners vs. non-
Southerners, 129–32; in country mu-
sic lyrics, 114
Domestic workers, Social Security Act,
86
Dominant elite, 236
Du Bois, W. E. B., 4
Durham, North Carolina, 239
"Durham Statement," 272

Economic growth and distribution: historical, 33–40; contemporary, 35–46;
future, 56–60, 62–67
Economic libertarianism: persistence,
231; among migrants to the South,
231
Economic recessions, 47–48
Economy: cotton, 106; tobacco, 106;
plantation, 107; influence on gender
relations, 107–09, 145–47; agrarian,
107; after World War II in South, 109
Education, 55, 59–61, 229, 275; Southern antebellum women and slaves,
108; and Southerners, 112, 114;
women, 114; women's election to
school boards, 129; by region, gender,
race, 133, 136–39
Educational reform and Southern Regional Educational Board (SREB), 276
Eisenhower administration, 188, 247
Elders: concentrate in Florida, 5; as a
major social category, 71; support
systems, 88, 90, 91; seasonal migration, 90; migration patterns, 90–91;
in rural areas, 91–92; income strata,
93–94; effect of heterogeneity on statistics, 94; effect of federal programs
on poor, 95; care of the frail, 97;
problems, 284
Elected black officials: by region,
190–94; increase in number, 190–94,
217; state legislators, 192–94, 216;
underrepresentation, 190–94
Elite, 236–42, 246–47, 249, 251, 253

Employment, 195, 197; of black vs.
white women, 121; by region, gender,
and race, 132–33, 136–43
Enduring South, The, 229–31; revised
edition, 233–35
England, 32
English, John W., 114–15
Enrollment: undergraduate, graduate,
281
Environment, 32, 40–41, 48, 53, 62; environmental problems, 284
Equality: denial for women and blacks,
106–09
Equal Rights Amendment, 122–23,
124–25; by region and date of
ratification, 123, 126–28
Estimated rates of population growth,
13, 15
Ethnic discrimination, 151, 186–87,
188–89, 196; against blacks, 173–74;
against Hispanics, 160, 172–73,
182–83; relation to size and growth
of minority, 173–74
Ethnicity: of Southerners, 107. See also
Race
Evangelical Protestantism, 230
Executive order: creating Fair Employment Practices Committee, 187, 196;
desegregating the armed services,
187; to provide equal opportunity in
federal employment, 196

Facilities for higher education, 275
Fair employment policy, 6–7
Fair Employment Practices Committee,
187, 196. See also Executive order
Falwell, Jerry, 250
Familism, 231
Family in Southern culture: care of the
elderly, 89–90; Southerners' orientation, 107, 114–15; among pre-
emancipation blacks, 106, 117–18;
marital status by region, race, and
gender, 129–32; household composition, 129–32, 134–35; changes from
1960 to 1980, South vs. non-South,
129–32
Federal programs for the elderly, 95,
96–97

Femininity and Southern white women, 133
Fertility, 35–36, 63; rates of Southern women, 133
Fisk University, 271
Florida, 71, 73, 76, 81, 90, 128, 152, 247; economic characteristics, 82; elderly population characteristics, 72; in-migration, 82; Jewish elderly, 92–93
Florida Committee on Aging, 96
Folger, John K., 276
Food, Tobacco, Agricultural and Allied Workers' Union of America, 244
Frasier, E. Franklin, 272
Frey, Fred C., 272
Frontier Idea, 232
Fund for the Future of the South, 280

Gaston County, North Carolina, 279
Gender gap, 122–23
Gender, gendering: Southern-style, 103, 104–06, 145–48; definition, 103; regions, 103; fictional accounts, 104; as a social construction, 104; and slavery, 108; roles and ideology, 116–17; norms, 117; social, political, economic, and cultural influences, 107–12, 145–48; geographic and demographic influences, 111–13, 148; in recent past and into future, 145–49
Gender relations, 103–04, 113–14; among antebellum white Southerners, 105; effects of Civil War, 104–06; in South, 109–13; between Southern white men and women, 108, 116–17; between Southern black men and women, 117–21; traditional, 110–11; opinions by gender, region, and race, 121–23, 124–25
Geography, 111–13, 147–48
George Mason University, 284
George Peabody College, 271
Georgia, 32, 73, 81, 128
Godwin, Winfred L., 276
Gore, Albert, 220
Graduate education, 282
Grady, Henry, viii

Graham, Bob, 247
Grandfather Clause, 186
Great Depression: influenced change of region, 6–7. See also World War II
Greensboro "sit ins," 240. See also Protest actions
Greenville, South Carolina, 251
Grenada, Mississippi, 244
Griffin, John A., 272
Grigg, Charles M., 272, 276
Grisham, Vaughn L., 279
Growth and Environmental Management, 279
Growth rates of Southern states, 14

Habitat for Humanity, 284
Hall, Tom T., 231
Hancock, Gordon B., 271
Harriet-Henderson Mills, 244
Health and Public Education, 273
Helms, Jesse, 249–50
Herrman, Margaret S., 284
Hightower, Jim, 252
Hill, Mozell, 272
Hispanic, 44, 66; elderly population, 92
Hodges, Luther, 239, 244
Homogeneity of ethnicity in the Old South, 111–12
Honor among antebellum Southern white men, 109–10
Hood, Tom, 285
Households, 13; by race and region, 129–32
House of Representatives, 169. See also United States Congress
Housing industry: retirement communities, 90
Human relations councils, 279
Hunt, Jim, 246–47, 250

Immigration, 44, 61, 63, 66; of Cubans, 155, 158; of Mexicans, 155, 159; of Puerto Ricans, 155, 158; policies of Bracero program, 159–60. See also Migration
Immigration Reform and Control Act, 183
Imprisonment of men by race and region, 119

Income: earnings by gender, race, and region, 1960 to 1980, 133, 139, 140–41; by race and region, 205–08; median family income of blacks, 205; ratio of black to white, 205, 208; influence of racism, 208

Incumbency, 129; and women political candidates, 128–29

Index of dissimilarity, 202–05

Individualism: Evangelical Protestantism, 230; persistence, 230–31; origins, 231–32; effect of history, 232; future, 232–35

Indocumentados, 155

Industrialism, 226

Industrial mix, 46

Industrial Revolution, 257–58

Industries: extractive, high-tech, and service, 7–8

Infidelity, 114

Infrastructure, 49, 50, 53, 61, 67. *See also* Transportation

Institute for Political Participation, 273

Institutional care, 90; provided by religious groups, 88–89. *See also* Nursing homes

Institutional structures: based on age policy rather than on need, 94–95; effect on elderly, 70, 71–72

Interracial Commission, 270

Interracial committees, 271

Interstate banking movement, 279

Interstate compacts, 274, 275

Isolation: of Southern women, 108, 112

Ivey, John E., Jr., 274

Jackson, Jesse, 253

Jackson, Maynard, 253

Jackson, Mississippi: Chamber of Commerce, Urban League, 241

Jewish elderly: migration to Israel, 92–93; as risk-takers, 93

Jim Crow Laws, viii, xii–xiii; and practice, 236, 238–43

Johnson, Charles S., 271, 272

Johnson, Guy B., 272

Jones, Thomas Jesse, 270

Jordon, Vernon, 273

Julius Rosenwald Fund, 270

Justice Department, 190

Kennedy, John F., 188, 196, 212, 240, 269

Kennedy-Johnson Administration, 212

Kentucky, 73, 80, 81, 129

Key, V. O., 236, 245, 247, 252

Kin, kinship, 121

King, Martin Luther, Jr., 111, 120, 188

Korea, 53

Ku Klux Klan, xii, 240

Labor markets and Southern women, 116–17, 146

Labor organizations, 242

Labor relations, 236–38, 245, 250

Land-use legislation, 230

Legal aid to blacks, 270

Lewis, Hylan, 272

Lewis, John, 273

Liberalism, 236–37, 251–53

Liberals, 236, 247–52

Libertarianism, economic, 231

Life care communities, 89

Life-course perspective, 89, 91

Literacy tests, 186

Little Rock, Arkansas, 238–40, 279

Local insight, 279

Localism: persistence, 231; changes in non-Southerners, 234

Louisiana, 33, 73, 128–29

Louisiana State University, 271

Lying and Southern white men, 114

Lynchburg, Virginia, 250

Lynchings, 118

Maclachlan, John, 272

"Making a Difference": by persons and professions, 269; by education and social scientists, 277; strategies for the future, 280–83

Marriage, marital status: dissatisfactions among black men, 118–19; and income, 118; rates, by race and gender, 118; opinions of women by region, 122–23; by households, gender, region, and race, 129–32

Marshall, Ray, 245

Martin, Jim, 249

Maryland, 128
Masculinity and violence, 110; and Southern white men, 113–14. *See also* Violence
Mass media, 229
Medalia, Nahm Z., 276
Median age: Southern states, 81
Medicaid, 70, 82
Medicare, 70, 71, 72, 84, 96
Men in the South: differences from Southern women, 103; changes in recent past, 103; in antebellum era, 105; in planter class, 106; control over women and blacks, 108; traits and stereotypes, 113–15; white and blue collar, 114; ego, 109–10; violence, 107, 110, 139, 144; black and Southern, 117–19, 129–32; white and Southern, 113–15, 129–32; relations between white men and black women, 110. *See also* Violence
Metropolitan, 58–59. *See also* Urbanization
Mexican Americans: education, 160–61; future structural assimilation, 184–85; historical contact with majority, 158–60; household structure, 176–80; income, 167–71; labor force participation, 161–67; language used, 180–81; political conditions, 169, 172; population size and growth, 54–57; return of human capital, 182–84; spatial concentration, 174–76
Mexico, 61
Michigan, 90
Middleton-Kern, Susan, 116
Migration, 35, 37, 40–45; to South, 229. *See also* Immigration
Minority status, 150–51
Misogyny, 106, 114–15
Mississippi, 33, 73, 81, 82, 128, 129, 239, 241, 246–47, 251
Mississippi College, 271
Mitchell, Broadus, 226
Mitchell, George S., 272
Modernizers, 238–53
Mondale, Walter, 84
Montgomery Bus Boycott (1955–56), ix. *See also* Protest actions

Moral Majority, 250
Morehouse College, 271
Motherhood and black women, 120–21
Murder, 118; and gender, 144; in South vs. non-South, 144; future rates by Southern men, 147
Music: gender and country lyrics, 114
Mutual aid societies and black women, 119–21
Myths about the Southern "lady," 115–16

National Assessment of Educational Progress, 277
National Association for the Advancement of Colored People (NAACP), 4, 186, 219
National Congressional Club, 250
National economic trends: loss of jobs and national deficit, 216
National Urban League (NUL), 4
National War Labor Board, 243
National Youth Administration (NYA), 7
New Christian Right (N.C.R.), 250–51
New Deal, viii, 7, 86, 238
New England Board of Higher Education, 275
New Jersey, 90, 92
New Market, Tennessee, 279
New Mexico, 151
New Orleans, 59, 241
"New South," 6–7, 225–26, 236, 272; characteristics, 6; began in New Deal, viii, 6; rediscovery, 7; economic development, viii
New York City, 33, 58, 72, 158
Nineteenth Amendment, 109, 145; opposition by white Southern men, 109; and racism, 108–09; by region and date of ratification, 123–28
Non-academic employment, 283
Nonviolence: confrontation, 188; strategies, 217; approaches, 218
North Carolina, 32, 80, 81, 128, 239–40, 244–47, 249–50
North Central Region, 192, 194, 210
Nursing homes, 70

Oak Ridge National Laboratory, 285

Occupational dissimilarity and issues of inequality, 202–05

Occupations: by sex, race, and region (1980), 139, 140–43, 197–205; service occupations, 197; white collar, 198–99; blue collar, 202; unemployment, 208; ratio, 199; national changes, 214, 216

Odum, Howard W., viii

Oklahoma, 34, 128

Older Americans Act, 73, 84

Old South: regional model, 14; women's legal and political status, 123, 126–29. See also South

"Operation Dixie," 243

Operation Opportunity, 273

Organizations Assisting Schools (in 1955–62), 273

Page, Walter Hines, 230

Park, Robert E., and Ernest W. Burgess, viii

Parks, Rosa, 120

Paternalism, 106, 109, 112

Patriarchy, 109, 112; definition, 105; and slavery, 105–06; and children, 105

Peacemaking and Conflict Resolution, National Conference, 284

Pearsall Plan, 239

Peculiar institution, 112. See also Slavery

Phelps-Stokes Fund, 270

Philadelphia, 33

Phoenix, 49

Physicians: ratio in Southern states, 81

Plantation legacy, 232. See also Economy

Planter class, 108, 113–14; and pretensions of aristocracy, 111. See also Economy; Social classes

Political consequences of population change, 16

Political economic elite, 236–38

Political economy, 82–87

Political power, 193

Political predictions: black elected officials, 190–92, 217; state legislators, 194, 217

Politics: women's, 128–29; and legal codes, 107; and Southern gender relations, 107–09, 123–29, 145–48; and Southern women, 146–47. See also Equal Rights Amendment; Nineteenth Amendment

Poll taxes, 186, 244

Poor whites, 3

Population: birth rate and death rate, 81; elderly by age, region, division, and state, 77–79; increase by migration, 80–81; median age, 76; rural areas, 80–81

Population, growth and distribution: historical, 32–41; contemporary, 46–50; future, 14, 51–55, 58–62; median age, 81. See also Fertility; Immigration; Migration; Race Relations; Urbanization

Population-based adaptations, 27–28; change and Southern character, 30–31

Population study problem and method, 13–14

Populist movement, 4

Post-World War II South, 237, 245

Poverty, 3; historical, 35, 59, 61; contemporary, 49–61; future, 60–62; rate and ratio by region, 212. See also Unemployment; Working poor

Power, 2–3, 101; traditionalist and modernizers, government and outside sources, emergence of countervailing power, pluralistic power structure, 262. See also New Deal; World War I; World War II

Prayer: as a coping mechanism, 88; and health, 87–88

Prediction, viii; definition, vii, 263–64; developmental, x; developmental summary, 263–64; types, leading statements, detailed predictions, increase of problematic conditions, 263, 264–65

Predictions: black elected officials, 190–92, 216–17; state legislators, 194, 217; occupational trends, 206, 218, 219

Preface to Peasantry, 271

Prejudice: racial, 229; religious, 229

Pressure from blacks, 196, 205, 214

Price, Daniel O., 276
Private household workers, 197
Problematic changes, 266–68
Problem of study: Hispanics and Anglos, 149
Project on Segregation and Christian Academies, 274
Protest actions: 1950s to 1970s, viii, 186–217
Protestantism, in the South, 106
Puerto Ricans: population size and growth, 155–57; historical contact with majority, 158; education, 160–62; labor force participation, 161, 163–67; income, 167–69; political conditions, 169, 172; spatial concentration, 174–76; household structure, 176–80; language used, 180–81; return of human capital, 183–84; future structural assimilation, 185

Race, xii–xiv, 35, 41, 45–46, 63–66; conflict, lessened after World War II, 7–8
Race relations, 237–39, 242, 245, 248–50, 270–74; study of, 271; improvement of, 272, 273. See also Race, conflict
Racial inequality, 205, 216; tension reduction, 272; planning, 284
Racism, 106, 107, 109, 112, 113–14; on earnings of men and women by region, 138–39; individual and institutional, 188; on income and employment, 205, 208
Raleigh, 239
Randolph A. Phillip, 187
Rape, 118, 144, 147
Ratios: occupation, 199; income, 208; unemployment, 208–10; poverty, 212
Reagan, Ronald, 84, 247; Supreme Court, 205, 216, 218; Administration, 219; ideological conservatism, 220
Reconstruction, 106, 107, 112
Region: and religion, 106; and race, 107; and opinions about women's rights, 122–23, 124–25
Regional pride, 90
Regional sociology, 227

Reid, Ira De A., 270, 272
Religion: effect on health, 87–88; elderly and the family, 87–89; as a factor in southern states, 95–96, 106–07, 110–11. See also Protestantism
Republicans, 189, 246–51
Research: on gender, 104; on Southern women, 104; need for study of Southern gendering, 147
Research Triangle Park, 72, 239
Retirement communities, 90; as surrogate families, 91
Richmond, Virginia, 272
Riley, Richard, 246–47
R. J. Reynolds Tobacco Company, 120, 244
Roanoke Rapids, North Carolina, 245
Roosevelt, Franklin D., 3, 86, 187, 196, 243, 269
Rosenwald Schools, 3
Rurality: labor market conditions, for Southern women, 116–17; black men, 118; black women, 121; and women's success in politics, 129
Rural populations, 70

St. Augustine, 240
Sanford, Terry, 240
San Francisco, 34–35
Sauer, Carl O., 7
Schietinger, E. F., 276
School desegregation, 212–14, 215; the Supreme Court Decision, 1954, 212, 214; the Civil Rights Act of 1964, 214; by region, 214; institutions of higher learning, 214
School Drop-out Prevention Project, 274
School segregation, 106, 244; enforced by state laws, 186; impact of, 188; supported discrimination, 186, 187, 212, 214
Segregation: of blacks, 174–75; of Hispanics, 175
Service occupations, 197
Sex-age population ratio increases, 16
Sexual activity: of Southern white men and black and white women, 113–14; of Southern black men, 119

Sharecroppers All, 271
Shift-share analysis, 46
Slavery, slaves, 1, 104–06, 108, 111–12;
  apologies for, 110; families and role
  of men, 117–18
"Snowbirds," 90
Social change, of region, 7–8; of organization, 259–60; of stratification,
  260–61; of power structure, 262–63
Social classes, 104, 114; of early
  Southerners, 112; Southern white
  men, 114; women's sense of self,
  115–16; gender relations, 113–17;
  and white women, 116–17; post-
  Civil War, 260. *See also* Social stratification
Social organization: mode of change,
  99; aspect of societal transformation,
  259; leads to urban industrial society,
  260
Social planning, 270; for education,
  276, 278, 280; problems, 284; for the
  elderly, 284; for environmental problems, 284–85
Social Sciences, viii
Social scientists: making a difference,
  277
Social Security, 7, 70, 71–72, 82, 96;
  benefit levels, 84; poverty index,
  93–94; welfare state, 85–86
Social stratification: postbellum
  classes, 10–11; blacks and women
  excluded and poverty-impotence
  widespread, 11; in 1960s, 260–61;
  criteria, new structure, sources of
  change, and new urban classes, 260.
  See also Social classes
Social structure, 10–12
Societal transformation, 258–59; dimensions of, types predicted,
  transformation of society, 258
Sociological mission, viii
Sociological Spectrum, 115
Sojourner Truth, 120
South, x–xi, 121–23, 124–25, 126–32,
  145–48; as a U.S. region, 106–07;
  and religion, 106; characterized, 270,
  272; growth and development, 281;
  folk culture, 283; reintegration in the
  nation, 283. *See also* Southern states
South Africa (comparison), 239

South America, 61
South Carolina, 73, 80, 81, 128, 240,
  244–47, 249, 251–52
Southern Changes, 272
Southerners: definition of, ix, x;
  qualities and values of, 106–07; and
  education, 106; history of gender re-
  lations among, 104; self-
  identification, 107; as ladies, 108;
  stereotypes of, 107, 113, 114–15,
  116–17
Southern Frontier, 271–72
Southern Growth Policy Board, vii,
  278–80; Ten Regional Objectives,
  278
Southern International Perspectives,
  279
Southern Justice Program, 273
Southern Labor Institute, The, 273
Southern Legislative Research Project,
  The, 273
Southern Politics, 236, 252
Southern Regional Council (SRC), viii,
  270–74; Equal Opportunity program,
  272
Southern Regional Education Board
  (SREB), 274–77; Academic Common
  Market, viii, 276; students educated,
  275; programs, 275; mental health
  program, 275
Southern Sociological Society, viii, 87
Southern states: as an agricultural region (1935), 86; collective solutions
  for the elderly, 98–99; defined as Administrative Region IV, 73; definition
  from Census usage, 73; demographic
  patterns, 73–82; demographic trends,
  71; economic issues, 72; effect of
  U.S. government, 72; family roles,
  89–90; future as a region, 95–96; future for the elderly, 95–99; paradox of
  modernization and regional culture,
  97–98; political economy, 82–84; political parties, 83–84; population by
  Census usage definitions, 76; statistical comparisons of population's
  characteristics, 80–82; traditional
  care of the elderly, 97. *See also* South
Southern Technology Council, 279
Southern Voices, 272
Spain, 159

Spartanburg-Greenville, 245
Spatial concentration and intergroup relations, 174–75
State Councils on Human Relations, 272
State legislators, 192, 194, 217; underrepresentation, 190, 192, 218
Status of women in U.S. South, 109
Stevens, J. P., 245
Structural assimilation, 149–50
Struggle, 187, 188, 189, 196, 217, 218, 220. See also Conflict; Race, conflict
Subregional cultures, 283
Suitt, Steve, 273
Supreme Court decisions, 186, 187, 188, 212, 214; Reagan Supreme Court, 206, 216, 218, 241–42
Survey research on Southern distinctiveness, 227–28; disappearance of traditional values, 228–29; in individualism, 230; in Evangelical Protestantism, 230–31; in attitudes toward violence, 231; in localism and familism, 231; in economic libertarianism, 231; effect of collective history, 232; future, 232–35
Swann v. Charlotte-Mecklenburg Board of Education, 241

Taft-Harley Act, 243
Tampa, 240
Teacher education: Southern Regional Educational Board (SREB), 276
Technology transfer, 280
Teenage unemployment rate, 210, 218
Tennessee, 128
Tennessee Valley Authority (TVA), 6–7, 274, 278, 279
Texas, 34, 49, 128, 151, 252
Textile industry, 72
Thurmond, Strom, 249, 252
Tobacco industry, 72
Tradition: orientation and gender relations, 110–17; behavior of northwestern vs. Southern women, 115–16
Traditionalists, 238–46, 248–50, 253
Traditional value orientation: disappearance of, 228–29; among blacks, 229
Tragedy of Lynching, The, 271

Transportation, 33–35, 40, 46, 53, 58. See also Infrastructure
Travel effect, 229
Truman, Harry, 187, 196
Tuskegee Institute, 4

Underclasses, 61–62, 212. See also Poverty
Underrepresentation: black elected officials, 190–92; state legislators, 192–94; by occupation, 199, 202
Unemployment, 59, 61; by race, age, and region, 208–12; rates, 194, 205, 208–12, 217–18; ratios, 208, 210, 212. See also Poverty
Union activity and black women, 120, 242–46
United States Congress: Southern power, 86. See also House of Representatives
University of Mississippi, 279
University of North Carolina, 271, 274
University of Tennessee, 285
University of West Virginia, 274–75
Urbanization, 107, 112, 145–48; historical, 33–35, 57–58; contemporary, 46–50, 57–58, 60–62; future, 57–58, 61–62, 66–67
Urban life effect, 229
Urban Planning Project, 273
"Urban villagers," 70

Vance, Rupert, 274
Veterans Services Project, 272
Violence: among Southern men, 108, 110, 139, 144; in the South, 112, 139, 144; against women, 139, 144; attitudes toward, 231–33. See also Masculinity; Men
Virginia, 32, 73, 128–29, 239, 244–45, 250
Virginia Medical College, 274
Virginia Union University, 271
Vocational education, Southern Regional Educational Board (SREB), 276
Voter registration, 190, 273; Education Project, 273
Voting Rights Act, 188, 189, 190

Wagner Act, 243
Wallace, George, 87, 252

War on poverty, 212
Washington, Booker T., 4
"Way of the folk," 69
Welfare state: conflict with Southern ideologies, 97–99; defined, 84–85; problems, 85; social market, 84
Western Interstate Commission on Higher Education, 275
West Virginia, 80, 128
White Camelias, 4
White Citizens Councils, 239, 241
White-collar occupations, 198–99, 208
White elite, 241–43; majority, 241
White primaries, 186
Wife beating, 110, 113, 139, 144, 147. See also Violence
William R. Kenan, Charitable Trust, 276
Williams, Harry, 276
Williams, Robin M., 272
Winter, William, 246–47
Woman Suffrage Movement, 120; and black women, 120. See also Women's rights
Women: historical studies of, 103; in antebellum era, 104–06, 115; as property, 104; myths of purity, 110; relations between white and black, 110; views, 114; qualities, 116–17; opinions on women's rights, 122–23,

124–25; and state Supreme Court justices in the South, 128; marital status by region and race, 129–32; white Southern, 104, 115–17, 129–32; black Southern, 104, 119–21, 129–32; dependence on Southern men, 108; perceptions of Southern men, 109
Women's rights, 121–29, 145–48; Southerners vs. non-Southerners, 122–23; to vote for President prior to 1918, 123, 126–28; state level Equal Rights legislation, 122, 123, 126–28. See also Woman Suffrage Movement
Working poor, 189. See also Poverty; Unemployment
Works Progress Administration (WPA), 5
World War I, 4–5; South discovered, structural change, challenge legitimacy of war, 4; change of race relations, 5
World War II, 5–7, 159–60, 186; cured Great Depression, economy at peak level, 5; rediscovery of South, began economic development, began cultural change, altered race relations, 6. See also Great Depression

Young, Andrew, 253